PILGRIMAGE
IN IRELAND

Pilgrimage in Ireland

The Monuments and the People

PETER HARBISON

Syracuse University Press

Copyright © Peter Harbison 1991

First Edition 1992

92 93 94 95 96 97 98 99   6 5 4 3 2 1

Simultaneously published in the United Kingdom by
Barrie and Jenkins Limited
20 Vauxhall Bridge Road, London SW1V 2SA

Harbison, Peter.
Pilgrimage in Ireland: the monuments and the people/ Peter
Harbison. — 1st ed.
p.   cm. — (Irish studies)
Includes bibliographical references and index.
ISBN 0-8156-0265-0
1. Christian pilgrims and pilgrimages—Ireland.   2. Ireland—
Religious life and customs.   I. Title.   II. Series: Irish studies
(Syracuse, N.Y.)
BX2320.5.I73H37   1992
263'.042415—dc20   91-5052
CIP

Design by David Fordham

Typeset by SX Composing, Rayleigh, Essex

Printed and bound in Great Britain by   .
Butler and Tanner, London and Frome

Fig. 1 *The magnificent Romanesque west doorway of
Clonfert Cathedral, County Galway* (SEE PREVIOUS
PAGE), *where St Brendan lies buried*

Contents

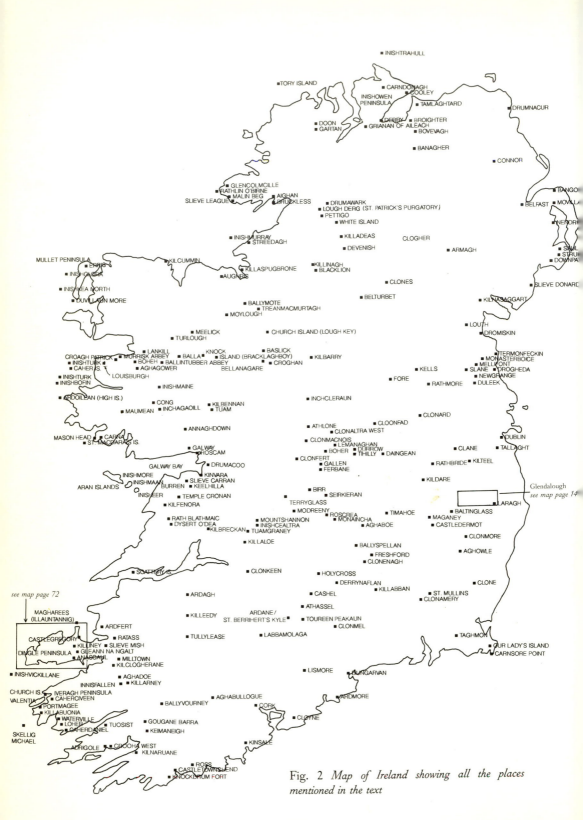

INISHTRAHULL

TORY ISLAND

CARNDONAGH
INISHOWEN COOLEY
PENINSULA TAMLAGHTARD

DRUMNACUR

DOON DERRY BROIGHTER
GARTAN GRIANAN OF AILEACH
BOVEVAGH

CONNOR

BANAGHER

GLENCOLMCILLE
RATHLIN O'BIRNE
MALIN BEG AIGHAN
SLIEVE LEAGUE DRUCKLESS

BANGO

BELFAST MOVILLA

DRUMAWARK
LOUGH DERG (ST. PATRICK'S PURGATORY)
PETTIGO
WHITE ISLAND

NENDR

SAUL
STRU
DOWNPA

CLOGHER

KILLADEAS

INISHMURRAY
STREEDAGH DEVENISH ARMAGH

KILCUMMIN KILLINAGH SLIEVE DONARD
KILLASPUGBRONE BLACKLION
AUGHRIS CLONES KILTASAGGART

MULLET PENINSULA
ENNIS
INISHGLORA BELTURBET
INISHKEA NORTH LOUTH
DUVILLAUN MORE BALLYMOTE DROMISKIN
TREANMACMURTAGH
MOYLOUGH TERMONFECKIN
MEELICK CHURCH ISLAND (LOUGH KEY) MONASTERBOICE
TURLOUGH MELLIFONT
LANKILL BASLICK SLANE DROGHEDA
CROAGH PATRICK MORRISK ABBEY KNOCK ISLAND (BRACKLAGHBOY) KILBARRY KELLS NEWGRANGE
INISHTURK BOHEH BALLINTUBBER ABBEY CROGHAN DULEEK
CAHER IS. BALLA BELLANAGARE FORE
AGHAGOWER CROGHAN RATHMORE
INISHTURK LOUISBURGH
INISHBOFIN
ARDOILLAN (HIGH IS.) INISHMAINE INCHCLERAUN
CONG KILBENNAN CLONARD
MAUMEAN INCHAGOILL TUAM
ANNAGHDOWN ATHLONE CLONALTRA WEST DUBLIN
MASON HEAD CARNA CLONMACNOIS CLANE TALLAGHT
ST. MACDARA'S IS. GALWAY LEMANAGHAN
ROSCAM BOHER DURROW DAINGEAN RATHBRIDE KILTEEL
GALWAY BAY DRUMACOO CLONFERT THILLY
INISHMORE KINVARA GALLEN KILDARE
INISHMAAN SLIEVE CARRAN FERBANE
ARAN ISLANDS BURREN KEELHILLA
INISHEER TEMPLE CRONAN BIRR SEIRKIERAN Glendalough
KILFENORA TERRYGLASS see map page 14
RATH BLATHMAIC MODREENY TIMAHOE LARAGH
DYSERT O'DEA ROSCREA MONAINCHA BALTINGLASS
KILBRECKAN MOUNTSHANNON AGHABOE MAGANEY
TUAMGRANEY INISHCEALTRA CASTLEDERMOT
KILLALOE CLONMORE
BALLYSPELLAN AGHOWLE
FRESHFORD
SCATTERY IS. CLONENAGH
CLONKEEN HOLYCROSS CLONE
ARDAGH DERRYNAFLAN
see map page 72 CASHEL KILLABBAN ST. MULLINS
MAGHAREES KILLEEDY ARDANE / ATHASSEL CLONAMERY
(ILLAUNTANNIG) ST. BERRIHERT'S KYLE TOUREEN PEAKAUN
CASTLEGREGORY RATASS TULLYLEASE LABBAMOLAGA CLONMEL TAGHMON
KILLINEY SLIEVE MISH
DINGLE PENINSULA GLEANN NA NGALT OUR LADY'S ISLAND
ANASCAUL MILLTOWN CARNSORE POINT
KILCLOGHERANE LISMORE DUNGARVAN
INISHVICKILLANE AGHADOE
INNISFALLEN KILLARNEY ARDMORE
CHURCH IS. IVERAGH PENINSULA AGHABULLOGUE
VALENTIA CAHERCIVEEN BALLYVOURNEY CORK
PORTMAGEE CLOYNE
KILLABUONIA
WATERVILLE GOUGANE BARRA
LOHER TUOSIST KEIMANEIGH
SKELLIG CAHERDANIEL
MICHAEL KINSALE
ADRIGOLE CROOHA WEST
KILNARUANE
ROSS
CASTLETOWNSEND
KNOCKDRUM FORT

Fig. 2 *Map of Ireland showing all the places mentioned in the text*

PREFACE

I T WAS THE SIGHT OF A CROSS-DECORATED OGHAM STONE LOCATED AT OVER 2000 feet on the slopes of a mountain overlooking the Atlantic Ocean on the westernmost tip of Europe which first set me thinking about the subject of the present book. Why should an Ogham stone be placed so high up on a mountain, where it is unlikely to have acted as a grave marker, which most Ogham stones are considered to have been? Surely, I said to myself, its location must have had something to do with the age-old pilgrimage to Mount Brandon, on whose slopes the stone was located in the townland of Arraglen. But the more I looked into the question of pilgrimage in early Ireland, the more I realised how little we knew about the subject from early historical sources, and also how little had been written about it in modern secondary literature, with a few honourable exceptions such as Daphne Pochin Mould's *Irish Pilgrimage* of 1955.

But the fact that so little is known about early Irish pilgrimage need not mean that it scarcely existed. A look through the old Irish annals convinced me that it certainly did exist, and had a tradition going back as early as the 6th century. I then started looking at the early ecclesiastical sites to see if the ancient monuments surviving on them could shed any further light on the matter. If all the sites had only been peopled by monks, one could well ask how much room was left for a lay population, and where did they fit into the picture if they were scarcely ever mentioned in connection with pilgrimage? The great majority of pilgrims today consists of lay people, as was also the case in earlier times, and the problem lies in the fact that they were obviously unaccustomed to writing down their experiences. Ireland had no Chaucer to provide a native version of *The Canterbury Tales*. The only well-documented Irish pilgrimage was that to St Patrick's Purgatory in Lough Derg, County Donegal, but as most of the early sources describing it are of foreign origin, they are of little help in ascertaining the nature of pilgrimage among the early Irish. It was only when the meagre historical information listing sites of pilgrimage was expanded to cover the monuments surviving *in situ*, and the reliquaries which had originally come from them, that a number of dislocated pieces of a jigsaw puzzle emerged. When put together with a degree of imagination, these began to provide what seemed like a more coherent and consistent, if far from complete, picture.

It is the purpose of this book to present and assemble those pieces of the puzzle so that, like the tesserae of a mosaic, they will create a picture which will shed new light on a much neglected aspect of life in early Christian Ireland, and by populating the monuments with a host of pious pilgrims, unfold a rather different view of those ancient ecclesiastical sites, which hitherto have been considered as having been purely monastic in character. Even if some of the views expressed in the following pages have to be more in the nature of conjecture than fact, given the sparsity of historical source material, I hope that the tentative conclusions drawn will encourage fresh discussion about the religious atmosphere in early Christian Ireland, a period which can be seen as the zenith of achievement in the country's long cultural history.

PART ONE

PILGRIMAGE PEOPLE

Fig. 3 *St Brendan's Oratory at Kilmalkedar, County
Kerry in G.V. Du Noyer's watercolour of around
1860*

Fig. 4 *The Church of the Holy Sepulchre in Jerusalem,*
as sketched in Konrad von Grünenberg's description of
his visit to Jerusalem in 1487

CHAPTER 1

PILGRIMAGE: THE HISTORICAL
BACKGROUND IN ASIA AND EUROPE

PILGRIMAGE MAY BE AN IRRATIONAL RELIGIOUS EXERCISE, BUT IT IS ONE WHICH has been filling a deeply felt human need and providing a form of popular self-expression since long before the development of the Christian, Islamic and other religions which practise it today.

Being usually more an act of personal piety than an event of historical significance, pilgrimage was not something which normally wrote itself into the history books. Thus, the earliest pilgrimages probably went totally unrecorded, whether they were in Mesopotamia, Egypt, or the Holy Land. Even the early history of Palestine is shrouded in mystery, but long before the time of Christ pilgrims were certainly going to Jerusalem, which was considered to have been the cradle of mankind. According to Jewish tradition, it was on Golgotha that Adam was created, and it was his skull which was often represented beneath the cross of Christ in medieval representations of the Crucifixion. It was in Jerusalem, too, that Abraham was prevented by the angel from sacrificing his son Isaac, as recounted in the Book of Genesis. But Jerusalem had its downs as well as its ups, and the lamenting prophet Jeremiah bemoaned the fate of the city when none came to her solemn feasts.

At the time of Christ, Jerusalem probably had around 55,000 inhabitants, but it is estimated that, on high feast days, more than double that number must have thronged into the city from far and wide to participate in and be present at the ceremonies. This pilgrimage to the centre of their faith gave the Jews a great sense of togetherness, a consciousness of being one race and one people, with a religion and a God better than all others – but it was also a social occasion when friends and families could meet together in harmony and trust to honour the Lord in and around his temple, and to celebrate the harvest of the crops he bestowed. There were, in addition, lesser pilgrimages for purposes of seeking a cure, to such places within the city walls as the pools of Siloah or Bethesda, which are mentioned in the Gospels. Great respect was also paid to the graves of the prophets and the patriarchs – and to these the people came in number to make what can fairly be called a pilgrimage.

Further west, in the Greek world, pilgrimages were undertaken too, for a variety of reasons. One of these was to find something out about the future, for which pilgrims went across the sea to the blessed island of Delos in search of advice from the god Apollo, or trundled up the slopes of Mount Parnassus to consult the oracle at Delphi, which invariably gave an ambiguous answer. Those who wanted to find solace in what might befall them after death were more attracted to the mysteries at Eleusis. Another, perhaps more restricted, form of pilgrimage practised in the lands bordering the eastern Mediterranean was that to the Hellenistic sanctuaries such as Ephesus in Asia Minor or Epidauros in the Peloponnese, undertaken by those in search of a cure for their ailments. In the world of Classical and Hellenistic Greece, Asclepius was regarded as the great god of healing, and intercession could be sought through him for a cure at over 200 sanctuaries dedicated to his honour. The island of Kos was one of the most celebrated of these, but his cult spread as far as Rome; in the land of the Pharaohs, Serapis was his near equivalent. As at a modern spa, the cure often meant staying for weeks or even months at a sanctuary, preparing oneself and being prepared psychologically for the cure, sleeping in the temple or curing place, and being analysed with methods which can count as the forerunners of those used by psychiatrists in our own century. Again reminiscent of modern religious practice, lamps were lit in sanctuaries – which, in the case of those dedicated to Asclepius, were usually round buildings – and people who were cured sometimes had descriptions of their cure carved in stone to impress and give hope to those coming after them. Frequently, too, they left behind them as a gesture of thanks some small symbol representing the part of the body cured – an eye, ear, leg

Fig. 5 *The Mosque of Omar and the Dome of the Rock*
in Jerusalem by David Roberts, 1839

or arm – and similar *ex votos* can be seen today in present-day places of pilgrimage in Greece, as at the shrine of the Virgin on the island of Tea.

When Christian pilgrimage began to develop in the centuries after the Saviour's death, it drew on both the older Jewish and Greek traditions of pilgrimage and, even if its outer form differed, it was to the centre of Jewish pilgrimage that the first Christians flocked – to the great and holy city of Jerusalem, for it was there that Christ had suffered his Crucifixion, where he was buried and from whence he had ascended into heaven. It was also the city where the core Christian community had been formed; it was the same Saint Paul who had been drummed out of Ephesus who came on pilgrimage to Jerusalem to renew his bonds of association with the community of Christ by going up to the city on great feast days. But this nascent form of Christian pilgrimage came to an abrupt end when the Romans sacked the city in AD 70, after which the notion of the 'new Jerusalem' began to develop. For more than two centuries afterwards we have little documentary evidence about pilgrimage to Jerusalem.

Despite a probable revival of pilgrimage during the 3rd century, the most dramatic change came about when the Emperor Constantine declared Christianity to be the state religion of his empire. He was the first to rekindle and encourage Christian enthusiasm for the holy places, and after his mother, Helena, moved to the sacred city in 326, members of the imperial court began to follow in her footsteps. It was not long before bishops, monks and the common people flocked to the city from all over the Orient, to gaze in wonderment at the new churches and other buildings which the emperor had built to decorate the holy places. With Helena's discovery of the True Cross in 326, a new era of pilgrimage to Jerusalem began, and the Cross quickly came to need protection from the thousands who wanted to take a piece of it back home with them.

Pilgrims began to arrive even from the far ends of Europe, and it is indeed from the western travellers of the 5th and 6th centuries that we discover most about Jerusalem and its holy places at the time of the emerging Byzantine empire. Sometimes anonymous authors provide us with descriptions, but women travellers, such as the intrepid Aetheria and Melanie, were also punctilious about recording their experiences of the holy places, and of the items which they saw relating to the life of Christ. Their accounts are valuable too in repeating the stories told by their guides, and were useful to other travellers in giving tips about where to go. From these accounts it becomes clear that, by the 5th and 6th centuries, items other than the Cross which had been associated with Christ had come to be venerated in Jerusalem: the lance which pierced Christ's side, and the chalice into which the sacred blood flowed from the wound in his side. The relics venerated were not confined to Christ alone, and included those of St Stephen, the first martyr, whose death was recounted in the Acts of the Apostles. Nor did the travellers who had come from afar restrict themselves to Jerusalem, for they took the opportunity to visit other places of importance mentioned in the Old and the New Testaments. Bethlehem had already become popular at the time of Constantine, and the cult of the Virgin developed as far away as Ephesus, along with that of John the Baptist.

One particularly popular place had nothing to do with the Bible, however, and, it has been suggested, attracted more pilgrims in its heyday than Jerusalem itself. That was Kala'at Simaan, in what is now Syria. Comparatively little-known in the West nowadays, its church (Fig. 6) became a major centre for pilgrims from East

Fig. 6 At the centre of the great church at Kala'at Simaan in Syria is the stump of the pillar on which Simeon the Stylite sat for thirty years

and West, including Spain, Gaul and Britain, because of one remarkable man who sat upon a pillar there for thirty years – Simeon the Stylite (390-459). He was attracted by the life practised by the ascetics in the Egyptian Thebaid and in other areas of the Near East, and after a short period in a monastery he withdrew to a hill half a day's ride from Antioch. At first he chained himself to the hill as part of his spiritual exercises, but he abandoned this when his bishop told him that his own strength of will should be a sufficient chain for him. Whereupon he set up a pillar on which he sat, but it was not high enough for him, so he finally chose one which was apparently about 60 feet (20 metres) high – of which only the stump remains, since the numerous visitors chipped away at it after his death. People flocked to him from far and near, and he is credited with numerous miracles during his lifetime. Anything which had come in contact with him was much sought after, from the lentils of his half-eaten soup to earth from the site partially mixed with water; even while he was alive these 'relics' of his were more highly prized than those of the martyrs. He was followed by other stylites, but none was as famous as he, and on his death his mortal remains were accompanied by an imperial military escort to Antioch. The people of that city were incensed when, subsequently, the emperor had them translated to the Byzantine capital at Constantinople.

With emperors of the calibre of Constantine and Justinian, this great city on the Bosphorus came to possess a great treasure of relics, as we know only too well from the vast number which were carried away as booty after the participants in the Fourth Crusade had disgracefully sacked its churches in 1204. When Jerusalem was taken by the Persians in 614, and access to the holy places was made much more difficult, the Holy Cross and other relics were brought to Constantinople, which thereby became a more important place of pilgrimage for western travellers who, until then, often visited it only as a stopping-off point on their way to Palestine.

But long before the rise of Constantinople, the West had its own place of pilgrimage in Rome, which contained the graves and relics of Christ's apostolic martyrs, Peter and Paul. The church over the grave of St Peter became too small for the vast flow of devotees, and Constantine built a large five-aisled basilica instead (Fig. 7), which was only replaced in the 16th-17th centuries by the present basilica. Because the streets leading to the tomb of St Paul were too narrow, his remains were removed outside the city walls, where another great basilica, St Paul's-without-the-walls, was built around 384. It survived until destroyed by fire in 1823, though it was rebuilt in the same style shortly afterwards. Particularly on the combined feast day of Saints Peter and Paul, 29 June, the pilgrims flocked to Rome to pray, but often in a festive spirit.

Many of the martyrs who followed Peter and Paul to death were buried in the catacombs, and already in the 2nd century AD pilgrims had access to their tombs, though they were forbidden to remove any of their relics. The most one could do would be to touch them, but many of the pilgrims also scratched their names on the walls seeking the intercession of the martyrs, graffiti which still remain today, though they are now scarcely legible.

As with so many other things, the cult of the martyrs had begun earlier in the East than in the West, but in Rome it had certainly become established to some degree by as early as the mid-3rd century. By 500, Rome outshone Constantinople in having the finest collection of churches in Christendom (despite the havoc wrought by the Germanic tribes when they sacked the city in 410 and again in 453). This led the African, Fulgentius, to exclaim, 'What must the heavenly Jerusalem be like when earthly Rome radiates such brilliance?' It was, apparently, not until the 6th century that Rome began to distribute actual relics, but these were largely only given to visitors of exalted station. The common people brought home with them such items as oil from the lamps that burned so brightly in the churches, poured into small containers. When the Pope gave presents of this oil, he may have used vessels known as ampullae which had contained similar oil brought from the Holy Land but which were refilled with less valuable oil from Roman lamps. Some of these Palestinian ampullae are still preserved at Monza; fragments of others came to light early this century in the church of St Columbanus at Bobbio.

In the 4th and 5th centuries, most of the non-Italian pilgrims who visited Rome would have come from Gaul. Already by the 6th century, Britain was sending pilgrims to the Eternal City, and it would not be surprising if the Irish too followed in their footsteps, though we have no contemporary evidence to prove this.

By the 7th century, Rome's political power was on the wane, and the star of Byzantium was again in the ascendancy, so the numbers going to Rome may have correspondingly decreased. Nevertheless, for the Western world, Rome was to remain the most important centre of European pilgrimage. It was from here that relics were obtained, and it was through pilgrimage that this centre of Christendom was able to keep in contact with the fledgling Christian communities beyond the borders of Italy. There were other Italian places of pilgrimage – Nola in Campania, where St Felix was venerated, and Monte Gargano in Apulia, where the cult of St Michael the Archangel was promoted from the 6th century onwards – but none ever came close to Rome in popularity.

One centre outside Italy did rival Rome in attracting Western pilgrims, and that was Tours, on the Loire. The object of devotion there was St Martin who, though born in Hungary around 316 or 317, became bishop of Tours in 371, a position he retained until his death in 397. He may not have rivalled Simeon the Stylite in asceticism, but he did present a Western parallel to him in that he had been a monk and a hermit, and was a living person who was credited with so many miracles (including the curing of animals) during his lifetime that people flocked to him for help and for his blessing. Apostle of the Franks, he was the first of a number of bishops who were venerated in Gaul, a country which – unlike Rome – had few martyrs to show for its conversion to Christianity. St Martin's fame, and the accounts of the miracles he worked, came through the pen of his admiring biographer Sulpicius Severus, and the miracles which happened after his death at Tours, and at places like Marmoutier where he had also spent some time, were faithfully recorded by his successor as bishop, Gregory of Tours. Many of the later miracles, which took place largely on the feast day of his episcopal ordination (4 July) or of his death (11 November), were cures for various ailments, achieved with the help of dust from his grave and oil from the lamps of his church, both of which were frequently mixed with water and even wine. The relics used in such cures were thus not the actual bones of the Saint but material which had come into contact with them. They also included pieces of cloth which had been laid on his grave, and these as well as the dust mixed with water were obtained by the pilgrims who often visited Tours on their way to Rome and Jerusalem, and brought away by them to their homelands in Gaul, Britain and Spain. Although early Irish visitors to Tours are not reliably recorded, there may have been many for, as James Kenney noted, 'It seems certain that in Ireland there was a peculiar veneration for Martin as a kind of national apostle'. In this context it is interesting to note that the Book of Armagh, an early 9th-century manuscript which contains some of the most important early texts relating to the country's number one national apostle, St Patrick, also preserves one of the most faithful copies of *St Martin's Life* by Sulpicius Severus, in a version which some think may have reached Ireland as early as the 5th century.

St Gregory of Tours was also responsible for the dissemination of another popular French cult, that of St Julian, the martyr of Brioude in the Auvergne, but neither his cult nor that of other Gaulish saints was ever able to rival that of St Martin of Tours.

In Britain, the cult of saints was initiated in the 3rd century with the martyrdom of St Alban, to whose grave St Germanus of Auxerre came in 429 in gratitude for the success of his mission against the Pelagian heretics. The early Anglo-Saxons may have honoured other martyrs from the Roman period, but the evidence is far from secure. Relics certainly came to England in the wake of Augustine of Canterbury's mission, and were kept carefully in churches where special altars were probably built to house them. But the English also had their own saints, whose relics they made a practice of exhuming and enshrining, though leaving the whole

Fig. 7 *The earliest surviving representation, in an 11th-century Farfa manuscript, of the old St Peter's Basilica in Rome* (OPPOSITE), *built in the 4th century and replaced by the present structure consecrated in 1626.*

body entire and unfragmented. Such relics appear to have been used for the aggrandisement of the churches and of the regal families connected with them. But St Cuthbert of Lindisfarne requested that his bones be kept away from the public and be largely available for visitation only by his own community, though pilgrimage to them at Lindisfarne was well promoted in the century after his death, doubtless partially for reasons of territorial enrichment. The relics of Oswald, the martyr-king of Northumbria, seem to have been held in particular regard by the lay population, but that may have been the exception rather than the rule. Most of the literature written about the lives of the early English saints appears to have been largely for ecclesiastical consumption, rather than being designed for kings or laity, at least until the 10th century. Indeed, in England there was apparently little encouragement for the common people to go on pilgrimage in the pre-Viking period, and those recorded as having gone to Rome were mostly either high ecclesiastics or members of royal families.

On their arrival in Rome they probably found that Rome's popularity as a centre of pilgrimage had continued undiminished, but that attitudes were changing towards the relics which pilgrims came to venerate. After the Lombards had besieged the city in 756, Pope Paul I (757-67) felt it necessary to appeal to the martyrs of Rome for assistance, and he started to bring up their relics from the catacombs and distribute them among the various churches in the city. Hitherto, the Roman Church had largely succeeded in keeping the assemblage of each martyr's bones together, and had only distributed 'second relics' (ie. those which had come in contact with saints' bones and graves) to relic-seekers who, by the 8th century, included those who had private collections of considerable size. But now, with the removal of the martyrs' relics from the catacombs, it became increasingly difficult to keep the relics intact, particularly after the Second Council of Nicaea had decreed in 787 that new churches required relics for their altar dedications. Moreover, following Charlemagne's annexation of Lombardy, the increasing number of Carolingian churches north of the Alps created a greater demand for relics as they themselves had none, especially as the Synod of Frankfurt in 794 had ordered that 'no new saints might be venerated or invoked, and only those chosen by authority of their passion or by the merit of their life should be venerated in church.' With much of Europe (with the exception of the north and east) already Christian, the supply of new saints was drying up, and not even the Vikings' monk-slaying incursions on places like Iona in the following century produced any martyrs who would generally be recognised as saints. Relics wherewith to work miracles or to consecrate altars had to be selected from those of martyrs, bishops and Church founders of earlier generations – and so the race was on for the increased supply of older relics.

Rome, that inexhaustible treasure house of relics, proved to be the only place which could keep pace with the demand, and this it did by shamelessly plundering the catacombs for remains, many of doubtful authenticity, which were then sold northwards across the Alps. One of the most notorious perpetrators of such activity was Deusdona, who denuded the catacombs of many dubious relics and brought them in caravan-loads across the Alps in the second quarter of the 9th century, there to sell them to the highest bidder. From him and others, the Carolingian churches of central Europe bought relics by the score in order to increase the stature of their foundations and to encourage pilgrims to visit the relics because of the miracles attributed to them. As Paschasius Radbertus, a 9th-century abbot of Corbie in northern France, remarked at the time:

> *Nor would I say that it is without reason that miracles of saints long asleep in Christ have recently begun to flash forth. Never before have so many and so great things been done at one time by the relics of saints since the beginning of the world, for everywhere saints in this kingdom and those brought here excite each other to song even as cocks at cockcrow.*
>
> [GEARY'S TRANSLATION]

As in England, there is little documentary evidence at this stage for the participation of the peasantry in pilgrimages to those places with sacred relics. But this does not mean that the lower classes did not go on pilgrimage. It was merely that the accounts of these great foundations were written by ecclesiastics who were more interested in bolstering up the importance of their foundations by writing about the saint whose relics they possessed than in giving details about the amount of lay participation in pilgrimage. Miracles were carefully recorded and declaimed publicly, thereby advertising the shrines and attracting more pilgrims – and money – but lay people, often illiterate, never documented their own pilgrimages. It is only from the latter part of the 10th century onwards that we sense a greater literary interest in lay pilgrimage on both sides of the English Channel, coming to the fore because of the cures experienced by the laity with the help of relics.

At the close of the 8th century, but above all in the 9th, the pilgrimages which had grown up to the various shrines in Europe, encouraged by the well-organised Carolingian church, suffered a severe setback as a result of the onslaught of the barbarous peoples on the edges of the empire and Europe. The Magyars established themselves in Hungary, the Arabs raided southern Europe and the Vikings descended in menacing hordes upon the coastlines of northern and western Europe. During the 10th century, Arab penetration as far as the Alps made pilgrimage to Rome such a hazardous undertaking that a monk named Bernard was moved to write that it was safer to travel in the lands of the Caliph of Baghdad than it was to traverse the roads of southern Italy. The horror stories which would have circulated after the numbing speed of the earliest Viking raids around AD 800 in Britain, France and Ireland, must have led the keepers of relics, to which pilgrims had flocked, to remove them out of harm's way. There is a touching parallel in the fate of the relics of St Martin of Tours and St Cuthbert of Lindisfarne at this period: those of St Martin did the rounds of various inland churches before finally being returned to Tours when danger had passed, whereas St Cuthbert's relics were devotedly carried around by members of his community to different locations in Northumbria before finding their present resting place in Durham.

Despite gloom among some people because certain preachers were foretelling that the world would end in the year 1000, things began to look up for those wishing to travel to Jerusalem. The overland route was re-opened at the end of the 10th century, which not only allowed the great and rich to reach their goal, but also enabled the common folk to travel to the Holy Land at a cost they could afford.

The world happily survived the arrival of the new millennium, though the relief turned to lamentation when Jerusalem was overrun by the Caliph Hakim in 1009. But this proved to be only a momentary hiccup, and a new wave of pilgrimage to the holy places started shortly afterwards, particularly from southern France. The easing of long-distance travel encouraged a mass pilgrimage to Jerusalem on what was taken at the time to be the 1000th anniversary of the death of Christ in 1033, though here again the fears of the world ending revived because of the storms and tempests which appeared like the heralds of doom at the beginning of the year.

The dawn of the new millennium brought renewed desires for pilgrimage to holy places in the west of Europe, but the reasons were different, if still somewhat obscure. A new spirit was abroad; there was a growing consciousness among Christians of the burden of their sins, and the need to expiate them by whatever means were available. The Church, and even the lay courts, laid down pilgrimage as a kind of public penance for sins committed, and the impression was created that one could be forgiven one's sins, or at least obtain some remission of the time that the soul would spend in purgatory, by going on pilgrimage to a particular shrine, and preferably to Rome. This notion had already developed in the 9th century, as is witnessed by an Irish penitential of the period which recommended that a parricide should be sent to Rome to receive pardon from the Pope in person, but it did not gain universal acceptance until the 11th century. This was an age of spiritual intensity and religious sensitivity, and the physical hardship provided by pilgrimage gave the participant the feeling that he was really working off his sins, though he could also help to do so by donating alms in appropriate measure.

This spirit was enshrined in the teaching of the great Burgundian abbey of Cluny, whose monks continually stressed the importance of obtaining remission for sins. They crusaded against the luxurious way in which the rich went on pilgrimage, calling forth from Peter the Venerable the remark that 'salvation is achieved by holy lives and not by holy places'. Cluny emphasised the necessity of going on pilgrimage in the proper spirit which, it was felt, gave the truly penitent pilgrim a kind of 'second baptism', an opportunity to renew his life and, as it were, have a second bite at the celestial cherry. The final arbiter on the Last Day would be Christ, whose cult was now in the ascendancy as a judge not terrible but merciful. This humanitarian approach was reflected in the sculpture adorning the many churches influenced by Cluny and its teaching.

> Some three years after the year 1000 there was a sudden rush to rebuild churches all over the world, and above all in Italy and France. Christians everywhere vied with each other to improve them. It was as if the world itself had thrown aside its old rags and put on a shining white robe of churches.   [SUMPTION'S TRANSLATION]

It was Cluny, to which Raoul Glaber, the author of these words, was for a time attached, which brought this post-millennium building fever to new heights through the development of the Romanesque style in church construction. An ideal method of disseminating ideas and architecture in combination was adopted by Cluny in promoting – and projecting to pan-European fame – the pilgrimage to Santiago de Compostela in northwestern Spain. There, in 813, the remains of the

Fig. 8 *This 12th-century carving of* Christ on the road to Emmaus (OPPOSITE) *in the Spanish monastery of Santo Domingo de Silos shows Christ wearing the pilgrim's satchel with the shell, emblem of the pilgrim to Santiago de Compostela*

apostle James (Sant' Iago) had been miraculously 'discovered' in a field of shells having, it was claimed, been miraculously carried to Compostela after his death. We now know that there was a Roman cemetery on the site, but the legend that St James had come to Spain and Christianised its inhabitants was only recorded many centuries after his death. The remarkable discovery in the field of shells provided Santiago with its internationally known 'logo', the immediately recognisable shell worn by those participating in the pilgrimage and shown on the bag carried by Christ the pilgrim in the Emmaus scene so magically carved on the cloister of Santo Domingo de Silos (Fig. 8), close to the pilgrimage road. Indeed, so distinctive is this symbol that a grave recently discovered at Tuam in County Galway could be identified as that of a medieval Irish pilgrim to Santiago through the scallop shell interred with the deceased.

No documentation survives of any pilgrim to the site before 950 and, as the town was destroyed in 997-8, it was not until the 11th century that circumstances were sufficiently propitious for the development of a pilgrimage to what was considered to be the only easily reachable tomb of an apostle outside Rome. In due course, Santiago de Compostela put into the shade the older Spanish pilgrimages to Sta Eulalia in Merida and St Vincent the Deacon in Valencia, and came to rival Rome, becoming the second most popular place of pilgrimage in Europe. The decline of the caliphate in Cordoba, and the increasing strength of King Sancho (970-1035) in leading Spanish recovery against the Infidel, encouraged the proliferation of pilgrims across the roads of northern Spain leading to this new and exciting place of pilgrimage. The movement to promote it was cleverly orchestrated by the monks of Cluny, who had obtained a firm grip on northwestern Spain and brought famous shrines in southern France, such as Vezelay and Moissac, under their control. The way was now open for developing the great pilgrimage road to Santiago, which became, in the words of one commentator, 'one of the busiest in all Christendom'. A great new church was built over the presumed tomb of the saint in the late 11th century, and kings and noblemen were encouraged to construct hospices and bridges, whilst the ecclesiastical authorities built a number of delightful smaller churches in the Romanesque style at suitable stopping places along the road. Various paths, from the English Channel and from the Rhineland, came together in France and then led across the arid country of northern Spain to Santiago. Along the road a number of subsidiary shrines leapt to fame and prosperity, and visits to them – and to Santiago – became one of the main preoccupations of 11th- and 12th-century Europe.

The shrines vied with one another for the available relics. Hitherto unknown specimens such as Christ's foreskin and his umbilical cord began to make their appearance, and the stealing of relics became a common occupation tinged more with glory than with shame. Pilgrimages to the various shrines in France and Spain in the first two centuries after the turn of the millennium established a pattern which was to continue for a further three centuries until the scandal of indulgences brought the practice into such disrepute that it scarcely survived the Reformation.

CHAPTER 2

REASONS FOR GOING ON PILGRIMAGE

T HE ACT OF GOING ON PILGRIMAGE IS COMMON TO MANY RELIGIONS, NOT ONLY Christianity but Islam, Hinduism and Buddhism as well, and one which spans millennia from ancient Egypt to the present day. Nomadic peoples feel no need for it, as they are on the move anyway. It is a phenomenon found only among settled communities, usually those which have a considerable cultural development behind them. Christians know that they can communicate their thoughts to God from a church, or indeed from anywhere. So why go on pilgrimage, and why have so many millions done so through the ages? Why do Christians feel themselves drawn to visit the places where Christ trod during his lifetime, where martyrs underwent a cruel death or even where the Virgin is said to have appeared? There is no one answer; the reasons vary according to place, time, religion – and the individual. But we can be sure that it is not just a desire to experience, and to have visited, places where certain historical/religious events took place, something which modern travel makes so easy, thus denying us the same thrill which the pilgrims of earlier ages must have felt when they reached their distant goal, Jerusalem, Rome or Santiago, after weeks and months of tedious travel by foot or on horseback. It must be more than that, a combination of factors including belief, faith, hope, inquisitiveness and the search for forgiveness or a cure, which has torn people away from their family and friends, from their homes and fields, to venture into the uncertain – and at times the unknown – to make a voyage to some faraway place.

The Jews of antiquity already felt that they could get closer to God by visiting the place of Adam's creation or the tombs of the prophets. The Greeks could come face to face with their pantheon by gazing upon the images of Pallas Athene or Apollo or Asclepius in the temples built to house them. What sparked off the first Christian pilgrimage was the desire felt by St Paul to stand on the same ground the Saviour had trodden, and to be united with the religious community which Christ had founded. The Christian pilgrims who followed in his footsteps wanted to see the place of Christ's entombment and from whence he had ascended into heaven. By the 2nd century, the pilgrims' route began to include other places associated with his life – Bethlehem, Nazareth, Cana and the Mount upon which he had given his sermon. The Holy Land was thus the kernel of Christian pilgrimage, and throughout the Middle Ages and down to our day, it has remained for Christians the most spiritual of all places on earth. There, the pilgrim felt that he or she could come closer to God than anywhere else.

Matthew 9:21 shows how people came to Christ, as on pilgrimage, to touch his gown. But people also wanted to come into contact with exceptional human beings whom they felt could provide help, solace and a cure for ailments. Chapter 4 of the Acts of the Apostles tells how the sick were brought out into the streets and laid on beds and pallets so that St Peter's shadow might fall on them as he passed, and chapter 19 relates how handkerchiefs and aprons which had come into contact with the person of St Paul were carried away to people whose diseases (or devils) thereupon left them. The value of having something which had been touched by a holy person is demonstrated by the case of Simeon the Stylite, to whom multitudes flocked during his lifetime in the hope of receiving even a hair from the animal skin on which he sat, or to seek mundane favours such as rain for their crops. Even if such an idea may seem foreign to many today, one need only think of Padre Pio in Italy or Therese Neumann of Konnersreuth in Germany to see that the same phenomenon is still alive in our own century. As a sidelight to this, one might mention two almost forgotten priestly figures to whom people flocked in the Irish province of Leinster during the early years of the 19th century. Fr Mullins, who served in Clonmore in County Carlow, was renowned for curing the deaf and dumb, the lame and the blind, and the faithful came to take earth from his grave even after his body had been transferred back to his own native heath at Daingean in County Offaly. Fr Moore of Rathbridge in County Kildare, who died in 1826, refused the offer of a parish from his bishop so that he could continue the relief of suffering which he was able to provide through fasting and prayer. The well he blessed in order to provide cures for those who made the pilgrimage to it in good faith was still, in our own century, surrounded by the crutches and walking sticks of those who had been relieved of their ailments at the spot.

The belief in a life after death led Christians by the 3rd century to believe that those mortals who worked miracles during their lifetime would continue to do so after their death. Thus developed the cult of martyrs, which led the holy pilgrims to visit the places where they had wrought their miracles, but more particularly where they had suffered their martyrdoms. At first, pilgrims concentrated on places associated with Christ's own band of workers, such as Peter and Paul in Rome, but it was not long before martyrs' graves in East and West became the haunt of pilgrims.

Relics had no part to play in the earliest Christian pilgrimages. Christ's tomb had none to show for the momentous event of the Resurrection. But with the development of the cult of martyrs, and more particularly with Helena's discovery of the True Cross in a cave beneath the Mount of Golgotha in 326, relics began to be of central importance in the reasons for going on pilgrimage. Through the Middle Ages, visits to relics developed into one of the main pilgrimage activities and held a fundamental place in the fabric of medieval life. Indeed, martyrs' relics came to be of greater significance than their places of burial, as can be seen in the case of Saints Cosmas and Damian. They were buried in Spain, but it was not to there but to Constantinople, where their relics were housed, that pilgrims came to venerate them. St Jerome was one of the first to argue the advantage of relics, pointing out that they were not worshipped in themselves but served as an aid in venerating those martyrs whose lives gave good example to the populace; 'and we honour them in honour of the Lord', as he said. One who disagreed with him was Claudius, the 9th-century bishop of Turin, who denounced all pilgrimages to the relics of saints, and whose destruction of crosses in his diocese, and his generally iconoclastic views, called forth a rebuttal from an Irishman living in Italy, Dungal of Pavia.

The 13th-century *Summa Theologia* of St Thomas Aquinas summarised the views of his contemporaries in favour of relics by arguing that they should be venerated as physical reminders and links with the souls of the saints of whom they formed part, and that by the very fact that they worked miracles God showed that he wished them to be venerated.

For someone from western Europe setting off to somewhere as far away as Jerusalem, pilgrimage was an arduous task not easily undertaken, and subject to many potential perils and constant discomforts. One type of pilgrimage which the Irish came almost to monopolise, though they were by no means the first to practise it, was the ascetic pilgrimage. This involved leaving behind forever one's country, kith and kin, forsaking them in order to go on a lifelong wandering pilgrimage as a self-imposed discipline. Jesus portrayed himself as the eternal wandering pilgrim of the earth, and when he said, 'Foxes have holes, and birds of the air have nests; but the Son of Man has nowhere to lay his head', he was giving the lead to the Irish ascetic monks to go forth from their country in his name, and to combine their journey with a missionary zeal in obedience to Christ's words, 'Go ye therefore and teach all nations, baptising them in the name of the Father, and of the Son, and of the Holy Ghost' (Matthew 28:19). But these were not pilgrims in the usual sense of the word, for they had no goal and did not intend ever returning home.

One who went halfway down this road, thus creating a separate reason for going on pilgrimage, was St Jerome, who forsook the bustling cities of Antioch and Constantinople to draw down the mercy of Christ upon himself in the solitude of the countryside, but then decided to go to Jerusalem, stay there for the rest of his life, and be buried near the entrance to the Church of the Holy Sepulchre. He can be said to have gone on pilgrimage with the intention of remaining at his goal, never to return home. He was followed, though doubtless also preceded, by many who travelled to the Holy Land and the deserts of the Near East to practise a form of asceticism in the footsteps of the great desert hermits, the argument being that to be buried near a saint's grave gave one a greater chance of rising heavenwards on the Last Day, a tradition which is still strong in the Ireland of our own day. In the West, such pilgrims went to Rome to take the monastic habit and be buried near the Prince of the Apostles.

Not far removed from this ascetic spirit was the penitential pilgrimage, which the Irish may have developed as early as the 6th century as one of the punishments for severe transgressions, or simply to bring the body into submission, as expressed in this short Middle Irish poem written around 900 or later:

> *A dear pure pilgrimage,*
> *subduing faults, a body chaste,*
> *a life of poverty lowly and secluded*
> *occur often to my mind.*

The translation is by P. L. Henry, who quotes two further stanzas relevant to the Irish desire for going on pilgrimage:

> *The gift of piety, the gift of pilgrimage,*
> *the gift of repentance for my soul,*
> *O Christ without reproach,*
> *grant them all to me*

and the efficacy of doing so:

> *Three steps designed for all,*
> *the best that any will ever take,*
> *a step to visit the sick,*
> *a pilgrim step, a step to church.*

But not until the 11th or 12th centuries did expiation of one's sin and guilt become the overriding motive for going on pilgrimage throughout many parts of Europe. At this period, the Church did not hesitate to impose rigorous pilgrimages on even the highest in station for crimes committed, as it did on King Henry II after he had murdered Thomas à Becket in Canterbury Cathedral; for him it even became politically opportune to be seen to carry out the ecclesiastical sentence.

There were, of course, other less murky reasons for going on pilgrimage in the medieval period. One was simply to express gratitude for a favour received, or the hope of having a wish granted, like the many barren women who set out in the hope of having issue. Rather more unexpected is what we find in the 9th-century poem *Liadain and Curithir*, an Irish precursor of Heloise and Abelard, where Curithir 'went in a currach upon the sea, and took to strange lands and pilgrimage' to get over a love-affair with Liadain, a lady from the Dingle Peninsula who had taken the veil after she had failed to find him. Perhaps the most straightforward reason was simply to pray, in the belief that prayers would be more effective when uttered at the tomb of some saint or in the presence of his relics. The pilgrim would usually bring some gift or *ex voto* offering to be laid at the point of pilgrimage and, in order to prolong the advantages emanating from the saint's relics, the pilgrim would often bring back home some secondary relic, a cloth, some dust, oil or water which had come into contact with the saint's remains, just as visitors will bring back a bottle of holy water from Lourdes today.

Each pilgrim would probably have been motivated by a number of reasons. But the quest for personal salvation would probably have been paramount, to provide for the comfort and well-being of the soul. In pilgrimage, man expressed his relationship to his maker and to religious activity in general, by combining prayer, sacrifice, devotion and an element of physical discomfort. Whilst the journey itself may have been exhausting, it gave the pilgrim a sense of satisfaction and fulfilment, and the feeling that God speaks to us better in some places than others. It is certainly one of the more unusual, and at times almost inexplicable, expressions of religious life and activity, yet one which has continued to hold its fascination down to our own day, as countless visitors to Lourdes or Knock – and even Mecca – amply demonstrate.

It is unlikely that the Irish pilgrim would have differed greatly from any of his other European counterparts in the motives which inspired him to go on pilgrimage either at home or overseas, even if he would appear to have laid greater emphasis on the penitential aspects. But in the sparse literary sources we have, one poem stands out in giving us access to the pilgrim's mind and his motivations. Giving the thoughts of one who is about to depart overseas on pilgrimage, it has come down to us in a number of versions, attributed to various authors including St Colmcille (521-97) and Cormac Mac Cuilleanain, king-bishop of Cashel, who was killed in battle in 908. In the *Annals of the Kingdom of Ireland*, by the Four Masters, it is ascribed to Celedabhaill, an abbot of Bangor who left Ireland in 926 and died on pilgrimage in Rome the following year, and it is with John O'Donovan's translation of this version that I bring this chapter to a close:

> *Time for me to prepare to pass from the shelter of habitation,*
> *To journey as a pilgrim over the surface of the noble, lively sea.*
> *Time to depart from the snares of the flesh, with all its guilt,*
> *Time now to ruminate how I may find the great son of Mary.*
> *Time to seek virtue, to trample upon the will with sorrow,*
> *Time to reject vices, and to renounce the Demon.*
> *Time to reproach the body, for of its crime it is putrid,*
> *Time to rest after we have reached the place wherein we may shed our tears.*
> *Time to talk of the last day, to separate from familiar faces,*
> *Time to dread the terrors of the tumults of the day of judgment.*
> *Time to defy the clayey body, to reduce it to religious rule,*
> *Time to barter the transitory things for the country of the King of heaven.*
> *Time to defy the ease of the little earthly world of a hundred pleasures,*
> *Time to work at prayer, in adoration of the high King of angels.*
> *But only a part of one year is wanting of my three score,*
> *To remain under holy rule in one place it is time.*
> *Those of my own age are not living, who were given to ardent devotion,*
> *To desist from the course of great folly, in one place it is time.*

CHAPTER 3

IRISH PILGRIMS IN JERUSALEM AND ROME

THE INTERNATIONAL PILGRIMS WHO FLOCKED TO JERUSALEM, ROME AND TOURS during the early centuries of Christianity must certainly have included many Irish people. Among them we know of no women – in the early 8th century the Venerable Bede warned English women not to go to Rome, as too many before them had ended up as prostitutes on the streets of north Italian towns. But even the Irishmen who reached Jerusalem we do not know very much about. Dicuil, the famous Irish geographer who worked at the Carolingian court, mentions having met a presumably Irish monk named Fidelis who had been to Jerusalem before 767, but he tells us only of his wanderings in Egypt – the first recorded Irishman to have described the Pyramids! Almost a century earlier, Adomnan, the ninth abbot of Iona who died in 704, gave us one of the most detailed accounts of the Church of the Holy Sepulchre in Jerusalem, but he derived his knowledge not from personal experience but from a Gallican bishop named Arculf who was shipwrecked on the coast of Britain. When Arculf came to Iona on a visit, Adomnan used the opportunity to note down carefully the details of his itinerary, which also included Alexandria, Constantinople and Sicily. Other Irish pilgrims are scarcely known to us even by name, but in the 11th century we do know of Ua Cinn Fhaelad, King of the Déisi in the southeast of Ireland who, according to the *Annals of Inisfallen*, went to Jerusalem in 1080 – presumably on pilgrimage.

We are better informed about the Irish pilgrims to Rome, though again we cannot always rely on written sources with any confidence, as many of the saints' lives recording pilgrimages to Rome were composed centuries after the alleged events. That said, it may be that the Irish started going to Rome on pilgrimage not long after Christianity had been implanted among them. If the heretic Pelagius was

Fig. 9 *The cross-decorated stone inscribed VII ROMANI* (OPPOSITE) *at Temple Brecán, Inishmore*

indeed an Irishman, he may have been one of the first Irish pilgrims to Rome in the later 4th century. St Ailbhe is said to have gone to Rome, but as the *Life* which tells us this probably dates from no earlier than the 12th century, we cannot place too much reliance on it. An obscure 6th-century saint named Briac is claimed by Kenney to have been the son of an Ulster prince and, as well as having founded a monastery in Brittany, is said to have made a pilgrimage to Rome. Probably slightly later was Dagan, a bishop likely to have been of Irish origin who is described in the *Life* of St Molua of Clonfert-mulloe, as having visited Rome in the reign of Pope Gregory the Great, around AD 600. St Molua himself, who died in 609, expressed the strong desire to go to Rome, according to the same *Life*, which was written many centuries after his death. When his master pointed out how difficult the journey was, Molua is said to have replied, 'If I don't see Rome, I will die immediately.' Die he certainly did, but we may never know if he ever got to Rome. A visit to Rome was made by a delegation from Ireland at around 630 in connection with the controversy over the date of celebrating Easter, but the members of the delegation went to Rome on business, and not as pilgrims in the normal sense.

James F. Kenney, who had an unrivalled knowledge of early Irish ecclesiastical sources, stated:

> In the 9th and 10th centuries the usual route for pilgrims from Ireland to Rome was across Wales and England to the Straits of Dover, through the Low Countries to the Rhine, and then up-river to Switzerland and the passes of the Alps. Liège was a convenient stopping-place on this road.

Kenney quoted letters to a Bishop Franco (854-901) of Liège, in which reference is made to 'a poor Irish pilgrim returning wearied from Rome' and to an old Irish priest who, because of the infirmity of his feet, could not continue the journey to Rome. A further Irish saint on the Continent who is said to have made a pilgrimage to Rome was St Findan (died 878) who, after abduction by the Vikings, escaped from them in Orkney and made his way to the Rheinau on Lake Constance.

Some time later, in 1012, an Irishman named Colman, who was on his way to Jerusalem, was martyred in Stockerau near Vienna because the local population took him to be a government agent. Nevertheless, Colman became one of the patrons of Austria, and is revered at the monastery of Melk on the Danube, where his remains are preserved. The *Life* of another Irish saint on the continent, Marianus of Ratisbon, states that he and two Irish fellow countrymen set out on a pilgrimage to Rome in 1067, but never reached there because they stayed in Bavaria.

By far the richest source for the names of Irish people who went on pilgrimage to Rome is the series of old Irish annals. The list they give does not, however, start until the 10th century:

926–7	*Celedabhaill, abbot of Bangor*
1024	*Fachtna, lector of Clonmacnois, who died in Rome on pilgrimage*
1026	*Mael Ruanaid Ua Máil Doraid, king of Cenél Conaill, who likewise died on pilgrimage in Rome*
1028	*Flannagáin Ua Ceallaigh, lord of Brega, and Sitric, son of Amhlaeibh, and others went to Rome*
1030	*Flaithbheartach Ua Néill ('of the pilgrim's staff')*
1034	*Amhlaeibh, son of Sitric, was slain by the Saxons as he was going to Rome*

1036	Cellach Ua Silbaig, an abbot, died, 'who had made a pilgrimage to Rome'
1038	Cairbre Ua Coimhghilláin, successor of Cainnech, died in Rome
1051	Laidchenn, son of Mailán Ua Leocáin, and his wife went to Rome on pilgrimage, and died on their return
1064	Donnchadh, son of Brian Boru, went to Rome after he had been deposed as king of Munster. He died in the monastery of St Stephen the Martyr (San Stefano Rotondo), where he lies buried
1095	Eógan, head of the Irish monks in Rome, died of the pestilence
1134	Imhar Ua hAedhagáin, who had erected a church in Armagh, died on pilgrimage in Rome.
1175	Conor mac Concoille went to Rome to confer with the Pope, and died there.

Dr Chris Lynn, who assembled this information, has pointed out that pieces of porphyry, an exotic stone usually of Greek origin and much used in imperial Rome, have been found in isolated instances in Armagh, Downpatrick, Movilla (County Down), and Kilteel (County Kildare) as well as in the excavations of the old Viking city of Dublin, and may have been brought from the ruins of ancient Rome by pilgrims to serve as parts of portable altars.

One further interesting sidelight on the journey to and from Rome by Irish pilgrims is that the name Rome came into the Irish language as a common noun *rómh*, meaning a holy burial ground, and the *Life* of St Colman mac Lúacháin tells us that soil from St Peter's tomb and from the graves of other apostles and saints in Rome was brought back to Ireland and spread in Irish graveyards.

The upper echelons in Carolingian society on the Continent lavished favours on the *peregrini*, the wandering Irish monks, and bishops of Liège, Cambrai and Metz are recorded as having given them help. In the mid-9th century, the Irish were dispossessed of their foundations on the Continent; those who usurped the administration of these foundations refused to admit travellers and drove out the monks who had long been living there. As the Council of Meaux put it in 845:

> *The hospices of the Irish, which holy men of that race built in this kingdom and endowed with property bestowed on them because of their sanctity, have been entirely alienated from that service of hospitality: and not only are newcomers not received in those hospices, but even the very men who from infancy have in the same places been serving the Lord in religion are sent forth and compelled to beg from door to door.*[GOUGAUD'S TRANSLATION]

The council of Meaux called for the restoration to the Irish of these hospices, and the Emperor, Charles the Bald, responded willingly to the call to restore these *hospitalia*, which were obviously pilgrims' hostels.

Yet even after this, things were not ideal, for in 858 bishops demanded that the establishments of the Scotti (Irish) should revert to the uses for which they had been intended. From the mid-9th century such hospices multiplied, particularly outside the borders of the Frankish kingdom. In 850, Donatus, bishop of Fiesole, bestowed the church of St Brigid on the city of Piacenza, to which a hospice was attached where two or three pilgrims could be received. In 883, Charles the Fat, one emperor who was a great friend of the Irish, erected a *monasterium Scottorum* on the Viktorsberg in Rhaetia, and two years later he gave money for the upkeep of a hospice at the monastery which would give hospitality to ten or twelve pilgrims. Thus the Irish pilgrims to Rome would appear to have had a network of hostels to which they could repair on their way to and from Rome. In Rome itself there was a small hostel dedicated to the Trinity and intended for the use of the Scotti.

CHAPTER 4

PEREGRINATIO: WANDERING IRISH *PEREGRINI* ON THE CONTINENT

T
HE 9TH-CENTURY GERMAN MONK WALAHFRID STRABO SPOKE OF 'THE IRISH
people with whom *the custom of travelling to foreign lands* has now become
almost second nature.' For the words indicated by italics he used the
Latin *consuetudo peregrinandi*, and the many Irish *peregrini* he must have
seen on the Continent in his day were the successors of many more who had
trodden the same ground in preceding centuries, for the Irish had, by that time,
already been going on *peregrinatio* for two hundred years. The word *peregrinus* was
used in Roman law to describe a stateless person, or one who had lived without any
civil rights in the Roman provinces. In time, it came to refer to a stranger who had
left his own country, and it was in that sense that the word was applied to many
Irish pilgrims in the early centuries of Christianity. The first person we know to
have applied it to himself in Ireland was none other than St Patrick, who had left his
own country, Britain, to come to Ireland to preach the gospel to the heathen Irish.
Others followed in his footsteps some centuries later: the Venerable Bede mentions
Englishmen in the 7th century who came on pilgrimage to Ireland, men such as
Egbert and Wigbert, and also St Willibrord, who later founded the famous
monastery at Echternach in Luxembourg. Another, unnamed, pilgrim from Wales is
recorded in the Annals of Ulster as having come to Munster, in the south of the
country, in 913.

In early historic Ireland, leaving the country could be either a forced or a
voluntary exile. Old Irish law provided for expulsion from one's own territory, but
more particularly expulsion from the country, as an appropriate sentence for the
most heinous crimes, so that the evil committed would not infect the other members

Fig. 10 *In a wood near Ballyvourney, County Cork*
(OPPOSITE), *St Abbán's grave is flanked by three
Ogham stones and accompanied by a bullaun and
modern devotionalia*

of society. According to one 7th-century source, a man who had tried to murder St Patrick was banished by being put into a boat without oars and left to the whim of the waves as to where he might land. The wind, as it happens, brought him to the Isle of Man, where he is said to have become a bishop. Many others in similar circumstances might well have landed up on the many islands around the coast. The Irish penitentials of the 6th and 7th centuries prescribed exile, too, for clerics of the Church who had committed fratricide or incest.

But the *peregrinatio*, the going on pilgrimage, that we have come to associate most with the early Irish Church was a purely voluntary exile. Perhaps the earliest saint whose name is linked with *peregrinatio* is Colmcille, or Columba, though in his case we cannot be sure that a certain amount of pressure may not have been exerted on him to leave Ireland because of his involvement in the battle of Culdreimhne in 561, two years before he left to found that beatific monastery on the Hebridean island of Iona.

Probably the first clear case of an Irishman going on *peregrinatio* was St Columbanus, the person who set the whole Irish pilgrimage movement in train. His biographer Jonas points out that St Columbanus first departed from his family and people in order to take up his cross at the monastery of Bangor in County Down, but that he subsequently practised what Jonas describes as the highest form of asceticism in leaving his native country forever, following the Lord's advice to Abraham in the Book of Genesis (12:1ff.): 'Get thee out of thy country, and from thy kindred, and from thy father's house, unto a land that I will shew thee'. These are the same words which had earlier inspired Saints Paul and Anthony to seek a life of solitude and prayer in the Egyptian desert. Jonas reports that the desire to leave his country burned in St Columbanus like a fire, and that he may have been inspired to leave by a lady ascetic whom he had encountered as a young man. She had told him that she had toiled on *peregrinatio* away from home (but obviously in Ireland) for fifteen years, and that were it not for her sex, she would have sought out a place of more potent *peregrinatio*, that is, much further away and presumably overseas. As we know, Columbanus went to the Continent, where he founded a number of monasteries, including Bobbio in Italy where he died in around 613. In the course of his wanderings, he was encouraged by the Merovingian royalty of Gaul to preach the word of God to some of the people of central Europe who were still pagans.

But, although we often think of Columbanus and those who followed in his footsteps as essentially missionaries, to preach and engage in missionary work were not necessarily the prime aims of those who went on *peregrinatio*; this seems also to have been true of St Columbanus. Their purpose was, much more, to aspire to a place in heaven by practising a solitary life of hardship, poverty and penance, by turning their backs on home and country, and by travelling to another land where they would not be known and where initially they would not even have known the language. Though Columbanus attempted to return home, and was frustrated by contrary winds, his original intention was certainly to stay away forever, because to return home would have meant a diminution in the value of going on *peregrinatio* and, conversely, the further you went, the more effective your journey would be in attaining its celestial goal. Some, such as St Fursey, did return home, but he did so because he had become involved in missionary work; he returned mainly to garner more workers for the apostolic harvest.

The 6th and 7th centuries were the start, but also the high point, of such *peregrinatio*, when the ideal and the practice of the ascetic pilgrimage were one and the same. But during the 8th century, both the Continental and the English attitudes towards these Irish *peregrini* brought about a change, which has been splendidly chronicled by the late Kathleen Hughes in a compact article entitled 'The changing theory and practice of Irish pilgrimage', one of the few works, along with Pochin Mould's *Irish Pilgrimage*, which deals with early Irish pilgrimage. Hughes pointed out that it was, initially, the English who played an important role in changing the Continental attitude to the 8th-century Irish *peregrini* on the Continent. St Boniface, leader of the English mission there, desired valid orders for those bishops serving in his newly organised dioceses, and he seems to have had little use for the wandering Irish bishops, probably doubting the validity of their ordinations. Furthermore, in order to administer their territories efficiently, the Carolingians encouraged the Benedictine rule, which required a stability running counter to the Irish desire to wander freely. As early as the 730s, efforts were being made on the Continent to restrict the activities of the Irish *peregrini*, and these culminated in edicts issued at various councils in 813, the year before Charlemagne's death. The most specific of these in declaiming against the wandering Irish bishops was the Council of Châlon-sur-Saône. Kenney translated Canon 43 of this Council as follows:

> *In some places there are Irishmen who say that they are bishops and ordain many irresponsible persons as priests and deacons without having any authorisation from their lords or the magistrates. The ordination of these men, since it frequently results in the heresy of simony, and is liable to many abuses, we have all unanimously decreed ought to be regarded as null and void.*

But Irish *peregrini* continued in the form, not of wandering bishops, but of pilgrims, particularly to Rome, and with the official encouragement of later councils and of the emperor himself, as discussed in Chapter 3.

It was probably as a reaction to the Continental pressure to abolish the Irish episcopal *peregrini* that the Irish turned towards pilgrimage in their own native land – a change which was to have a great effect on the subsequent development of Irish pilgrimage. Already at the end of the 8th century, the ascetic Maelruain of Tallaght, who died in 792, was discouraging pilgrimage overseas and exhorting people to stay at home. He is reported to have heard the elders saying that 'any one who deserts his country, except to go from east to west, and from north to south, is a denier of Patrick in Heaven and of the Faith in Erin'. The *Life* of the 8th-century Saint Samthann puts into her mouth the words, 'Since God is near to all those who call on him, we have no need to cross the sea. One can reach the kingdom of God from every land,' echoing the words of the Byzantine St John Chrysostom that there was no necessity to go overseas, and that it is better to pray at home. It is in this context that Kathleen Hughes quotes the pithy phrase of a 9th-century poem, 'To go to Rome, much labour, little profit', which itself is somewhat reminiscent of St Jerome's remark that people were not any better because they were in Jerusalem (whither he had gone himself). Nevertheless, such pious sentiments did not prevent Irish abbots and even kings from going on pilgrimage to Rome a century and more later, when the waning Viking terror had once again allowed safer passage by sea.

The Carolingian edicts probably turned the thoughts of the Irish more to pilgrimage at home than overseas, and doubtless reduced drastically the numbers of those Irish monks who left the country to go on an indeterminate wandering and ascetic pilgrimage. That they turned instead to going to the Continent as teachers is shown by the great Irish scholars, including Johannes Scottus Eriugena, who peopled the schools of the Carolingian court. Those Irish who did travel to the Continent henceforward settled for longer periods at already established monasteries, or stayed as normal pilgrims in those hospices set up for their support, which the Carolingians were instrumental in maintaining.

For the 9th-century Irish, the old-style ascetic wandering *peregrinatio* became a thing of the past, something to be dreamed of more than to be realised. An Irish monk of the period penned a brief poem on the margin of his manuscript: 'All alone in my little cell, such a pilgrimage would be dear to my heart.' It was just such anchorites who became the spiritual heirs of the 7th-century *peregrini* and, as we shall see in Chapter 5, in the solitary's fantasy their place was taken by the navigators, who were shortly to be imperilled by the advent of the Vikings. As Kathleen Hughes put it: 'The Irish *gyrovagus* was no longer welcomed: his wanderings had to be concentrated on other seas and stranger lands.'

CHAPTER 5

NAVIGATIO: SEA PILGRIMAGE AND ST BRENDAN

GOING ACROSS THE SEA ON PILGRIMAGE DID NOT ONLY MEAN GOING TO THE Continent, or even just as far as England, as St Comgall of Bangor is said to have done. Another entirely different world of sea-going pilgrimage is associated with the Atlantic west coast of Ireland, largely centred around the *Navigatio Brendani,* the story of the famous voyage of St Brendan the Navigator. St Brendan (Plate I) was born somewhere near Ardfert in County Kerry (Fig. 11) towards the end of the 5th century and died in 577 or 583 at one of his monastic foundations at Annaghdown, County Galway, though he was buried at another of his foundations, at Clonfert in the same county (Fig. 1). It was probably more than 200 years after his death that the great tale of his voyage, the *Navigatio Brendani,* was composed. The earliest known manuscript dates from the 10th century; it is itself a copy, and most scholars would agree that the original probably dates from some time in the previous century, perhaps from the second half. Where the Latin version which we know was first written down is disputed by academics, but Carl Selmer, who edited the definitive edition of the text, believed that it was written on the Continent, perhaps in Lotharingia, or what is now Lorraine in eastern France.

Yet the origins of the tale are clearly Irish, for it continues a tradition of Irish voyage tales of a more or less fabulous character. The earliest of these were the *echtra,* literally 'outing'. In these a Celtic hero such as Conle goes overseas into an island Fairyland, an Elysium where constant happiness reigns and which knows neither age nor death. This island can be traced back to the Promised Land of the Old Testament, or even further to the land of Utnapishtim where Gilgamesh sought eternal youth in the Sumerian epic of the third millennium BC. The island of the Echtraí is thought of as being in the western sea, and thither the hero is lured in a glass boat by a beautiful girl, either never to return or to come back and immediately be turned to ashes – for he has been away for hundreds of years. One of the best-known examples of the genre is *Echtrae* (or *Immram*) *Brain,* in which

Fig. 11 *The Romanesque arcades of a 12th-century church were left in place when a more extensive Gothic Cathedral was built in the 13th century at Ardfert, County Kerry, centre of the cult of St Brendan the Navigator*

Bran son of Febal sets out to visit various islands, one of women, another full of people who laugh constantly; and on the waves he encounters the Celtic sea god Manannán mac Lir. One of the members of his crew conceives the desire to return to Ireland, and they land at a place named Srub Brain. The people who assemble on the shore to find out who had arrived are told that it is Bran, son of Febal. 'We know him not,' they reply, 'but *The Voyage of Bran* is one of our ancient stories.' The man who wanted to return to Ireland goes ashore and is immediately turned to ashes. Thereupon, Bran tells all his adventures to the assembled company, writes his quatrains down in Ogham, and departs, never to be heard of again.

The Voyage of Bran does contain certain Christian elements, and others are found in a further development of the voyage tale known as the *Immram* (literally, 'rowing about'). Its best-known example is the *Immram Curaig Maíle Dúin*, which dates from around the 8th century. It has found for itself a curious niche in English literature because of a rather free rendering of it composed by Alfred, Lord Tennyson. It starts with Maíl Dúin, having unsuccessfully tried to find his father's murderer, setting sail with seventeen companions, allowing their boat to sail wherever God might guide it. He visits a total of thirty-one islands, including the island of Fruit, which Tennyson describes in the following verses, which show perhaps why the poem has remained in comparative obscurity:

And we came to the Isle of Fruits: all round from the cliffs and the capes,
Purple or amber, dangled a hundred fathom of grapes,
And the warm melon lay like a little sun on the tawny sand,
And the fig ran up from the beach and rioted over the land,
And the mountain arose like a jewelled throne through the fragrant air . . .
And the peak of the mountain was apples, the hugest that ever were seen,
And they prest, as they grew, on each other, with hardly a leaflet between.

Another island lay under the sea, according to Tennyson:

and we past
Over that undersea isle, where the water is clearer than air:
Down we looked: what a garden! O bliss, what a Paradise there!
Towers of a happier time, low down in a rainbow deep
Silent palaces, quiet fields of eternal sleep!
And three of the gentlest and best of my people, whate'er I could say,
Plunged head down in the sea, and the Paradise trembled away.

On another island Maíl Dúin encounters a pilgrim who had come out floating on a sod which grew year by year into an island, where he is fed by angels. On yet another, the sailors find an old monk who is the last survivor of fifteen disciples of St Brendan of Birr (who died in 565), who had set out on pilgrimage and landed there, and who is not to be confused with his younger contemporary, Brendan of Ardfert, the subject of the *Navigatio.* Finally Maíl Dúin returns home and, in an anticlimax, finds but spares his father's murderer. Another of the *immram* type of tale is that of Snédgus and Mac Riagla, which tells of two monks from Iona who set out on an ocean pilgrimage. Another (11th-century?) example is *The Voyage of the Uí Chorra,* which contains a quatrain explaining the reason for going on such a voyage:

We went on our pilgrimage
At the blast of the whistling wind
To obtain forgiveness of our sins
There is the cause of asking.

The Uí Chorra had set out in two boat loads, but only one survived, its crew living on the Island of Promise until doom, as the Litany of Pilgrim Saints tells us. This poignant account reminds us that many of those who set out by boat on their *peregrinatio* never returned, having presumably perished at sea. We hear only of those who returned home safely to a hero's welcome, now entered in the pages of legend. Many others doubtless lived alone as hermits on offshore islands, their heroic asceticism going unrecorded because they chose to be solitaries on the wide ocean.

The visitation of islands in the western sea, which is found in both the *echtra* and the *immrama* – the *Voyage of Bran* specifically mentions 'thrice fifty' islands, each of them two or three times the size of Ireland – is also the central theme of the *Navigatio Brendani,* for the main island sought by Brendan is the Promised Land of the Saints. He hears about it initially from a monk named Barrind, whose son Mernóc found an island near Slieve League in County Donegal called the Delightful Island, from whence father and son sailed westwards to the Promised Land of Saints. This was a land full of fruit and precious stones, where a year seemed like a fortnight, where food and drink were unnecessary, and where Christ was light. Barrind's tale arouses more than mere curiosity in Brendan, who decides there and then to set out with fourteen of his brethren in search of this Paradise of God in the wide sea. First, he fasts for forty days and pays a visit to St Enda in Aran. Then he goes to a remote part of the region where his parents live but, avoiding them, sets up his tent on the top of a mountain which extends far out into the ocean, at a place called Brendan's Seat. There he builds a light boat with a wooden frame and ribs, covered with ox-hide smeared with fat and provided with a mast and sail, and presumably a rudder with which to steer. He is then approached by three further brethren of his community who ask to join him as they have decided to go on pilgrimage (*peregrinari*) for the rest of their days – a request which Brendan grants, thus showing that the voyage he is about to undertake is very much in the nature of a *peregrinatio*. All eighteen then set sail 'against the summer solstice'. When the wind drops after fifteen days, Brendan decides to ship all the oars, leave the sail up and let God do the navigating for them. They come to an island with high cliffs and only one landing place with a single opening flanked on either side by cliffs. There follows a succession of islands with individual characteristics, which they visit one by one, staying at each for a while to celebrate the liturgy of important feast days such as Christmas, Good Friday, Holy Saturday, Easter and Pentecost, as well as the feast of St Peter; throughout the seven years of what is described as their pilgrimage, attention is paid each day to saying the divine office at the prescribed hours: matins, lauds, terce, sext, nones, vespers and compline.

For their first Paschal feast at sea, St Brendan and his brethren land, suitably, on an island full of sheep and lambs; Pentecost they spend on a neighbouring island which is, equally symbolically, a Paradise of Birds (the remnants of Lucifer's fall).

In between, they land on a flat island without grass, and set a fire with driftwood. But when the fire begins to burn under their pot, the island begins to shudder beneath them, and they all beat a hasty retreat back to the boat. St Brendan then explains to the brethren that they had lit a fire on the back of a whale; they encounter this whale a year later with the pot remaining exactly where they had left it. On another island they are greeted by eleven brothers with reliquaries (*capsis*), crosses and hymns. They declare that they belong to the community of Ailbe (who is also mentioned in the tale of the Uí Chorra), and that they have been there for eighty years without any sign of ageing, the only sounds they make being uttered in praise of the Lord. They worship in a square church with seven lights and a circle of twenty-four seats (preceding by many centuries the dictates of the Second Vatican Council), and with altars, patens, chalices and cruets all made of crystal.

Brendan and his followers continue their journey, visiting an island with a well whose water puts the brethren to sleep, then voyaging through a 'coagulated sea', safely passing a beast which was killed before it could attack them. The next island has three choirs, and one of the brothers remains on pilgrimage; then follows an island of grapes, a clear sea full of fish that takes eight days to cross, and a crystal pillar covered with a net and containing a window with a chalice and paten. Next comes an island of Smiths, one of whom throws a lump of burning slag at Brendan's boat but misses, so that the slag falls instead into the sea, which immediately begins to boil. There follows a mountainous island of fire, billowing smoke from its peak, followed by another where they encounter the unhappy Judas, whom Brendan saves from the fires of hell for the length of a day. On another sits Paul, the spiritual hermit, who is held up to Brendan's brethren as the ideal ascetic and who, though stated to be from the monastery of Abbot Patrick, bears a strong resemblance to the hermit of the same name in the Egyptian desert. Finally, Brendan reaches the Promised Land of Saints he has sought, and taking as many of its fruits and precious stones with him as he can, he returns home to tell those of his monks who remained behind the details of his wondrous voyage, and dies.

The *Navigatio* is a brilliant piece of imaginative literature, and obviously the product of a monastic environment. Unlike the other adventure and voyage tales, it had the advantage of having been written in Latin, the *lingua franca* of Christian Europe, so that it was accessible to a wide international audience. Throughout the medieval period, it was translated into a number of vernacular languages – English, French, Flemish, Dutch, German, Italian and Norse – and at least 120 different manuscript versions of the tale survive in libraries in various parts of Europe. One can say that it was not only read, it was devoured by a reading public fascinated by its imaginative rendering of an adventure narrated within a religious framework and appealing to the inquisitive through its search for new worlds beyond the boundless ocean. J. F. Kenney rightly described it as 'the epic – shall we say the Odyssey? – of the old Irish Church' and 'the chief single contribution of Ireland to the general literature of medieval Europe'.

It is not surprising that the *Navigatio Brendani* is fabulous, being as it is the culmination and high point of the otherworld and voyage tales of *echtra* and *immrama* type which are anchored in the Celtic Irish tradition of colourful storytelling. Yet it cannot be described as having no foundation in reality, for there are indications that the tale may represent an amalgam of sailors' yarns and lore, cleverly knitted together into a highly elaborate and coherent story. There are too many similarities between the places described in the *Navigatio* and what we now know of the many islands along the north Atlantic face of Europe for the resemblance to be merely fortuitous. It is not without reason that suggestions have been made that the islands of sheep and birds may be the Faroes (or even the St Kilda group in the Outer Hebrides, where a church was dedicated to St Brendan), the island of smiths and the mountain of fire Iceland, and the crystal pillar the iceberg of Greenland. It has even been suggested that the island of grapes could represent the mainland of North America.

Tim Severin, in his epic voyage in 1976-77, showed that it would have been possible for St Brendan to have achieved such a feat as reaching North America in the kind of boat described by the *Navigatio*. The vessel is a variant of the kind used nowadays on the west coast of Ireland and known as a currach, or in County Kerry as a *naomhóg*, a beetle, from its resemblance to that insect when it is being brought upside down to its launching by a team of four men. To guide him in the details of his reconstruction of the boat, which he called the *Brendan*, Tim Severin drew on a representation of what may seem like a currach on a stone pillar of around the 9th century at Kilnaruane, near Bantry (Plate II). This vessel has a set of four oars on each side, like the modern currach, which changed from an ox-hide to a canvas covering in the 19th century. But such a boat would have been too small for St Brendan's full complement of seventeen crew, brethren and himself. Nevertheless, we do know that there were much larger currachs, built on the same principle of a wooden frame of light lathes laid along and across the length of the vessel, and provided with a sail. An illustration of such a wickerwork vessel was drawn by

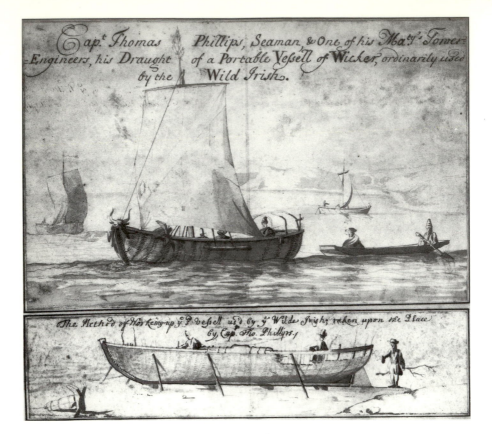

Cap.ᵗ Thomas Phillips, Seaman & One of his Ma.ᵗ.ˢ Tower Engineers, his Draught of a Portable Vessell of Wicker, ordinarily used by the Wild Irish.

The Method of Working up y.ᵉ Vessell used by y.ᵉ Wilde Irish: taken upon the Place by Cap: Tho. Phillips.

Fig. 12 *'Portable vessell of wicker, ordinarily used by the wild Irish' as drawn by Thomas Phillips c.1685, and preserved in the Pepys library in Magdalene College, Cambridge. It is larger than the modern currach, and was powered by sail*

Phillips in 1685, and was fortunately preserved for us by Samuel Pepys who put it in his scrapbook now preserved in Magdalene College, Cambridge (Fig. 12). That the boat must, however, have a history going back long before the time of St Brendan is illustrated by a small model boat made of gold from Broighter, County Derry (Fig. 13), dating from around the 1st century BC and now preserved in the National Museum in Dublin. This has a sail and a total of eighteen oars, significantly the same number as in Maíl Dúin's and Brendan's boats, and Detlev Ellmers has estimated that the full length of the currach-like vessel on which the model was presumably based must have been about 13-14 metres, or about 40 feet.

Another feature which rings true in the *Navigatio* is the account of how St Brendan gives the orders to ship oars and

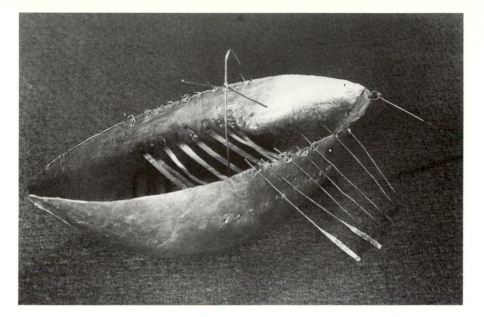

Fig. 13 *Gold boat-model from Broighter, County Derry,*
dating from the 1st century BC, and now preserved in the
National Museum in Dublin. It was modelled on a boat
about 40 feet in length with a crew of 18 men

let the boat be guided by the winds. We find this detail too in Christian pilgrimage literature of the 5th century, in which a lady known as Melanie the Younger lets her boat be guided in a similar manner in the Mediterranean as she sails on her way to Jerusalem – and ends up on the coast of north Africa! And in addition to the tale related above of St Patrick's attempted murderer, whose oarless vessel drifts him to the Isle of Man, the English Chronicle of Alfred the Great tells how three Irishmen landed on the coast of Cornwall in 891 and were brought to King Alfred's court, where they explained that they had left Ireland secretly in a boat without oars because they wished for the love of God to be in exile. *The Voyage of Snédgus and MacRiagla* repeats the same theme when the two monks on their way to Iona say, 'Let us leave our voyage to God, and let us put our oars into the boat.'

The idea of monks setting out to seek a life of solitude on an island in the ocean is even documented in certain Irish historical sources. The earliest of these is the *Life of St Columba* by Adomnan, Columba's ninth successor as abbot of Iona. Adomnan describes how a man named Cormac Ua Liatháin undertook three voyages in an unsuccessful search for an earthly solitude on the ocean. In one, he set off from Erris in County Mayo but failed because he was accompanied by a monk who had not obtained permission from his abbot to travel. His second attempt brought him after some months to the Orkney Islands. On his third and most frightening attempt, a southerly wind drove him northwards bringing him 'beyond the bounds of human discovery and endurance', where return seemed impossible. There he was attacked by strange stinging creatures as large as frogs, which most would identify as large jellyfish such as the Portuguese man-of-war, but which T. C. Lethbridge suggested were Greenland mosquitoes. Through the prayers of St Columba, however, Cormac Ua Liatháin was enabled to return safely to Iona. If Adomnan is to be believed, this voyage must have taken place before St Columba's death in 597, and therefore some time during the 6th century. Some, indeed, have seen Adomnan's account, and the story it tells, as the initial stage of development of the *immrama* tales and ultimately of the *Navigatio Brendani*. Adomnan, incidentally, also mentions another, comparable case of a Briton named Baithín who also unsuccessfully sought solitude on the ocean, and returned thereafter to a life in the monastery.

The other important historical source is the Irish geographer Dicuil, who worked at the Carolingian court on the Continent, and who wrote a treatise entitled *Liber de mensura orbis terrae* in around 825. In it he describes certain islands to the north of Scotland, generally identified as the Faroes, where there was so little darkness at the time of the summer solstice that it was possible for a man to pick lice from his shirt in the middle of the night. More important for us, he tells of Irish solitaries who had lived on these islands during the previous hundred years, but who had had to abandon them because of the rapacious northern Vikings. He also mentions religious men who in 795 lived in what he calls Thile, which has frequently been identified as Iceland, though Professor Gordon Donaldson, the Historiographer Royal of Scotland, suggested recently that the island of Foula might fit his description better.

Almost exactly three hundred years after Dicuil's treatise, the Icelandic historian Are Thorgilsson wrote his *Islendingabók*, in which he refers to *papar* (Irish Christian monks) having lived in Iceland, but who left because they did not want to remain there any longer with heathens (Vikings); as they wanted it to be known that they were Irishmen, they left behind them Irish books and bells and croziers. Some Icelandic place-names still retain elements of the word *papar*, including Papey, the island of *papar*, on the east coast of Iceland. There, between 1967 and 1981, the late President of Iceland, Kristján Eldjárn, conducted archaeological excavations at a number of sites including Írskuholar ('Irish knolls') and Papataettur ('Papa-ruins'), in the hope of discovering some physical remains of the *papar*. Sadly, the features he uncovered seemed to have had nothing to do with Irish monks on the island. Given the simple lifestyle of the hermit, it is perhaps not surprising that his quest remained fruitless. As Eldjárn pointed out, the same name is found in place-names such as Papa Westray in Orkney and Papil on Burra in Shetland. We can see, therefore, that the historical sources show that Irish hermits were undertaking voyages of *peregrinatio* in search of solitude to places as far away as the Orkney Islands in the 6th century, the Faroes in the 8th and Iceland in the 9th.

Even if St Brendan may not have reached all the islands recognisable in the *Navigatio*, which was written more than two centuries after his death, we know that he had a reputation as a voyager in his day. One independent source, Adomnan's *Life of St Columba*, written only a century after Brendan's death, tells us that he visited St Columba on Iona; one of the many lives of Brendan recalls another voyage, probably to Wales, where he met Gildas. The undatable *Life of St Fintan* or

Fig. 14 *Was St Brendan ever lured by such a vain mermaid with comb and mirror* (OPPOSITE), *carved in the 15th-century Cathedral marking his burial place?*

Munnu mentions a settlement of Brendan in the Land of Promise, but this is probably a reflection of one of the Lives of St Brendan dating from some centuries after his death.

Of the numerous Lives of St Brendan – of which there are many versions of various dates – one, known as the First *Life*, is uncontaminated by the content of the *Navigatio* and was written independently of it, and very probably earlier. Certain of its details correspond to, and may well be contemporary with, the Litany of Pilgrim Saints, written probably in the monastery of Lismore in County Waterford, and normally ascribed to the period around 800, though Sarah Sanderlin has argued for a date closer to 900. This First *Life* differs from the *Navigatio* in certain important respects, particularly in the details of the saint's youth and the preparations for his voyage. He was, it appears, baptised with the name Mobhi, but a white mist which appeared at the same time mysteriously ensured that he was thenceforth called by the name which had made him internationally famous: Brénainn or Brendan. Furthermore, there are important differences in relation to a mountain somewhere near where his parents lived in County Kerry. The First *Life* says that having left his parents, he went to a mountain of his province from which he saw a beautiful island, which he thereupon decided to find. The *Navigatio* says that, avoiding his parents, he set up his tent at a place called Brendan's Seat on the summit of a mountain that extends far out into the sea, where his brethren built their boat. Another *Life* gives the name of the mountain as *Aitche*, but this cannot otherwise be identified, while the *Life* of the saint preserved in the Book of Lismore says that he built his boat in Connacht.

The importance of this divergence in the various versions is that there would appear to be no old and strong tradition as to where the mountain was, what St Brendan did there and where he built his boat. The First *Life*, which is likely to be marginally earlier than the *Navigatio*, gives few details of the mountain, and it is only the *Navigatio* which gives sufficient detail to permit a conclusion that it could be identified with Mount Brandon on the Dingle Peninsula, and which adds the note about St Brendan's Seat on the top of the mountain. Given that none of the sources mentioning the mountain is likely to be earlier than 800, well over two hundred years after St Brendan's death, it may be relevant to note for the discussion below (pages 80-2) that there is nothing written earlier than 800 to associate St Brendan with the Dingle Peninsula. Saints' Lives in the medieval period were rarely designed to give facts or dates; instead, they wished to impress upon the reader the sanctity of their subject and his facility to perform supernatural miracles. There may have been many purposes in writing such Lives; most were written to promote the cult of the saint, and the motives of power and material gain were never too far away. With the writing of the First *Life* of St Brendan, we get the strong impression that here was some excellent propaganda developed to promote the cult of the saint which, as we know from church dedications of uncertain date, ranged from Brittany to Wales and Scotland, and even as far north as the Faroes. Kenney has argued that it was the Ciarraige, the people of Kerry (including St Brendan's own population group, the Altraige), and other peoples of the west of Ireland who were responsible for spreading St Brendan's cult outside Ireland. He believed that the First *Life* only contained the saint's voyage to Britain, and that the fabulous island voyages were inserted. Its presentation of an island in the ocean whither Brendan might withdraw on pilgrimage Kenney saw as being linked up with the impulse to voluntary exile.

Its insistence that Brendan should not remain on the island, but return home to teach the way of life to the Irish, was a version adopted by the religious community associated with St Brendan 'to promote both the fame of their patron and the authority of his monastic rule'. In contrast, he believed, the *Navigatio* was not written from the point of view of Brendan's own community, having a tone more cosmopolitan than any other Irish hagiographical document.

The only island mentioned by name in the Brendan sources which we can clearly identify is the Aran island of Inishmore, where St Brendan visited St Enda. One might be justified in asking whether the first island the saint visits on the actual voyage, the one with only one entrance having tall and steep sides where Brendan and his companions find an uninhabited *oppidum*, could possibly be identified with the island of Inishmurray (see pages 99-105) off the Sligo coast, which has only one landing place and a large stone-walled oval enclosure, which may have been temporarily abandoned after the Viking attack of 807. On the opposite side of Donegal Bay is Slieve League (see page 71), near which was the island (Rathlin O Birne?) which was sought out for life as a solitary by Mernóc, son of Barrind, from whom Brendan first learned of the Island of Saints. This mountain also features in the story of St Munnu of Taghmon, who was told that if he ever experienced an unbearable trial or temptation, he should go to Slieve League in Tír Bogaine in south Donegal and there embark upon his voyage. Inishglora, an island off the Mullet Peninsula in County Mayo, has a settlement associated with the name of St Brendan, where a beehive hut was popularly called St Brendan's house; it is interesting to note that it was from the same area that Cormac Ua Liatháin set off on the first of his three voyages in search of an island solitude.

Inishglora is the most northerly of a number of islands situated off the west coast of Connacht where we may presume that hermits sought a life of solitude from as early as the 6th century onwards. It would not be surprising if these hermits were sought out during their lifetime, like Simeon the Stylite in Kala'at Simaan, or that their graves became hallowed with time and were visited by pilgrims, as St MacDara's Island off the south coast of Connemara is today (see pages 96-9). These and other islands along the western and northern seaboard of Ireland present ideal stopping-off points for an undocumented but likely maritime pilgrimage along these coasts, and beyond them to the islands of Scotland, of which the *Navigatio* would seem to be a literary reflection. Support for the existence of such a maritime pilgrimage comes from both the Dingle Peninsula (see pages 71-86) and Glencolmcille (see pages 105-110), whose importance as places of pilgrimage really only makes sense when it is presumed that pilgrims approached both of them from the sea rather than the land. The fact that the tradition of visiting Atlantic islands in a Christian context of *peregrinatio* coalesced not around Cormac Ua Liatháin, who is the first recorded example, but around St Brendan, could suggest that such a maritime pilgrimage may have been associated with the cult of St Brendan, who was known as a sailor.

But he may not have been the first or only one whose name could have been associated with a maritime pilgrimage. Heinrich Zimmer expressed the opinion that the story of the Brendan Voyage was originally attached to St Brendan's older namesake, Brendan of Birr, who died in 565, and it is interesting to note therefore that the account of *The Voyage of Maíle Dúin*, which may have influenced the *Navigatio*, describes a monk of the community of Brendan of Birr who had gone on pilgrimage into the ocean and came to an island. The *Navigatio* also mentions that its Brendan came upon pilgrims from the community of Ailbe, and taking this in conjunction with the pilgrimage of Glencolmcille, which makes most sense when understood in relation to the sea, and the dedication to St Colmcille (Columba) of a church on the island of Inishkea North close to Inishglora, we may suppose that the names of Ailbe and Colmcille may also have been associated with maritime pilgrimage along the western and northern coasts of Ireland.

The Brendan who is noted in the Litany of Pilgrim Saints, dating probably from around 800, as going out with 150 men to seek the Land of Promise is almost certainly to be identified with the Kerry St Brendan, as this account corresponds in detail with the First *Life* of St Brendan. The same is probably also true of the *egresso* of the *familia* (or community) of Brendan mentioned in the early 10th-century *Martyrology of Tallaght*. The spread of the cult of St Brendan and the pilgrimage probably associated with it, as implied by his inclusion in the Litany of Pilgrim Saints of around 800, fits in well with Kathleen Hughes's belief discussed above that in the middle of the 8th century there was a turning away from *peregrinatio* to the Continent in favour of a pilgrimage within Ireland. Such a movement would help to explain the emergence of a Litany of Pilgrim Saints around 800; the sudden rise in interest in the voyages of St Brendan and others could support the notion that pilgrimage within Ireland could have included pilgrimages not only to islands like Inishglora associated with St Brendan but also to other islands off the west and north coasts of Ireland that housed the remains and the relics of those solitary hermits who had practised the ascetic way of life on them from the 6th century onwards.

The maritime pilgrimage proposed here would only just have been getting into its stride when the Vikings made their appearance on the west coast of Ireland, their first recorded raid there being on the island of Inishmurray in 807. Their arrival heralded the end of what E. G. Bowen aptly named the 'Celtic thalassocracy' of the west coast of Europe that had prevailed since Roman times, yet the Vikings may only have succeeded in dampening but not destroying the determination of the Irish to go on pilgrimage to islands off the country's western coastline. This is, perhaps, the message to be learned from an interesting passage about boat-building in the First *Life* of St Brendan. It tells how the saint sets out on a first voyage in three skin-covered currachs with thirty men in each, and not the single currach with his seventeen companions described in the *Navigatio*. This first voyage is not a success, and St Brendan subsequently returns to St Ita, of Killeedy in County Limerick, who fostered him as a child. She tells him that he failed because he had ventured forth in a boat made from the hides of dead animals, and she recommends to him instead that he should build a wooden boat for his next voyage, which he does. This account could suggest that the Irish quickly came to realise the superiority of the wooden sailing craft of the Vikings, and that the only way to counter like with like was to abandon their large skin-covered currachs in favour of wooden vessels. It could also be taken to imply that the First *Life* of St Brendan may not have been written until after the first descent of the Vikings upon the west coast of Ireland in the first decade of the 9th century.

PART TWO

PILGRIMAGE PLACES

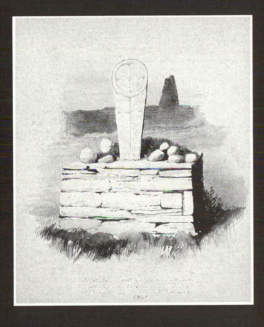

Fig. 15 Altóir Beg ('the small altar') inside the
Caiseal *on Inishmurray, County Sligo, as sketched
by W. F. Wakeman in 1890*

Chapter 6

Early references to places of pilgrimage in Ireland

I T IS NOW TIME TO TURN TO WHAT IS THE CENTRAL THEME OF THIS VOLUME, EARLY
pilgrimage sites within Ireland, including the islands off the west coast. The
importance of this internal Irish pilgrimage has almost certainly been
underestimated by scholars, with honourable exceptions such as Daphne
Pochin Mould and Kathleen Hughes, doubtless because information about it in
early literary sources is sparse and sporadic when compared to the richer and more
coherent material available on the monastic life of Early Christian Ireland, with
which it is connected. So meagre is our information in most cases that we know
little more than the names of places known to have been the goal of a pilgrim.

Lough Derg in County Donegal, Croagh Patrick, Monaincha and Glendalough
were given as the four chief places of pilgrimage in Ireland in the Third Irish *Life of
St Kevin*, which was assuredly written long before the oldest surviving manuscript
version dating from the 18th century. Our main source of information about early
pilgrims in Ireland is, however, provided by the entries in the early Irish annals
which mention where a pilgrim died, thus giving us a likely indication of at least
some of the places of pilgrimage during the Early Christian period. The earliest
recorded place of pilgrimage in the country is Clonmacnois, County Offaly, where
according to the *Annals of the Four Masters* (AFM) a pilgrim died in the year 606.
Pilgrims to the site are mentioned in the local *Annals of Clonmacnoise* under the years
617, 754 and 832, while the *Annals of Tigernach* (ATig.) contribute one more for the
year 722. The *Annals of the Four Masters* list a further instance in 834, after which
there is a long gap before the same Annals relate the death of another pilgrim there
in 1100 and another in 1118. The *Annals of Tigernach* mention yet another around the

Fig. 16 *The texture of granite weaves a spell* (OPPOSITE)
at Reefert Church in Glendalough

year 1167. Remarkably, the Annals do not associate any other site with pilgrimage before the middle of the 10th century, when *The Annals of the Four Masters* record the death of a pilgrim at Glendalough (in 951), adding further examples for the years 1030 and 1122. The Annals do not feature Armagh as a place for pilgrims before 976, when it is mentioned in *The Annals of the Four Masters*, which add further instances under the year 1004, 1012 and 1151. The *Annals of Ulster* (AU) record the death of other pilgrims at Armagh in 989, 1004, 1043, 1063, 1073 and 1103, while the *Annals of Inisfallen* (AI) list another example in 1029. The following sites are first mentioned in the 11th century as places where pilgrims died: Cork in 1025 and 1028 (AI), Clonfert in 1026 (AI) and Clonard in 1052, 1070 (both AFM) and 1092 (AI), as well as 1185 (AFM). The list of sites is further extended in the 12th century as follows: Aghaboe in 1100 (AFM); Derry in 1122, 1173 and 1188 (all AU); Lismore in 1123 (AU), 1126 (AI, which may possibly include another instance in 1116) and 1136 (*Annals of Loch Cé*); Monaincha in 1138 (AFM); Killaloe in 1142 (ATig.), 1159 (AFM) and 1165 (ATig.); Cong in 1150 (AFM), 1168 (AU) and 1183; Tuam in 1170 (AFM); Drogheda – meaning probably Mellifont – in 1186 (AU) and finally, Inchcleraun in Lough Ree, which is mentioned twice in the *Annals of Loch Cé* under the year 1193.

In addition to these early annalistic references to places where pilgrims died, one further source for places of pilgrimage may be mentioned, even if it is outside the period generally being considered in this book. This is the Register of Primate Dowdall of Armagh, which lists the following (not all satisfactorily identifiable) places which one Heneas MacNichaill was told to visit to atone for having strangled his son in around 1543: Glendalough, Ross, the Skellig, Aran of the Saints, Crock Brandain (i.e. Mount Brandon) in Kerry, Killaloe, Croagh Patrick, Lough Derg, Inis Gorain at Gort, Cornancreigh in the land of MacSwine, Tyrebane in the land of O Donnell, Holy Cross, the Rock of Cashel, Downpatrick, Saul and Struell.

To this can be added the list of places of popular devotion to which Pope Paul V granted concessions of indulgences in around 1607 on certain specified days of the year: Monaincha (on St Michael's Day and Palm Sunday); Fore (Corpus Christi and the Annunciation); Inishcealtra (second quadragesima Sunday); the Skellig; Aran; Croagh Patrick; Modreeny near Birr (Seir Kieran?); Clane; Armagh; Clonmel, and Our Lady's Island in Wexford.

Returning to the annalistic entries given above concerning pilgrims who died at places listed prior to 1200, it is not surprising that the annals record almost exclusively only kings – and the male and female members of their families – together with higher ecclesiastics as going on pilgrimage. References to pilgrimage in Irish monastic rules and penitentials would suggest that many of the more humble monks would also have gone on pilgrimage, voluntarily or otherwise. But it would be reasonable to assume that pilgrim numbers would have been considerably swelled by the lay population who would not have been important enough to earn a mention in historical sources. It is, of course, idle to speculate on how many places of pilgrimage in early Ireland went unrecorded in the annals simply because no one of particular note happened to have died there.

The reduction in annalistic references to the deaths of pilgrims during the 9th century, when compared to the marginally larger numbers recorded for the previous two centuries, need not be taken as evidence for the failure of the movement to retain pilgrims in Ireland noted by Kathleen Hughes. It is more likely to be a reflection of the likely effect the Viking invasions had on pilgrimage traffic, for there is a noticeable absence of references to the deaths of pilgrims between 834 and 951. It is only after the middle of the 10th century that Irish pilgrimage traffic takes up again, to reach even greater heights than ever before in the 11th and 12th centuries, as shown by the annalistic entries, which mirror a similar tendency in Continental Europe.

Other than the rather bald notification of the death of a pilgrim at a particular spot, the old Irish annals do occasionally mention the particular type of self-mortification practised by the pilgrim. One such rare instance is the case of an abbot of Louth who, according to the *Annals of Tigernach*, died on pilgrimage at Clonmacnois in around 757 after having lived there for a year on the water from St Finghin's Well. Among other aspects of self-mortification involved in pilgrimage, we should probably also include the physical hardship of travelling long distances to reach one's goal, particularly to offshore islands such as the Skellig or Aran Islands visited by Heneas MacNichaill in the 1540s. Almost equally arduous were the climbs to the peak of Mount Brandon or Croagh Patrick.

If pilgrimage in early Ireland was not as easy or as comfortable as it is made today, it was not of short duration either. Whilst not everyone went on pilgrimage for the remainder of their earthly existence, as Celedabhaill, abbot of Bangor, did, some spent many years on their pious peregrinations, as exemplified by entries in the *Annals of the Four Masters* for the years 704 and 987, which tell us of two separate instances of people dying after having spent twelve years on pilgrimage.

Though the annalistic entries mentioning pilgrimage are generally very short, they provide us with a valuable, and indeed the only, list of pilgrimage sites for the pre-Norman period in Ireland, whilst the penitential tour undertaken by Heneas MacNichaill in 1543, and the papal indulgences granted to various sites around 1607, add additional examples. In the order of their appearance in the historical record, they may be tabulated as follows:

SOURCE	YEAR	PLACE
Annals	606	*Clonmacnois, County Offaly*
	951	*Glendalough, County Wicklow*
	976	*Armagh*
	1025	*Cork*
	1026	*Clonfert, County Galway*
	1052	*Clonard, County Meath*
	1100	*Aghaboe, County Laois*
	1113	*Croagh Patrick, County Mayo*
	1122	*Derry*
	1123	*Lismore, County Waterford*
	1138	*Monaincha, County Tipperary*
	1142	*Killaloe, County Clare*
Henry of Saltrey	*c.1147-51*	*Lough Derg, County Donegal*
Annals	1150	*Cong, County Mayo*
	1170	*Tuam, County Galway*
	1186	*Drogheda/Mellifont, County Louth*
	1193	*Inchcleraun, Lough Ree, County Longford*
Heneas MacNichaill	1543	*Ross, County Cork*
	1543	*Skellig Michael, County Kerry*
	1543	*Aran of the Saints*
	1543	*Mount Brandon*

SOURCE	YEAR	PLACE
	1543	*Inis Gorain near Gort (Kilmacduagh, County Galway?)*
	1543	*Cornancreigh in the land of MacSwine (Glencolmcille, County Donegal?)*
	1543	*Tyrebane in the land of O Donnell (Slieve League, County Donegal?)*
	1543	*Holy Cross, County Tipperary*
	1543	*Downpatrick, County Down*
	1543	*Saul, County Down*
	1543	*Struell, County Down*
Pope Paul V	*c.1607*	*Fore, County Westmeath*
papal indulgence	*c.1607*	*Inishcealtra, County Clare*
	c.1607	*Modreeny, near Birr (Seir Kieran, County Offaly?)*
	c.1607	*Clane, County Kildare*
	c.1607	*Clonmel, County Tipperary*
	c.1607	*Our Lady's Island, County Wexford*

Obviously the first historical mention of a place is in no way the date of commencement of the pilgrimage, which in many cases is likely to have been many centuries older. Furthermore, as this book essentially confines itself to the period up to 1200, places are probably missing from this list that are in later medieval historical sources, which I have been unable to comb through in detail.

Some of the early sites, such as Clonard, have left scarcely a stone upon a stone dating from the pre-Norman period. Others, such as Armagh, Derry, Cork, Lismore and Tuam, have become towns and cities which have only small fragments of stonework surviving from the period before the arrival of the Normans. Others have retained considerable traces, and it is worthwhile looking at a selection of these in some detail to examine their present state and the features they have in common in order to speculate on what their relevance may have been to pilgrimage traffic. It must be kept in mind, however, that many of these sites – with obvious exceptions such as Croagh Patrick or Mount Brandon – were also early Irish monasteries, which would have been actively promoting pilgrimage to their particular sites.

CHAPTER 7

ST PATRICK'S PILGRIMAGES

LOUGH DERG, DONEGAL

Loch Dearg aonRóimh na hEireann
mar fuair sinn sa seinléigheann
Sreabh ó nach soibherte geall
Dár lean oilithre Eireann

Ar uaimh Phádraig léaghthar linn
don neach nigheas a inntinn
nach fuil teagh aithrighe as fhearr
aithnighe a chean ní chaitheann.

Loch Dearg, Ireland's chief shrine and ever called
Eire's Pilgrimage, is a lake which none other can
rival: so I find in the old lore.

Of Patrick's Cave I read that, for one who would
cleanse his soul, no better penance-cell exists;
it ceases not to wash away his sins.
[*Tuileagna O Maol-chonaire, early 16th-century Irish poet –*
TRANSLATION BY SIR SHANE LESLIE]

Every summer without fail sees the recurrence of two of the best-known Irish pilgrimages, which are associated with the country's national apostle: those to Croagh Patrick mountain in Mayo and to Lough Derg in Donegal. Both can be traced back historically until they get lost in the uncertain mists of time, and both are among the few surviving examples in Europe which give the present-day participant some idea of the true rigours experienced in going on pilgrimage in medieval times.

Of the two, the pilgrimage to St Patrick's Purgatory in Lough Derg was the only one internationally documented, and consequently the only one known outside Ireland, during the later Middle Ages. Indeed, at the time, Ireland was probably best known throughout Europe for the visions said to have been experienced there, tales of which spread quickly across many frontiers, not only by word of mouth but also through the medium of manuscript accounts, many written in a Latin understandable to most literate people throughout Christendom, others translated into European vernacular languages. In the words of Shane Leslie, who in 1932 assiduously collected all the earlier accounts of the pilgrimage:

> *St Patrick's Purgatory was the mediaeval rumour which terrified travellers, awed the greatest criminals, attracted the boldest of knight-errantry, puzzled the theologian, englamoured Ireland, haunted Europe, influenced the current views and doctrines of Purgatory, and not least inspired Dante.*

To explain how all this came about, we must go back roughly to the year 1184, and to an English Cistercian monk in the Huntingdonshire abbey of Saltrey, in the diocese of Lincoln. We know him merely through his initial H., but he is generally known as Henry of Saltrey. He was engaged in writing down diligently what he had heard from Gilbert, another Cistercian monk, who was formerly abbot of Basingwerk in North Wales, and who had been sent to Ireland some thirty-five to thirty-seven years earlier to found a new house of the order there, probably at Baltinglass in County Wicklow. But Gilbert had been faced with a problem: he did not know the language of the country, for Welsh and Irish were then, as now, quite distinct languages. In his plight he turned for assistance to a king, probably the Norman English king Stephen, who placed at his disposal the best interpreter he had, a young Irish knight who may have been called Eoghan, or John, but whom we know by the Welsh form of his name, Owein. Owein had served in Stephen's armed forces for some considerable time, and fulfilling the king's request to act as interpreter, he accompanied Gilbert to Ireland and stayed with him there for two and a half years. In the course of the numerous conversations they doubtless had during that time, Gilbert heard how Owein had committed some heinous crime, in remorse for which he had decided to undertake a pilgrimage to Lough Derg – probably in the 1140s – after which he joined the Crusades and went to Jerusalem, before returning to Ireland where he presumably spent the rest of his life as an exemplary Christian. What fascinated Gilbert above all was what Owein related about his pilgrimage to Lough Derg, and it was this account that Henry of Saltrey recorded in such detail for posterity, and which Yolande de Pontfarcy has recently translated into English.

Keeping us in suspense before relating Owein's experiences, Henry ruminates on what happens to the soul after death, and tells us how St Patrick's Purgatory came to get its name. St Patrick, he reports, was having difficulty in convincing the pagan Irish of the 5th century of the truth of his teaching about heaven and hell; they were not prepared to believe him unless one of them had experienced it themselves. To assist Patrick in his mission, Christ appeared to him and gave him a text of the Gospels and a staff (which – as the *Bachall Íosa*, Christ's staff – became one of the validating insignia of the Archbishops of Armagh until it was ignominiously burned by the Protestant Reformers in Dublin in 1538). Christ showed Patrick a dark pit in a deserted place and told him that whoever would enter the pit for a day and a night would be purged of his sins for the rest of his life. In the course of those twenty-four hours, he would experience both the torments of the wicked and the delights of the blessed. St Patrick immediately had a church built, which he handed over to the Augustinian canons (who did not come to Ireland until the 12th century), locked the entrance to the pit and entrusted the key to the canons, so that no one would enter rashly without permission. Already during the lifetime of St Patrick, according to Henry, a number of Irish entered the pit and were converted as a result of what they had seen. Thus the pit got the name of St Patrick's Purgatory.

Henry of Saltrey continues by setting out the condition specified by St Patrick that no one should enter the Purgatory without first getting permission from the bishop, who should do everything in his power to prevent the pilgrim from proceeding with his arduous undertaking. But should he persist, the pilgrim would be provided with letters for the Prior of the Purgatory, who would exhort him once more to desist, with the request that he consider the numbers of those who had gone on pilgrimage to the pit and never returned. Having received Holy Communion and been sprinkled with holy water, the pilgrim would then be led by the Prior to the entrance to the pit. The Prior would lock the door behind him, leaving him there for a full twenty-four hours. If he returned at the end of a day, he was to be welcomed by the Prior and community, and remain in the church for a further fifteen days. If he did not return, he would be presumed dead, whereupon the Prior would lock the door behind him and go away.

Having followed the procedures laid down by St Patrick, Owein duly entered the Cave; Henry of Saltrey gives us details of all the horrible torments which the knight himself experienced, and which he saw befall others. He was thrown into a pit of fire by ugly demons who sound like the inspiration for those painted by Hieronymus Bosch and others in the 15th century, and whom Owein saw nailing wicked souls to the ground by red-hot nails, or gnawing at their vitals. He also saw agonised beings immersed in molten metal, or freezing in icy water, while he himself was dragged unsuccessfully by the devils into a pit and a river beneath which, they said, was the entrance to hell. But, *mirabile dictu*, knight Owein was able to extricate himself from all of these perils by uttering in each case the name of Jesus, whereupon the devils retreated in powerless confusion and disarray.

As a reward for his courage, Owein was also shown the joys of that earthly Paradise from which Adam and Eve had been banned. It was full of flowers and perfume, and he was given heavenly food to eat there before returning the way he came to the mouth of the Cave, where he was greeted by the rejoicing canons. As told by Henry of Saltrey, Owein's is a gripping and chilling tale, which was read as far away as Italy, where it may have inspired Giotto's painting and Dante's *Inferno*. It was, in all likelihood, probably also the ultimate source for some of the details of the mid-14th century fresco recently rediscovered at Todi in Umbria (Fig. 17), showing the earliest known fresco representation of St Patrick. Almost half a millennium later, the story was still able to fascinate the English poet Robert Southey who, in 1798, was to use it as the basis of his ballad 'Sir Owen', which is well worth comparing with Henry of Saltrey's account.

Owein's story obviously need not be taken as a verbatim account, but probably represents a romantic amalgam culled from a variety of sources, including oral

Fig. 17 *The 14th-century fresco at Todi in Umbria*
shows St Patrick with his stick (RIGHT), *bending over the*
entrance to Purgatory with its Seven Deadly Sins

tradition and older tales of other-world visions, some of them of Irish origin, crafted together by Henry of Saltrey to create a bestseller of its day.

In the *Tractatus de Purgatorio sancti Patricii*, to give the account its full Latin title, Henry of Saltrey does not specify where the Purgatory lay. But his contemporary Gerald of Wales, better known to us as Giraldus Cambrensis, writing only a few years later, informs us that it is on an island in a lake on the bounds of Ulster, and subsequent chroniclers make it clear that St Patrick's Purgatory is on an island in Lough Derg.

There are two Lough Dergs in Ireland, the larger of the two being in the lower reaches of the river Shannon, bordered by Counties Clare, Galway and Tipperary. But St Patrick's Purgatory is in the smaller Lough Derg in County Donegal, which forms part of the old nine-county province of Ulster. The largest stretch of water in the southern part of the county, it is best reached today from the border village of Pettigo. The thousands – or, if we could but count them, perhaps millions – of pilgrims who have visited the Purgatory since Owein's sojourn in the 12th century probably reached it along the same road. One so-called ring-fort, Rathnacross in the townland of Drumawarke, is traditionally said to have been on the route to the Purgatory, and an old pilgrims' road is still pointed out bordering the south-western part of the lake and leading to the shore opposite Saint's Island, where an ancient wooden bridge formerly joined the island to the mainland.

The number of islands in the lake totals 46, but it was already clear from written sources as early as the 13th century that only two of these are of especial significance in the history of the pilgrimage: the larger Saint's Island, and the much smaller Station Island. But it is by no means absolutely clear from the various medieval and modern accounts which of these two islands contained the original cave which is traditionally said to have been visited by St Patrick. Both would appear to have played a part in the pilgrimage, one island being the site of the

Augustinian canons' foundation, from which the pilgrims were rowed across to the other island where the Cave was. But the majority of writers believe that the canons inhabited Saint's Island, and that the Cave was on Station Island, which is the centre of today's pilgrimage, which is now dominated by William Scott's basilica that was ceremoniously consecrated in 1931.

The medieval descriptions of the Cave vary considerably – the Hungarian George Crissaphan in 1353 made it out to be two miles long. But, literally, more down to earth and probably more accurate is the description by Guillebert de Lannoy, a Knight of the Golden Fleece, whose account of 1430 is translated by Shane Leslie as follows:

> The hole is nine feet long from east to west and then turns five feet towards the south-west and as a whole is fourteen to fifteen feet long. It was built with black stones and is about two feet wide and three feet high.

Two decades earlier, in 1411, the Italian Antonio Mannini said that it was high enough for a man to kneel in but not to stand upright, and vaulted overhead. Descriptions such as this have led to the suggestion that the Cave may have been a souterrain, one of those man-made subterranean passages that are often associated with Irish ring-forts of the pre-Norman period.

Towards the end of the century, in 1494, the lake was visited by a Dutch Augustinian from the abbey of Eymstadt. He was told that he could not enter without paying the usual fees to the clergy, but after prolonged protestations about his poverty, he was lowered on a rope into a deep pit, and next morning duly hauled up again, having experienced nothing of the visions which many before him since the days of Owein had claimed to have seen. He left in disgust, and later wrote to the Pope decrying the place as a sham, and accusing the clergy of simoniacal practices. The Pope, Alexander V, took the Dutchman's protest so seriously that he ordered the closure of the Cave. But the monk of Eymstadt's description is so different from that of the many previous visitors that the suspicion has been expressed that, because he had made himself so thoroughly objectionable, he was lowered into a cave which was not genuine, but another one on one or other of the two major islands. Fr Aubrey Gwynn thought that the 'Bishop' from whom the monk of Eymstadt got permission was none other than Cathal Óg MacMaghnusa who, as compiler of the *Annals of Ulster* of 1497, noted the destruction of the Cave, concluding with the wry remark ' . . . it being understood by everyone in general from the history of the Knight and other old books that this was not the Purgatory that Patrick got from God'. By this 'most ingenious paradox', the canons apparently succeeded in having the wrong cave closed down by Papal Order, and were thus able to keep open the genuine Cave, which is probably the one visited in 1517 by none other than the Pope's own Nuncio, Chiericati, who seems to have been blissfully unaware of the Pope's condemnation only twenty years earlier.

In the following century, the Protestant government in Dublin proved less tolerant. Because the Lords Justices found that the superstitions, ceremonies, pilgrimages and offerings were so extremely abusive 'as is not fit to be endured', they ordered that the Cave should be filled in. Revd John Richardson, rector of Belturbet and author of that splendidly titled tract *The Great Folly, Superstition and Idolatry of Pilgrimages in Ireland, Especially of that to St Patrick's Purgatory, together With an Account of the Loss that the Publick sustaineth thereby, truly and impartially Represented* (Dublin, 1727), related that in the 1690s a Breton named Louis Pyrrhus spent two summers trying to discover (or to rediscover) the true Cave. He searched in both islands for the passage to the Purgatory, but all that he found was a little bell, an image interpreted as that of a prehistoric monster, which St Patrick is said to have overcome in the Lake, and part of a window on Saint's Island. This window the Papists believed to have been the entrance to the Purgatory, as the parish priest said that it smelled strongly of brimstone, and shortly afterwards Pyrrhus ceased his diggings and returned to his own country. It is clear that, from some time in the second half of the 17th century, some kind of cave (known as the Prison) seems to have been visited by pilgrims to the lake, but it was closed in the 1780s due to the danger it presented to life and limb when occupied by a large number of pilgrims. Since then, the pilgrimage has taken place entirely above ground.

It is difficult to get an adequate idea, from the medieval and early modern descriptions, of the physical appearance of both islands as they were before 1632 when Bishop Spottiswoode of Clogher completely demolished all the buildings. Our first clear view of Station Island – the island to which modern pilgrimage takes place – is a bird's-eye view presented by Thomas Carve in the second edition of his *Lyra Hibernica*, printed in Germany in 1666 (Fig. 18). It shows the Cave to have been located near the centre of the island, close to the church. A Mr Coppinger, who visited the island in 1630, tells us that in the church (destroyed in 1632), suspended above the altar at the east end, was a statue of what must be taken to be a *Pietà*; to the right was a picture of the Adoration of the Magi and, to the left, a canvas of the Crucifixion. Close to the altar were three wooden statues: one, worm-eaten, of St Patrick, another of St Dabheoc (of whom more anon), and a third of an otherwise unidentifiable saint named Voluscius. Among other buildings on the island, according to the mid-17th century Protestant Bishop of Clogher, Henry Jones, was a house for the hearing of confessions, as well as various 'Irish houses covered with thatch but lately built' (obviously since the 1632 destruction). Indeed, the buildings seen on Carve's print are likely to have been constructed after 1632, when all the earlier buildings had been demolished.

Between the church and the Cave there was a heap of stones bearing a broken cross dedicated to St Patrick which was kissed by the pilgrims as they alighted on the island; another, to the east of the church, had a cross made of interwoven twigs; on it were three pieces of a bell said to have belonged to St Patrick. Dedicated to the same saint was a well on the island, which is also likely to have been blocked up in the demolition of 1632.

The erection of the present hostel, as well as the construction of the Basilica, have left little room on Station Island for earlier buildings. The only surviving features which are likely to date from earlier than the 19th century are the so-called 'beds' euphemistically termed 'mansions' by Henry Jones in the 17th century – round walls which were dedicated to various Irish saints, Patrick, Brigid Colmcille, Molaise, Brendan and Dabheoc, and to one non-Irish saint, Catherine, presumably of Alexandria. They get their name 'beds' because it was believed that the saints to whom they were dedicated had actually slept there. In his letter to the Protestant Archbishop of Armagh in 1632, James Spottiswoode specifically described breaking down 'Circles and Saints beds', so the surviving examples must be later, though they probably recreate the type of structure which existed before the 1632

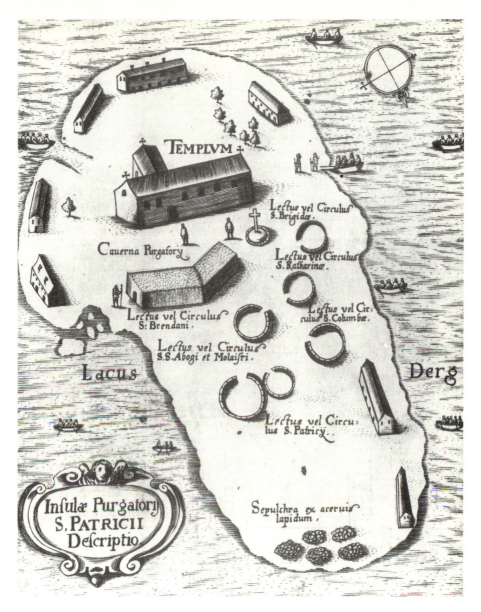

Fig. 18 *A bird's-eye view of St Patrick's Purgatory in
Lough Derg as illustrated by Thomas Carve in his*
Lyra Hibernica *of 1666*

destruction, and which have been compared in size and shape to beehive huts (see
page 181). These beds had been the centre of pious exercises, as we can see from the
detailed description of around 1600 by Michael O'Clery, one of the famous Four
Masters who wrote the Annals still bearing their name:

It is thus the Round of Lough Derg which is called the Purgatory of Patrick should be performed, according to the instructions of the wise men of the Purgatory.

First when beginning the Round, after entering the Chapel or Church, to kneel, to recite Pater, Ave Maria *and* Credo, *and to give a kiss to the Church door when going out, keeping the Church to thy right westwards and to give a kiss to the old Cross which is in front of the Church and keeping the Cross to thy right, northwards to the side of the Church and to give a kiss to the stone, which is at the side of the Church, and to go northwards hence to the Cross and to the Cairn, which are on the eastern side of the Church and to give a kiss to the stone which is on the northern side in the Cairn, and to take to thy right on the other side of the Cairn and to the Cross where is the Bell of Patrick, broken in three fragments, and to give a kiss to one of these, and to go from the north forward round the Church to the other Cairn, and to give a kiss to the round and wide stone, in which a Cross is carved and hence to the door, from which thou set'st out before, and to go seven times round the Church (and it is not needful to give a kiss to any one of the said objects except the first and last times, but to bend thy head at every spot where a kiss is given) and when the seventh time is performed, go to the Cross which is on the western side of the Church, as we have said, and give it a kiss and northward again to the other stone which is at the side of the Church, and give a kiss and go from the north again, retracing thy steps, between the Church and the old Cross we have mentioned, and go westwards directly from the Cross to Brendans Bed and give a kiss to a certain stone, which is in the door of the bed, and go three times sunwise round the Bed, reciting certain prayers, on the outside and go three more times sunwise inside and say three* Paters, *three* Ave Maria *and* Credo *on thy knees, and come out of it on to thy right hand, going out to Brigid's Bed, and do the same thing, and on coming out again, take to thy right hand on each side of the same Bed northwards to Catherine's Bed and do the same thing. And after leaving the same Bed, keep it to thy right hand northwards to Colum Cille's Bed, and do the same thing. And after completing thy prayers there, keeping the same bed to thy right hand and northwards around it to Patrick's Bed and give a kiss to the uneven stone which is near the door of the Cave. The two separate Beds close together and intertwined with Patrick's Bed are Da-Bheog's and Mo-Laisse's Bed. And go seven times round them all, and at the seventh time say five* Paters, *five* Ave Maria *and* Credo *on thy knees at the same stone which is at the door of Patrick's Bed, and take to thy right, and inside the Bed which is called Mo-Laisse's and Da-Bheog's Bed and say six* Paters *and six* Ave Maria *and two* Credo *and divide them in two parts, going round three times with each three* Paters *and one of the two* Credo *and go out, and with thy right hand to the same Bed to the Lake, to the rough sharp stones eastward directly which are called* An Chaorthannach *and retrace thy steps westward again on every side of the stone on which Patrick knelt and there is a small stone 'where Patrick was' on the west side of this stone and say* Pater *and* Ave *on it. And there is another stone some distance thence eastward in the Lake, and it is customary to say the same thing on it. And come to the land, to the Cairn that is on the eastern side of the Church and give a kiss to the black stone and to some fragment of the Bell, and go up southwards to the other Cairn and give a kiss to the round stone, in which there is a Cross, and go to the Church door and give a kiss to the door and walk in and say Mary's Psalter, fifteen Decades on thy knees, and* Credo *with every five Decades. And to do all those things three times a day for the space of nine days without taking but bread and water once a day during that time and to be twenty-four hours in either of the two Caves from morning to morning and from midday before going into the Cave to midday after coming out of the same Cave without taking any food, but it is allowed to give a drink of water to a man who would be in utter need of it. And after they have all come out of the Cave, they should all go three times under the water at the spot which is called Patrick's Pool.* Laus Deo

[TRANSLATED FROM THE IRISH SCRIPT OF MICHAEL O'CLERY, ONE OF THE FOUR MASTERS, BY FATHER GROSJEAN, SJ BRUSSELS, ROYAL LIBR. MS. 5057-59]

Fig. 19 *Lough Derg in 1836 (after P. D. Hardy's* Holy
Wells of Ireland*)*

What Michael O'Clery described almost four hundred years ago differs only in degree from the pious exercises practised by modern pilgrims, as laid down by an ordinance in 1813. What the pilgrimage scene looked like twenty years after this ordinance can be seen in Philip Dixon Hardy's illustrations (Fig. 19) to his book *The Holy Wells of Ireland* (Dublin, 1836). Today, the 15,000 annual pilgrims spend only three days on the island, doing their rounds on the beds in the traditional manner. Their first night is spent without sleep; only on the second night are they allowed to sleep in the hostel on the island. Nourishment is confined to bread and black tea, made from the waters of the lake.

Today's pious penitential practices, so little changed from those described by Michael O'Clery, stand in considerable contrast to the emphasis on visions in the accounts of Lough Derg visitors in the first few centuries after Owein's visit in the 1140s. The knights of the late Romanesque and early Gothic era, intent on purging themselves of the sins they had incurred through heinous crimes, did so by encountering the horrors of the other-world, and by talking to those who had already passed through the doors of death. It was their accounts that set on fire the imaginations of the literati and the European knights seeking adventure and wonder, and which were therefore promulgated by the early Norman conquerors in Ireland. These knight-errants were silent about the beds and the minutiae of the prayers to be said in doing the rounds. But so too were the Irish. The harsh penances of barefoot pilgrimage were presumably to be endured and not written about. Or, if the Irish wrote about them in the medieval period, their stories have been lost.

But the fact that the medieval descriptions of visits to Lough Derg are entirely dominated by foreigners' accounts of their encounters with the other-world need not mean that the Irish did not go on pilgrimage to the lake during the same period, in roughly the same manner as they do today. It is not inconceivable that the Irish only started to go on pilgrimage to Lough Derg after the visions said to have been experienced from the 12th to the early 15th century ceased to materialise. But is it not much more likely that the Irish were going on pilgrimage to Lough Derg at the same time that the impressions were being written down of the visits of the twenty-seven foreigners who are recorded as having visited the Cave between the 1140s and the end of the 15th century – and probably even before that as well?

There is enough evidence to suggest that this was indeed the case. Tuileagna O Maolconaire's early-16th-century poem quoted at the head of this chapter demonstrates that, even in his day, the pilgrimage was already ancient, and long established as the prime example of its kind in Ireland. It was probably in 1152 that Diarmit Mac Murrough abducted Dervorgilla after she had told him that her husband, Tiernan O Rourke of Breifne, had gone on pilgrimage to Lough Derg – thus leaving the way open for Diarmit to kidnap her, an act which later cost him his throne and led him to invite the Normans to Ireland in an effort to regain it. And surely the knight Owein himself would not have expressed the intention of going on pilgrimage to Lough Derg in the previous decade had the pilgrimage not already existed, and been well known throughout Ireland. Henry of Saltrey says that the pilgrimage went back to the days of St Patrick – though this we may take with numerous grains of salt, since, as we have seen, Henry brings St Patrick into contact with the canons of St Augustine, who only reached Ireland in the first half of the 12th century.

Of the religious orders who spread to Ireland from the Continent in the 12th century, the Augustinians were virtually alone in occasionally taking over earlier Irish monastic establishments and giving them renewed vigour, instead of creating completely new foundations as the Cistercians and others did. It is very likely, therefore, that when the canons took over one of the islands in the lake and established themselves there in around 1140, they gave a new life to an already existing pilgrimage – gave it a second wind, as the present Catholic Bishop of Clogher, Joseph Duffy, put it in 1975. At the same time, it is quite probable that rivalry between those dioceses which had been newly created by the Synod of Kells in 1152 may have led to further competition in promoting pilgrimage traffic to the lake in the decades after Owein's visit.

The beds, dedicated as they were to six early Irish saints, might seem to provide proof, and indicate a survival, of pre-Augustinian pilgrimage to the lake going back to the early years of Christianity in Ireland. But the dedication of one of the beds to a non-Irish saint, Catherine, must make us wary for, as the late John Hennig pointed out, the earliest evidence for her cult in Ireland is found in the *Martyrology of Gorman*, which dates from no earlier than 1166. This points to the dedications of the beds being finalised after the arrival of the Augustinians; this supposition could be supported by the remarks made by Revd Dominick Brullaughan in a Latin guide to the Lough Derg pilgrimage published in Louvain in 1735:

PLATE I *St Brendan the Navigator, as portrayed by Wilhelmina Geddes in the stained glass window at Curraun, County Mayo, attracted a lost koala bear in search of its owner*

PLATE II *The 9th-century cross-shaft at Kilnaruane, County Cork, may illustrate the kind of boat used by St Brendan and his companions on their pilgrimage voyage*

PLATE III *The Saint's Road in the Dingle Peninsula led to Mount Brandon*

PLATE IV *'The Priest's' or 'St Brendan's' or 'The Chancellor's' House, at Kilmalkedar, County Kerry, in a watercolour by G.V. Du Noyer c1860*

PLATE V *Ardmore, County Waterford is dominated by the 12th-century Round Tower. Nearby is St Declan's House, the tomb-shrine of the founder*

PLATE VI Opposite: *View of Croagh Patrick, County Mayo*

PLATE VII *The Cathedral* (foreground) *and Round
Tower form the focus at Glendalough, County Wicklow*

PLATE VIII *Joseph Peacock's* Pattern Day at Glendalough *of 1813*

This Island of Saints some call the Island of Saint Dabeoc: others of Saint Avitus. The Pilgrimage was transferred from that Island to the small Island of St Patrick; but by whom and in what year I could never discover, but the antiquity of the Chapel built there proves that the Pilgrimage began there many centuries ago. But what was the reason for which it was transferred? Firstly it appears on account of the fears of Pilgrims in entering the profound and terrible Cave shown to Saint Patrick. Secondly on account of the nuisance and annoyance to the Canons of St Augustine inhabiting the Island of Saints: and as St Patrick's Island was more suitable for mortification, prayer and penance they built the Chapel, Cave and penal beds there. It is clear that the first Cave was in the Island of Saints, because where the Cave was shown to St Patrick there he built the Monastery of the Canons of St Augustine: and the Monastery has been built on the big Island, that of Saints, as its remains show. The Pilgrimage therefore was started in the Island aforesaid. [TRANSLATION BY SHANE LESLIE]

Yet the testimony of an earlier writer named Fergal, quoted by Haren and de Pontfarcy, suggests that the dedication of a bed to St Catherine may not have been original, as he omits her name and instead mentions a bed dedicated to St Adomnan, the famous 7th-8th century abbot of Iona. It is therefore possible that the dedication of one of the beds to St Catherine may have been an Augustinian idea, and that the bed dedicated to her may originally have been dedicated to Adomnan. The dedication of the other beds to a variety of Irish saints does not sound like an Augustinian invention, and probably represents an older Irish pilgrimage tradition.

One fact which some modern commentators have had to admit with a certain degree of regret is that, although we know that St Patrick passed through County Donegal, there is no source earlier than Henry of Saltrey to connect him with Lough Derg. Indeed, if anything, Henry's association of St Patrick with the Augustinians could suggest that it was the Augustinians who were the first to forge the link between St Patrick and the Purgatory Cave, unpalatable though this view may be.

As Haren and de Pontfarcy have pointed out, there is a similarity in folk tradition between Croagh Patrick and Lough Derg. The tale concerning St Patrick being disturbed by black birds – demons in disguise – and throwing his bell at them in order to disperse them, is first developed in around 900 in the Tripartite Life of St Patrick in conjunction with Croagh Patrick, and only applied centuries later apparently to Lough Derg. The devil's mother, Caora, is said to have disappeared into a lake on the side of Croagh Patrick, only to emerge again on Lough Derg in the form of a monster known as the Caorthanach, which would suck 'men and cattle into its mouth at a mile's distance' in the words of Revd Richardson. The monster was finally overcome by one of the Fenian heroes (who only became popular in the 12th century) – or even by St Patrick himself, as later tradition would have it – and the red colour of the stones on the lake shore is said to have been caused by the blood of the Caorthanach gushing out after its head had been cut off. Revd Richardson says that 'the Caorthanach's bowels were metamorphosed into great stones. The image of this pretended monster is cut in stone, and kept in the island where pilgrims perform their devotion, to confirm them in the belief of this ridiculous fable'. There would appear to be a suspicion that, like the Caorthanach itself, Patrician lore was transposed from Croagh Patrick to Lough Derg. As for most of the other Irish saints who had beds named after them, not only Donegal's most famous saint, Colmcille, but also Brigid, Molaise and Brendan, there is nothing to indicate that they ever visited the island, though this need not be considered as ruling out invocations for their help in the course of a pilgrimage tradition going back long before the arrival of the Augustinians, and thus the existence of the beds prior to the 12th century.

Only one of the Irish saints to whom the beds were dedicated is likely to have any direct connection with the lake, and this is the somewhat shadowy figure of St Dabheoc. Shane Leslie, without any obvious justification, identified him with Aedh of Loch Gierg (another name for Lough Derg) mentioned under 1 January in the 10th-century *Martyrology of Tallaght*. In contrast Colgan, who was described by John O'Donovan in the 1830s as having had more materials before him than any man who wrote since his time (1647), says the following:

> St Dabheoc is the patron of a very celebrated church on a certain lake in Ulster called Loch Gerg, in which is that celebrated Purgatory of St Patrick . . . in the adjacent territory St Dabeocus is held in the greatest veneration among our people to this day.

Colgan continues that 'it is stated . . . that he had foretold several things about the holiness and virtues of St Columba/Colmcille before the latter was born in 521, from which it would follow that he flourished around the time of St Patrick. He is ranked among the chief saints of Ireland by Cuimmín of Condeire (Connor) in his book concerning them, and also in a 17th-century *Life of St Brendan*'.

Yolande de Pontfarcy pointed out that there were two saints named Dabheoc in early Ireland, of whom the one who lived in the 7th century was claimed by O'Connor as the patron saint of Lough Derg. But whichever of the saints he may have been, it is important for our purposes to note that the *Annals of Ulster* record for the year 1070 that the 'Termon of Daveoc was plundered', and that the *Annals of the Four Masters* tell of a similar fate befalling it in 1111. The termon was an area under the patronage of St Dabheoc in the period before the arrival of the Augustinians, when he was obviously regarded as the chief saint in the locality. As Gwynn and Hadcock put it, 'the dedication appears to have changed from St Dabheoc to St Patrick'. They are sufficiently cautious not to indicate a date when this is likely to have happened, but the evidence would point to a period some time in the 12th century. It was at this time, as de Pontfarcy pointed out, that genealogists were first at pains to establish St Dabheoc's family tree, and that historical sources made an effort to establish his connection with St Patrick. One can but surmise that it was the Augustinians who were responsible, in an effort to claim continuity with the older tradition of devotion to the local saint Dabheoc.

Philip O'Sullivan Beare, writing in 1629 but using older sources now lost, claimed that the island of St Dabheoc was venerable because of his tomb, which would help to explain why he was the early saint of the termon. A mid-13th-century manuscript records that on the smaller (Station) Island 'old men were always dwelling, living an anchoretic life, who were nourished on nothing but water mixed with milk and in the Lenten season they always fed on oaten bread containing one third part ashes'. This account, though written a century after Owein's visit, suggests an older anchoretic tradition of devotion in the lake, perhaps associated with St Dabheoc's tomb, though located on a different island.

Without any historical sources to guide us, we can only conjecture as to what was happening on the lake before the arrival of the Augustinians in around 1140, but reading between the unwritten lines one gets the distinct impression that there was a pilgrimage/anchoretic tradition there connected with St Dabheoc, who was probably the earliest saint associated with the lake. In the absence of a link between the lake and St Patrick dating from before the 12th century, it would not be unjustified to suggest that it was the Augustinians who first popularised St Patrick's connection with the lake, linked him to a Cave on one or other of the major islands, and possibly even created the legend of the Cave in order to increase the pilgrimage traffic. St Patrick, being well-known throughout Ireland, was perhaps considered a more likely draw for pilgrims than the local St Dabheoc. In the overshadowing of the local saint in favour of the introduction of the national saint apparently in the 12th century, we may have a parallel to what would seem to be a similar case in the Dingle Peninsula, where the local saints Malkedar and Manchán were overshadowed by St Brendan.

To the credit of the Augustinians, it can certainly be said that they vitalised the Lough Derg pilgrimage and paved the way for those international visitors who came to the lake in search of other-world adventures in the 12th to 15th centuries. But the fact remains that we have no documentation about any pilgrimage to St Patrick's Purgatory before that date. Even if the sources are silent, the hints that we get about an early devotion to St Dabheoc, whose grave may well have been the goal of pilgrims before the Augustinians came, could suggest that the pilgrimage practices first recorded in detail by Michael O'Clery in around 1600 may descend from a pre-12th-century pilgrimage in honour of St Dabheoc, and suggest an unbroken tradition of penitential pilgrimage to Lough Derg that has now lasted for much longer than eight hundred years. The form of pilgrimage surviving today probably gives us a better idea than any written sources of the atmosphere of Irish pilgrimages prior to the 12th century.

CROAGH PATRICK, MAYO

A link between Lough Derg and Croagh Patrick is provided by none other than the devil's mother, commonly known as the Caora or the Caorthanach. St Patrick finally managed to kill her off in Lough Derg, but that was only at the second attempt. His first attempt was on the summit of Croagh Patrick, where the hero Saint managed to confine her in a lake on the side of the mountain. But she managed to escape, and her turning up again in Lough Derg suggests the transference of a St Patrick myth from Croagh Patrick to Lough Derg. According to a tradition which had grown up by around 900, the devil's mother was only one of the adversaries which beset the Saint on the mountain. The others were a set of demon birds who attacked him. To get rid of them, the Saint rang a bell which St Brigid had given him; when that proved ineffectual, he resorted to throwing the bell at them. A piece fell out of the bell on impact but the desired effect was achieved: the demon birds fled. The missing piece doubtless helped to identify this bell with a suitably damaged bell called the Clog Dubh, or Black Bell, of St Patrick which was for long in the hands of its hereditary keepers, the Geraghty family, until the last traditional steward sold it to Sir William Wilde, through whom it came to its present home in the National Museum in Dublin. When John O'Donovan visited the Geraghtys in search of the bell during the course of his Ordnance Survey work in 1838, it had gone on its annual outing to Croagh Patrick, where every pilgrim ought to pass it three times sunwise around the body, and kiss three times a cross engraved on it. But the kissing seems to have been so intensive that not a trace of a cross can be found on the bell now in the National Museum – or can it be that Sir William Wilde bought a different bell?

The demon birds which St Patrick had to contend with according to the 10th-century tradition go back to earlier birds, which even older tradition says surrounded St Patrick when he went up the mountain to fast and pray for forty days and forty nights in imitation of the biblical Moses and Elias. It should be mentioned, however, that such a notable Patrician scholar as the late Bishop Hanson believed that St Patrick never set foot on the Reek, as the holy mountain is known locally.

By its very shape, Croagh Patrick (Plate VI) was cut out to be a holy mountain. Particularly when approached from the flat plains of County Roscommon, the sudden sight of the great quartzite cone many miles to the west creates an unforgettable first impression. Its sides are gradually seen to narrow symmetrically towards the summit, which is so often shrouded in mist that it could well be imagined as communing with the ancient gods above the clouds. It looks down in a benign yet patriarchal fashion over the drowned drumlins of Clew Bay, which raise their heads above the waves like the whale on which St Brendan's crew landed to light their fire. From Clew Bay it looks rather different, as it can be seen to have a lower ridge to the east, along which the pilgrims climb on their way to the top. They start close to the medieval Franciscan friary of Murrisk, and turn their back on the north (which medieval minds considered to have been the abode of evil) to walk southwards for a while (Fig. 20) before heading eastwards up the final slope to the summit. The sticks that pilgrims hire at the bottom are surely the continuation of an old tradition of the staff which pilgrims used internationally to help them on their

Fig. 20 *Pilgrims wending their way up the path to Croagh Patrick, with the islands of Clew Bay in the background*

arduous path. Although the pilgrimage to Croagh Patrick can be undertaken on any day in the year, it is particularly popular on the last Sunday in July. On that day, around 30,000 pilgrims come annually from all over Ireland, but largely from within a radius of about thirty miles from the mountain, to partake in the pilgrimage in honour of St Patrick. Only a small number now follow the age-old tradition of starting off at midnight and making the ascent of about three hours in the darkness, aided only by a lamp or candle – and doing it barefoot, which becomes extremely difficult on the scree stones near the summit. Our generation is becoming soft, and most people, including myself, are content to make the pilgrimage in daylight and with their shoes on.

The pilgrim says prayers as he goes seven times around the first station he meets on the climb – Leach Mionnáin – or St Benen's Bed. When he reaches the summit he says more prayers, walks around the modern chapel, hears Mass and receives Communion. In olden days he would have entered the ruin of the old medieval chapel and left a token offering such as a rag or a nail. Also on the summit is St Patrick's Bed, where further prayers are said. In the 19th century it was mainly visited by childless women, who slept in the bed at night in the hope of having children. Not everyone nowadays visits the last station on the pilgrimage – a small triangular area on the south-western side of the peak, which is called Roilig Mhuire (Mary's Cemetery) – where pilgrims go seven times around a cairn of stones (resembling an ancient burial mound), saying the customary prayers of seven *Paters*, seven *Aves* and one *Credo*.

In ancient times, the Reek was approached by those coming from the east along the old pilgrimage road, known as the Tóchar Phádraig, the word *tóchar* being used in Irish to denote a trackway. The track now starts off from the Augustinian abbey of Ballintubber, founded by the O Conor king of Connacht in 1216, and continues for many miles, passing through Aghagower. In this village there is a round tower, a holy well, St Patrick's Bed and his 'Bath' with a sacred tree growing above it, the soil from the base of which was said to have curative powers. It has been suggested that the monks of Aghagower were in charge of the pilgrimage to Croagh Patrick. But there are many other sites in Connacht that may have provided hostels for pilgrims coming from other directions than along the Tóchar Phádraig, such as Kilbennan with its round tower and Inishmaine, which has a church in the western late Romanesque style of the early 13th century. The not easily accessible Caher Island off the west coast of Mayo is said to have been the last station on the pilgrimage round to Croagh Patrick.

The modern pilgrimage to Croagh Patrick derives from the efforts made by Dr Healy, Archbishop of Tuam, to revive it in 1903; he was responsible for the building of the present church on the summit. The pilgrimage had almost come to an end during the episcopate of his predecessor Dr McEvilly, who had tried to transfer the centre of pilgrimage to the foot of the mountain. But his efforts were in vain, for the old traditions die hard in the West of Ireland. Yet how long the pilgrimage had gone on for is unknown. The *Annals of the Four Masters* refer to the plundering of the Cruach in 1079, so that even at that time Croagh Patrick must have had valuables, presumably relics, worth plundering. Thirty people fasting on the mountain were struck by lightning in 1113, according to the *Annals of Loch Cé*, and the annals also report the capture of a MacWilliam Burke while coming from Croagh Patrick in 1351. But Tirechán's reference to St Patrick on the mountain as early as the 7th century would suggest that it had been established as a Christian pilgrimage site even at that time.

Máire MacNeill has pointed to the great probability that the pilgrimage's roots go back to pagan times. In her splendid, beautifully written book *The Festival of Lughnasa*, this most perceptive folklorist argued persuasively in favour of seeing Croagh Patrick as one of the many places in Ireland where the festival of the Celtic god Lug was celebrated. The mainstay of the evidence is that the pilgrimage takes place on the last Sunday in July, traditionally the last day of summer or the first day of the harvest season, on which day the pagan festival was celebrated by the climbing of a number of Lughnasa sites, such as Slieve Donard in County Down. She also pointed out that local tradition says that the proper day for performing the pilgrimage is *Aoine Chrom Dubh*, the Friday of Crom Dubh. This Crom Dubh was almost certainly a pagan deity, whom we shall meet again in the Dingle Peninsula.

The Dindshenchas, a 10th-century collection of place-lore, relates that Crom Derg murdered his nephew Aigle in revenge for his having slain a lady named Cliara who was under his protection. From this Aigle, Croagh Patrick is said to have got the name by which Tirechán referred to it in the 7th century, Mons Egli, an Hiberno-Latinisation of the name Aigle. It would seem, therefore, that the present name associating the mount with St Patrick post-dates the late 7th century, and that we have here another example of the Church suppressing an older name – in this case one that was pagan – in favour of a Christian name, in order to promulgate the cult of the national apostle, interest in whom began to increase from the 7th century onwards.

CHAPTER 8

WESTERN MARITIME PILGRIMAGE PLACES

MOUNT BRANDON AND
THE DINGLE PENINSULA

CROAGH PATRICK IS GEOGRAPHICALLY THE CENTRAL MOUNTAIN OF THREE ON the western seaboard of Ireland which are associated with pilgrimage. Further north, on the northern side of Donegal Bay, is Slieve League (1972 feet, 650 metres) which is mentioned in the *Navigatio Brendani* as the place near which Mernóc saw the Delightful Island, and which was where St Munnu of Taghmon was recommended to begin a journey. Traces of a drystone church, a beehive hut, a cross-inscribed stone and about twenty-six penitential stations along the mountain ridge are all the physical remains surviving of what must once have been an important pilgrimage. We know little about it because it had already died out by 1800 and, despite an effort to revive it in 1909, it remains dormant. Very much further to the south, in County Kerry, is the third and perhaps the most fascinating of all the pilgrimage mountains – Mount Brandon, near the end of the Dingle Peninsula.

The Dingle Peninsula is the most northerly of the five fingers which stretch out into the Atlantic on the south-western corner of Ireland, and is regarded as the most westerly point of Europe. There are three main groups of hills along its thirty-mile length, massed around its three main peaks: Slieve Mish (2796 feet, 853 metres) at the eastern end, Beenoskee (2713 feet, 827 metres) in the centre and Mount Brandon (3027 feet, 953 metres) to the west. Of the two modern roads connecting Tralee at the north-eastern end with Dingle, near the south-western corner, that over the Connor Pass is of comparatively recent origin. The old road (followed by the now sadly defunct Dingle railway) went up Gleann na nGalt (Madman's Valley, whither all the lunatics of Ireland would resort if they were allowed to be at large, according to tradition) and over a 700-feet pass via Anascaul to Dingle. Another old road led westwards along the northern edge of the peninsula as far as Cloghane at the head of Brandon Bay. To the west of the Mount Brandon massif there is a lower ridge of hills joining it with the higher Mount Eagle (1696 feet, *c*.500 metres) close

71

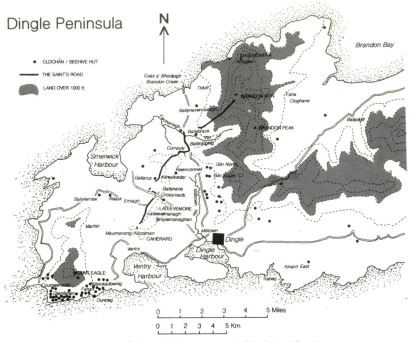

Fig. 21 *Map of the western half of the Dingle Peninsula, indicating the location of The Saint's Road and of* clocháin *(beehive huts)*

to the western tip of the peninsula. To the north and south of this ridge there are fine natural harbours: Smerwick and Dingle (in both of which foreign fishing boats are often seen at anchor as they ride out the frequent local storms) and Ventry, whose flat beach is useful for launching currachs. Ventry is the site of a famous mythological battle, the centrepiece of the medieval tale known as *Cath Finntrágha* ('The Battle of Ventry'), in which Fionn macCumhaill overcame an invasion by the army of the emperor of the whole world except Ireland. The area to the west of the Brandon massif (Fig. 21) is a magical world, full of small fields divided up by fuchsia hedges (only introduced in the 19th century), virtually woodless nowadays, but with a charm which attracts not only those who want to hear a dialect of Munster Irish still beautifully spoken, but also those who are interested in antiquities. For it has an unbelievably rich collection of these, which have a mysterious aura if for no other reason than that history records so little about them. But there may be something more than an antiquarian or even scenic and personal attraction; Mount Brandon in itself seems to possess some physical force which is known to disorientate the compasses of airmen. A German airplane crashed there during the Second World War, and its spars were subsequently used to create a cross on top of the mountain.

The name Brandon is shrouded in the mists of prehistory. It sounds similar to that of the famous navigating saint to whom the mountain pilgrimage is dedicated, but there is no proven connection between the two. It has been suggested that the name Brandon comes from the eponymous hero of the *Immram Bran*; at the end of his journey Bran arrived at a place called Srub Brain, which some would identify with the end of the Dingle Peninsula, though others locate it in County Donegal because of the name of Bran's father Febal, which may be related to Lough Foyle.

The pagan background suggested by the possible link with Bran of the *Immram* voyage tale is reinforced further by Máire MacNeill's researches published in her *The Festival of Lughnasa*, a book which should be read by every serious student of early Ireland. According to MacNeill, local tradition said that the pilgrimage to Mount Brandon took place on three different days: 16 May (the feast day of St Brendan), 29 June (the feast of Saints Peter and Paul), and the last Sunday in July (known as *Domhnach Chrom Dubh*, Crom Dubh Sunday). MacNeill was of the opinion that the first two are probably of recent origin, with the 29 June being the day chosen in 1868 by Dr Moriarty, the Bishop of Kerry, to revive the old pilgrimage on a great occasion which drew 20,000 pilgrims from all over the country, and even by boat from County Clare, on a gloriously fine day, though it failed to have any lasting effect on the pilgrimage, which has now virtually died out. The genuine old pilgrimage day, in MacNeill's view, was the last of the three – the same day on which the Lughnasa festival was, and the modern pilgrimage is, celebrated on Croagh Patrick. On the Dingle Peninsula it is centred around the pagan deity Crom Dubh, who is said to have lived at Ballyduff (*Baile Dubh*) about two miles from Cloghane, where a stone head (Fig. 22) in the ruined medieval church is locally claimed to represent him. In local folklore Crom Dubh was the god

Fig. 22 *A stone head, locally said to be that of the pagan god Crom Dubh, in the medieval church at Cloghane, County Kerry*

of harvest, worshipped by the pagans until St Brendan converted him to Christianity.

After the pilgrims had climbed to the summit of Mount Brandon, they descended on the eastern side of the mountain to assemble for a great 'patron' at Cloghane on Brandon Bay where games, athletics, vaulting over horses, dancing, singing and courtship took place, accompanied by feasting and faction-fighting. This last feature was doubtless the reason why the Catholic clergy tried to dampen enthusiasm for the pilgrimage in the 18th century. It seems paradoxical, then, that Bishop Moriarty tried to revive it again in 1868, but that was because, as Professor Jim Donnelly pointed out to me, the clergy would have wanted to divest the pilgrimage of its secular manifestations in order to make it into a purely religious event.

Crom Dubh was thus, in local eyes, the pagan who was overcome by St Brendan, the even stronger champion of Christianity. That St Brendan was taking on the mantle of his pagan predecessor is suggested by the name of his father, Fionn*lugh*, and it would seem, therefore, that the pilgrimage on Crom Dubh Sunday was nothing more or less than the Christianisation of an old pagan festival which celebrated the Celtic god Lug on that day at many places all over Ireland.

The Christian pilgrimage approached the summit of Mount Brandon from two sides. The more difficult climb started at Cloghane or Faha, and wended its way up the eastern side of the mountain, where steps had to be cut to assist the pilgrims. The climb from the western side was much easier, though anyone climbing the mountain from that side today should be warned of the mists which can suddenly envelop the summit; there is a steep drop of about 2000 feet all along the mountain ridge. In olden days, the *turas*, or pilgrimage, at the summit began at dawn, which implies that pilgrims undertook a night climb or a vigil on the hill. The rounds began with prayers at the ruined oratory on the summit dedicated to St Brendan; pilgrims then encircled it, and visited some mounds and a pillar stone called Leac na nDrom, the Stone of the Backs.

Pilgrims stood with their backs against this stone in the hope of obtaining a cure for backache – which many pilgrims, if they did not have it already, would have experienced after climbing 3000 feet, before descending the eastern flank of the mountain to participate in the festivities at Cloghane.

The easier climb, on the western side of the mountain, was the culmination of the walk along the old pilgrimage road, which is often considered to have started at Kilmalkedar, the focal point of a great arena which unfolds on to Smerwick harbour. But a look at the old Ordnance Survey maps shows that what is described there as the 'Saint's Road' – the saint being, of course, St Brendan – stretches further southwestwards. Its course is plotted on the map (Fig. 21). From Kilmalkedar, the road passes by the possibly 17th-century ruins known as the Chancellor's House and close to Gallarus oratory, continuing southwestwards along the edge of the plain that broadens out at the foot of what might be described as the Kilmalkedar arena (Plate III), climbing up over and down the other side of a ridge, and ending at an enclosure known as Kilcolman, in the townland of Maumanorig, in sight of Ventry harbour. The pilgrims would, of course, have gone on their pilgrimage in the opposite direction, starting at Ventry harbour and Maumanorig, and then proceeding northwestwards, stopping at Kilmalkedar, climbing the ridge behind it, dropping again to Currauly, and crossing the valley of the Feohanagh river (where the course of the road is uncertain) before making the final ascent via the small

Fig. 23 *The boulder at Kilcolman, Maumanorig, in the Dingle Peninsula, with two crosses and an Ogham inscription asking a prayer for Colman the pilgrim. In front of it is a bullaun*

settlement of Ballybrack to the summit, overlooking the sheltered valley of Ballinlochig.

It is possible that there was an alternative route further north, starting the climb at the hamlet of Tiduff, for there is a man-made road from there up through the bog, reaching a height of about 1800 feet, but some believe that this road was made in the 19th century to serve as a look-out post. The part of the Saint's Road skirting the plain southwest of the Kilmalkedar has recently been cleared by commendable local effort, which has made a walk along it a pleasure, to follow in the footsteps of a thousand years and more of pilgrimage.

If the Ordnance Survey map is anything to go by, that pilgrimage walk started at Maumanorig, in a small, almost circular earthwork about 135 feet (45 metres) in diameter and known as Kilcolman, which encloses an alleged church site, huts, and a cross-decorated Ogham stone (Fig. 23), with a bullaun stone in front of it. We can imagine pilgrims foregathering there to say initial prayers before starting the pilgrimage walk to St Brendan's Oratory on the summit. But if the enclosure at Kilcolman was the start of the pilgrimage road which led to Mount Brandon, the question must be asked, where did the pilgrims come from who foregathered there? If the pilgrims were approaching Mount Brandon from the southwest, they can only have come from the sea, and the beautiful sandy beach of Ventry harbour is the obvious place for them to have landed. Here again, we must use our imagination and picture large currachs coming in to land over the breakers on the last weekend in July a thousand years ago, with probably the same buzz and commotion which greets today's annual Ventry and Dingle currach regatta held nearby in August.

Maumanorig lies about 250 feet above sea level. Most of the ground around Ventry harbour is low-lying, at times marshy terrain. To the west, the land rises again at the foot of Mount Eagle, and along the coast at the southern flank of the hill, at about the same height as Maumanorig, that is, largely between the 200 and 300 feet contour, there are hundreds of round stone, corbel-roofed structures called *clocháin* in Irish, or beehive huts. These are perched on high ground overlooking the ocean; in the course of a few miles, Macalister counted a total of 414 such *clocháin* at the end of the 19th century. This is the most famous cluster of beehive huts in the country, and has given rise to speculation as to their use: whether they formed part of a prehistoric settlement, or were shelters for shepherds who came booleying there, that is, bringing their flocks in summer transhumance. The date of such structures is certainly unclear. Some were undoubtedly built within the last two centuries, but at least one example within an (?) Iron Age promontory fort at Dunbeg gave a radiocarbon date within the 9th/10th centuries.

It should not be forgotten that there are a further 150-200 examples scattered in the upper reaches of the valleys of the Milltown and Feohanagh rivers in townlands such as Ballynavenooragh, Ballybrack, Ballinlochig, Glin North and South, all of which lie at the western foot of the Brandon massif. There are, correspondingly, very few on the eastern side, though at least one is located at Faha, a starting point for pilgrims climbing the mountain from the east. The fact that so many lie at the foot of Mount Brandon would strongly support the notion that they were temporary habitations for seaborne pilgrims coming from the west and waiting for a clearance of the cloudy mist which often shrouds the summit from view, before attempting a safe ascent to the summit. As the mountain can often be clouded for

Fig. 24 *Gallarus Oratory in the Dingle Peninsula, County Kerry, with the view to Mount Brandon in the background*

weeks at a time, even in late July when the pilgrimage formerly took place, there would have been an obvious need to house the pilgrims until the all-clear for the ascent could be given. The Milltown river reaches the sea at Milltown on Dingle harbour, while the Feohanagh river flows into Smerwick harbour at Feohanagh, and it would make sense to envisage that, in addition to landing in Ventry Harbour and approaching Mount Brandon along the Saint's Road starting at Maumanorig, pilgrims coming by sea could have landed in Dingle harbour and gone up the Milltown valley past Reenconnell, or have landed in Smerwick harbour at Feohanagh and reached the foot of the mountain by the Feohanagh valley. When we consider that almost all the beehive huts lie west of the Brandon massif (as shown in the map, Fig. 21), and when we remember that even as late as the revived pilgrimage of 1868, people came by boat from Clare, it seems natural that the great majority of pilgrims who participated in the Mount Brandon pilgrimage in earlier centuries must have come by sea, an idea reinforced by the almost total lack of such huts on the eastern and less accessible side of the mountain. It could, of course, be argued in contrast that the pilgrims ascended the western side, and the beehive huts were on the same side, simply because it was the easier to climb.

The great concentration of huts in Glenfahan, Fahan and Coumeenole to the west of Ventry (Fig. 21) could be explained as shelters on higher ground for those who landed in Ventry harbour. But these hut groupings also look out towards the Skelligs, and it is eminently possible that they could also have served as resting places for pilgrims awaiting the right weather to make the journey to the Skelligs as part of an extended pilgrimage. If we accept the idea that beehive huts were pilgrim shelters, then we should understand the Mount Brandon pilgrimage as having been made, at least in good part, by seaborne pilgrims. This fits in admirably with the view put forward above that there was formerly a maritime pilgrimage along the whole west coast of Ireland and reaching up to the islands west and north of the Scottish mainland – and beyond, perhaps, too – which found its literary reflection in the *Navigatio Brendani*.

The same corbel construction used in the beehive huts is also found in what is perhaps the most famous monument in the Dingle Peninsula: Gallarus oratory (Fig. 24). This is a small building, measuring internally 15 feet 3 inches by 10 feet 2 inches (6.86 by 5.75 metres), having its north and south walls not upright but gradually curving inwards in the corbel technique until they meet in a ridge at the top. Various suggestions have been made to explain the Irish name, Gall Aras. If slightly ungrammatical, perhaps it is simplest to take it as meaning something like 'The House or Shelter for Foreigner(s)'; we might not go too far wrong in seeing the foreigners as being those pilgrims who had come from outside the Peninsula. It should be noted that the oratory does not lie on the Saint's Road, but about 200 metres from it down an old laneway (which is not the same as the modern access path). Perhaps the reason for the original choice of location only a small distance from the Saint's Road was to enable a view of the summit of Mount Brandon, which would have been virtually impossible from the nearest point on the Saint's Road.

The corbel technique was designed for a round building, and the danger of adapting the system to a rectangular structure is that the roof collapses in the middle, as has happened at most of the corbelled oratories. There are signs of sagging in the roof of Gallarus oratory, but the expert and carefully bedded masonry of the oratory (Fig. 25) has, thank heavens, prevented it from collapse so

Fig. 25 *The beautifully-bedded masonry around the
doorway of Gallarus Oratory in the Dingle Peninsula*

far. It is not always realised that Gallarus is by no means unique: there are about
twenty other examples in the country, less well-known simply because their roofs
have fallen in. Most of these are associated with the Dingle Peninsula, but others
occur on the next peninsula to the south, including the Great Skellig, and even as far
north as the Mayo coast. One of the collapsed examples on the Dingle Peninsula is
in Ballymorereagh townland, and it is called Teampull Mancháin or Temple-
managhan, the church or oratory of St Manchán, the little monk – a name which
was so common in early medieval Ireland that it is impossible to identify the saint
after whom the oratory was named.

It is curiously sited high up in a sloping field on the south-eastern flank of Lateevemore hill, presenting a splendid vista of Dingle harbour. To the east, a view of Mount Brandon presents itself on a clear day (Fig. 26). In the opposite direction, the Skelligs are visible just above a low saddle joining the high ground of Lateevemore and Caherard to the south. Had the oratory, like most others of its kind, been located on lower ground – even further down the same field – it would not have been possible to see the Skelligs. The only rational explanation for the choice of this location by St Manchán, who is presumably buried there, and the building of the oratory on a levelled man-made platform, is that it was purposely chosen so as to give a view of both Mount Brandon and the Skelligs. It underlines the importance of a visual link between the site and the pilgrims' goal, as suggested by Gallarus and Mount Brandon, and the Glenfahan beehive huts looking out at the Skelligs. Teampull Mancháin is important in visually connecting the two in one.

Another example of a collapsed oratory of Gallarus type was discovered at Reask, the only fully excavated site on the Dingle Peninsula. The oratory, of which only the lower wall courses remain, was found to overlie an earlier structure made of wood; while neither were able to provide a satisfactory date, the find is an important demonstration that wooden structures preceded those of stone in Early Christian Ireland. Beside the church was what the excavator, Tom Fanning, took to be the grave of a founding saint, who cannot be identified because the place-name indicates damp and marshy ground and not a personal name. The place is certainly not marshy nowadays, but there may once have been marshy ground not very far away, overlooking Smerwick harbour. The site includes a number of beehive huts, among them two sets grouped together. Similar groups are found in the clusters of huts in Glenfahan, west of Ventry (e.g. Fig. 78) where, as at Reask, they are

Fig. 26 *Teampull Mancháin with Mount Brandon in the background*

79

contained within an irregularly shaped cashel, or stone wall. The fine collection of cross-decorated pillars (e.g. Fig. 27) on the site could argue in favour of Reask having played a role in sheltering pilgrims landing on the nearby beach, though it is some considerable distance from the Saint's Road. Not far away, there is a roughly circular rath or fort (as it is marked on the Ordnance Survey half-inch map) in Emlagh townland, possibly with a collapsed stone structure within; it may have had some connection with pilgrimage traffic because the sightline from it to Gallarus oratory continues to the top of Mount Brandon, indicating an intentional rather than random choice of site.

One of the rarely visited oratories of Gallarus type is at Kilmalkedar (Fig. 3), and it is dedicated to St Brendan. It lies only a few fields away from the main church at Kilmalkedar (Plate XII). on the Saint's Road from Ventry and Maumanorig to Mount Brandon. This church is dedicated not to St Brendan but to a lesser-known Saint Malkedar (Maolcethair), son of Ronan, a king of Uladh. *The Martyrology of Donegal* records the saint's death in the year 636. It is noteworthy that the only real church on the Mount Brandon pilgrimage – and indeed the most distinctive church of the whole Peninsula – is dedicated not to the saint in whose honour the pilgrimage was held, but to a comparatively insignificant saint, about whom nothing is known other than his parentage and the date of his death. It was argued above that it is in the *Navigatio Brendani* that we first come across evidence of an association of St Brendan with the Dingle Peninsula, through the description of a tongue of land, stretching far out into the sea with a mountain at the end of it, in the remoter parts of the area from whence the saint sprang. The marginally earlier (about 800) First *Life* of St Brendan is in no way specific about associating the saint with the Dingle Peninsula. It would seem, therefore, that it was only around the time of the composition of the *Navigatio*, probably around the 9th century, that St Brendan began to be associated with the Peninsula and the pilgrimage which has ever since been linked with his name. The same first *Life* of the saint pointed out that his original name was Mobhi, and a story was invented to relate how he came to the name by which he is generally known. The association of St Brendan with the Peninsula and the Mount bearing a name sounding adventitiously like his own may have only come about when the Ciarraige (the people of Kerry) grafted their saint on to the old mountain festival associated with Lug and Crom Dubh, and started to promulgate the cult of St Brendan along the Atlantic seaboard, perhaps some time not too far removed from the year 800.

But as St Malkedar/Maolcethair was obviously already well established as the local saint, his cult was retained when St Brendan was made the central saint of the Peninsula's pilgrimage as his church lay directly on the Saint's Road from Maumanorig and Ventry harbour to Mount Brandon. Local traditional veneration must have been stronger than that of St Dabheoc in Lough Derg, but both cases present us with instances where an earlier local saint had the cult of a more important saint imposed upon his own, although the association of the lesser-known saint with the locality was probably better founded than that of the saint of

Fig. 27 *The stone with a cross of arcs at Reask on the Dingle Peninsula* (OPPOSITE) *had a hole on the upper left-hand corner when Du Noyer drew it around 1860, but it has since been broken out*

Fig. 28 *The cross-inscribed Ogham stone standing at*
about 2000 feet on the Brandon massif at Arraglen,
County Kerry. The ringed cross (LEFT) *is the east face,*
and the unringed cross (RIGHT) *the west face*

more national importance. The change of name from Cruach Aigle to Croagh
Patrick is likely to have been closer in time to the linkage of St Brendan with Mount
Brandon than to the linkage of St Patrick with Lough Derg.

The dating of oratories of Gallarus type is a notoriously difficult, not to say
insoluble, problem. There is no carved decoration by which to date them
stylistically, nor mortar by which to obtain a radiocarbon date. For many years,
such oratories were seen as a halfway-house, architecturally, between the beehive
hut and the church with upright walls, in what was seen as a Darwinian line of
development from the seemingly primitive to the seemingly more sophisticated. In
such a scheme, oratories of Gallarus type had to be placed at the beginning of
church development, and therefore some time before the 8th century, when the first
annalistic references to a stone church in the eastern part of Ireland are found. But
the oratories can equally well be seen as an adaptation of the idea of the rectangular
stone church of non-Irish origin to the local methods of corbel construction
practised in the beehive huts. Thus, these oratories could be seen as coming at the
end of a line of development, which would thus allow us to place the oratories
anywhere between the 9th and the 12th century, or say between 800 and 1200. One
could argue that they developed around the time, in the 9th century, when the
Ciarraige were cultivating the Brendan cult, but as the finial from Teampull
Mancháin/Templemanaghan is similar to a type found on the 12th-century church at
Kilmalkedar, one could equally well argue for a construction date in the
Romanesque period. It may be that the oratories, like the beehive huts, were built
over a number of centuries.

When we look at St Brendan's Oratory (Fig. 3) and the Romanesque church of Kilmalkedar (Plate XII), the latter looks much more developed and recent, which could give the impression that St Brendan's is the older foundation. But, as was the case with the oratory at Reask, St Malkedar's church as it stands at present is only the most recent church on the site, having been preceded, presumably, by one or more churches of wood, the oldest perhaps going back to the time of the saint himself in the 7th century. Nothing survives of these wooden structures, and disturbance through building and burial down the centuries would probably have destroyed most of the evidence to indicate their former existence.

Close to the church is a curious two-storey roofless building, recently repointed, known as St Brendan's, or the Priest's, or even the Chancellor's House (Plate IV). This is a rare survival of a possibly 17th-century stone house, which may have been the residence of the administrator of the pilgrimage. Close by are two holy wells dedicated to St Brendan, and beside the road a large bullaun with four depressions has been placed leaning up against a wall.

Kilmalkedar (Plate XII) is the only church in the Romanesque style on the whole Peninsula. It is characterised by *antae*, projections of the north and south walls out beyond the east and west gables of the nave. There is fine chevron ornamentation on the doorway and chancel arch, and the interior north and south walls have blind arcading which Leask suggested were modelled on Cormac's Chapel in Cashel, dating from 1127-1134, so that the Kerry church can be said to have been built no earlier than the middle third, or possibly even the final third, of the 12th century. The chancel is an addition, replacing a much smaller extension for the altar that was part of the original structure. In the grounds of the church are several interesting monuments. The largest is a stone cross six feet high; others of similar size are found throughout the Peninsula, as at Reenconnell, Killiney near Castlegregory, and the Magharees – the latter being an island site with a heavy stone cashel enclosing an oratory, beehive huts (Fig. 74), a bullaun and smaller cross-decorated stones. Kilmalkedar has a fragment of a cross-decorated stone which bears an old Irish alphabet that was dated by Bieler to around the 6th century, though it could well be later. In the burial ground surrounding the church there are small, undecorated stone crosses, an Ogham stone with a hole near its top (Plate XII), and a beautifully carved sundial – possibly dating from the 12th century – which has the face of the sundial on one side and an equal-armed cross of arcs on the other (Figs. 89-90).

This equal-armed cross greets us on another remarkable monument on the Peninsula – a pillar-stone over 6 feet (1.9 metres) high in the townland of Arraglen. It has what is virtually a cross of arcs in a circle on one face (Fig. 28), and on the other an equal-armed cross with a small extension at the right-hand end of the upper limb making it into a Chi-Rho, the symbol of Christ. On the corners of the pillar are Ogham characters read by Macalister as *Qrimitir Ron(an)n Ma(q) Comogann* – 'Ronan the Priest son of Comgan'. What makes this cross-inscribed pillar so remarkable is its location at a height of about 2000 feet on a saddle between Masatiompán (2509 feet) and the ridge leading southwards towards Mount Brandon. At that altitude, it can scarcely have been a burial monument or even a boundary marker, and the fact that it was erected by a priest so close in height to the summit of Mount Brandon would argue strongly in favour of its having had a connection with the Christian pilgrimage to the summit. It stands, in fact, where those approaching the summit from the most northerly route possible – from Brandon Bay on the east and Tiduff on the west – could have met before joining up for the final climb southwards towards the summit, going in the same direction as the initial part of the path to Croagh Patrick. Further support for the notion that this Arraglen pillar (re-erected in 1982, but since fallen again) was linked to the pilgrimage is found on the boulder at Kilcolman in Maumanorig (Fig. 23) near the other end of the pilgrimage road. Here, an encircled equal-armed cross and another without a circle are partially framed by an angular Ogham inscription which Macalister read as *Anm Colman Ailithir*, 'the name [or soul?] of Colman the pilgrim', a truly monumental reason for seeing the small enclosure at Maumanorig as being associated with the Mount Brandon pilgrimage.

The Peninsula houses many other examples of stones bearing crosses, too numerous to mention here individually. Suitable illustrations will be found in the invaluable *Archaeological Survey of the Dingle Peninsula*, published in 1986. Nevertheless, we may mention a few remarkable examples because of their relevance to the Mount Brandon pilgrimage. There are two, and possibly three, stones bearing crosses of arcs at Faha, where pilgrims approaching the summit from the east foregathered for the climb. At Currauly, on the Saint's Road in the valley of a tributary of the Feohanagh river, there is a stone (now broken) with two crosses one above the other; at Teampull Mancháin/Templemanaghan there is a stone with two simple crosses and an Ogham inscription, and not far away, at Kilfountan, is a stone with an equal-armed cross and a Latin as well as an Ogham inscription (Fig. 29). At Kilvickadownig, between Ventry harbour and the beehive huts at Glenfahan, there is a boulder with a fine equal-armed cross on a stem, and at Lateevemanagh, directly beside the Saint's road, a stone bearing an equal-armed cross leans perilously close to an incongruous water trough. Finally, at Reask, there are many cross-decorated slabs (some now preserved in the Heritage Centre at Ballyferriter nearby). The most famous of them is still *in situ*, and bears the letters *dne* (for *domine*, Latin for 'Lord') and a small perforation on the upper left side, now broken out (Fig. 27) but visible in its complete state in Du Noyer's mid-19th century watercolour.

About 350 Ogham stones are known from Ireland, and slightly more than one-sixth of these – totalling around 60 – come from the Dingle Peninsula. Only two of them are found east of Brandon; all the others are found to the south or west of the Brandon massif, a distribution which corresponds remarkably closely with that of the beehive huts. For monuments which are so often considered to be pagan, it is remarkable that approximately one quarter (more than fifteen) of the Ogham stones in the Dingle Peninsula bear one or more crosses; it is not possible to state for certain which was earlier – Ogham or cross – or whether, as would seem more likely on general grounds, both were contemporary. The crosses are usually of the Greek equal-armed variety (though differing in design from one stone to the next), but Latin crosses – those with the long stem – are also found. One unusual Ogham stone is that at Kinard East. It has a cross-design in a square, with a smaller cross within the two upper quadrants. For our purposes, the site is perhaps even more

Fig. 29 *Cross-inscribed Ogham stone* (OPPOSITE) *at Kilfountan, County Kerry*

interesting than the cross-design for, as Máire Macneill has noted, it was a place where people used to go picking bilberries on the last Sunday in July, Crom Dubh Sunday, on which day they would also go to Cloghane and partake in the great Patron there. The Kinard cross-decorated Ogham stone may thus provide a rather tenuous link between Ogham and the pilgrimage on the last Sunday in July.

Both Kinard and Maumanorig preserve examples of those mysterious stones, with man-made hollows like basins, known as bullaun stones. Their exact purpose has been the subject of much speculation, but their connection with pilgrimage is made at least plausible through the existence of a number of examples west of Mount Brandon, as at Kilcolman near where the Saint's Road started, as far as we can tell. They also occur at other places which may have been connected with the mountain pilgrimage, such as Kilmalkedar. Bullauns are known, too, from some of the offshore islands such as the Magharees (otherwise known as Illauntannig) and Inishvickillane. In most cases there is only one hollow on the bullaun stones of the peninsula, but the most easily acessible example – at the side of Main Street in the town of Dingle – has a total of seven depressions.

In the *Journal of the Royal Society of Antiquaries of Ireland* for the year 1960, Caoimhín O Danachair published a comprehensive and useful article on the holy wells of the Barony of Corkaguiney, which is roughly coterminous with the Dingle Peninsula. The visiting of holy wells is still an expression of ancient pilgrimage custom, though one which was apparently independent of the pilgrimage in honour of St Brendan, and it is interesting to note that there are three times the number of holy wells in this barony than in its neighbouring counterparts. Most of these retain their ancient characteristics and practices, though the annual visit on a particular day to these holy wells is largely a thing of the past. The practice of doing 'rounds', the drinking and application of water, differs little from the norm elsewhere in the country. What is of interest for us here is the dedication of the wells to saints who are associated with the Peninsula – St Brendan and St Manchán – but also to others who have no obvious connection with it, such as St Brigid, St Ciarán, St Enda, St Molaga and St Fionán, the last of whom is said to have come from Skellig Michael with the archangel Michael and landed at Kinard. The implications of these dedications are considered briefly below (pp. 180, 234).

The Dingle Peninsula, and its fascinating collection of ancient remains, can be said to represent a veritable microcosm of monuments which can be associated with pilgrimage traffic in early Ireland. Only two types of monument are missing. One is a special tomb-shrine for St Malkedar (for his tomb may well lie beneath the church at Kilmalkedar). The second is a round tower. But the Peninsula had no need of such a tower to act as a beacon to attract the pilgrim, for it had its own in the form of the mountain over 3000 feet (1000 metres) high, which could be seen from a much greater distance than any round tower.

SKELLIG MICHAEL, KERRY

Kinard, on the small inlet of Trabeg east of Dingle, has, as we have seen, a cross-inscribed Ogham stone, and on Crom Dubh Sunday people used to pick bilberries there, at Mary's Well. This is one of three wells at Kinard, the other two being dedicated to St Michael the archangel and St Fionán or Finan. Máire MacNeill records a local story which tells of the latter two returning from Skellig Michael and landing at Kinard, having lost their bearings in a fog. They fell to praying, whereupon two wells sprang up which ever since have borne their names. Fionán put the people of the district under his protection, and the Virgin Mary came to them, and praised their piety, so that a third well sprang up under their feet, which was dedicated to her. This naive legend connects the Skelligs and the Dingle Peninsula, and may echo an ancient practice of landing from the Skelligs on the southern side of the Dingle Peninsula. Further support for such a notion could be supplied by the beehive huts in the townlands of Fahan, Glenfahan and Coumeenole, which look out at the Skelligs and which may have been used temporarily by people who had landed at Ventry harbour after or preparatory to a visit to the Skelligs – one may presume, in the course of a maritime pilgrimage. It is not surprising, therefore, that some of the features we have met with in the Dingle Peninsula recur on Skellig Michael.

There are two Skellig islands – the Greater and the Lesser Skellig – the latter of which is almost impossible to land on unless you are a bird; it is one of the largest gannet colonies in these islands. The Great Skellig, commonly known as Skellig Michael, is a most remarkable island, rising steeply out of the Atlantic Ocean to a peak 714 feet high. Its conical shape makes it an obvious candidate for a holy island, and even if there are no obvious signs of prehistoric occupation, it may well have been a sanctuary in pagan times, as the 19th-century Cork antiquary John Windele argued when suggesting that it was used for the worship of the dragon which St Michael overcame.

Sacheverell Sitwell remarked that 'for emergency of site and drama of isolation there is nothing to choose between Aran or the Great Skellig and the rocks of Meteora or dales of Athos . . . yet, of all these, none is dramatic as the Great Skellig. It is the cauldron of the storm'. Certainly, the Great Skellig is not easily accessible. An hour-and-a-half sea journey in a big swell can be frightening to the point of panic for those not expecting anything of the kind on a pleasant day's outing, and a twenty-foot rise and fall in the water level at the landing place is only for those who are nimble of foot. Yet, for centuries, pilgrims have undertaken this hazardous journey. Perhaps the earliest reference to it as a place of pilgrimage is in the account of Heneas MacNichaill, who visited it in 1543 on his tour of pilgrimage sites in order to earn absolution from his sin. Two centuries later, a Franciscan named O'Sullivan from the friary at Muckross near Killarney mentions 'the great Skelike formerly very much noted for pilgrimage over most part of Europe'. Even if this were to be regarded as a piece of local hyperbole and pride, it does show us that the Skellig was an important place of pilgrimage. Yet, early historical references to the rock, which bring us back a thousand years earlier, make no mention of it as a place of pilgrimage. We know of a man named Eitgall, perhaps a hermit, who was carried away by the Vikings in 824, later to die of hunger and thirst. In 882, Flann, an abbot of Scelec, is referred to in the *Annals of Inisfallen*, and the *Annals of the Four Masters* mention the death of Blathmac Sgeillice in 950 and of Aodh ó Scellice Mhichíl – Hugh of Skellig Michael – in 1044.

These annalistic references bring out two important points, the first of which is the existence of an abbot of Skellig, thus implying the existence of a monastery of some sort there, unless the title were given to a person who may have been an administrator of the pilgrimage. The other significant item in the annalistic references is that it was only in 1044 that the name of the archangel first became attached to the island, which had previously been referred to, in one spelling or another, simply as the Skellig. The dedication to St Michael is in no way surprising, as he was the patron saint of high places, as demonstrated, for instance, by Monte Gargano in Apulia, Mont St Michel in Normandy, and St Michael's Mount in Cornwall. Nevertheless, 18th-century tradition in Kerry ascribed the foundation to St Finan, who is also associated with sites on the nearby Iveragh Peninsula, most notably St Finan's Bay, which is more accessible from the sea than from the landward side, and which looks out directly at the Skelligs. There are many St Finans in early Ireland and Scotland, and it has proved well-nigh impossible to differentiate between them satisfactorily. But we may speculate that our St Finan may have been a local Kerry saint associated with the western end of the Iveragh Peninsula, and that he was the first Christian saint to whom the island sanctuary was dedicated. We may have here yet another instance where the Church superimposed a better-known saint on a site associated with a lesser-known saint of purely local significance, as seems to have been the case with saints Brendan and Maolcethair (Malkedar) on the Dingle Peninsula. If this supposition is correct, we could surmise that the superimposition took place within fifty years of the turn of the millennium, between the annalistic entry for 950, which refers to Sgellice, and that of 1044, which describes the place as Sccelice Mhichíl, or Skellig Michael. But the story referred to above shows that local tradition in the Dingle Peninsula connects both saints with the island, though Françoise Henry's discovery of a 16th-century reference to the island as being 'of the Holy cross' may provide an alternative dedication.

Fig. 30 *The beehive huts on Skellig Michael may have provided accommodation for both monks and pilgrims*

The main cluster of buildings on the island is found largely on a man-made platform over 500 feet (170 metres) above sea level. From the present-day landing stage, this cluster is reached by an open stone stairway, which is probably a 19th-century replacement or embellishment of a much earlier one. Coming in to the earlier enclosure, which is surrounded by a stone wall, the visitor comes first to the 'monks' garden' and then emerges into the space containing the main group of buildings (Fig. 30, Plate X). These comprise five beehive huts and the ruins of a sixth. These huts are almost square inside but round outside, constructed in the corbelling method already encountered on the Dingle Peninsula. The largest of the huts has a series of stones protruding at regular intervals on the exterior, of a kind found on one of the beehive huts of comparatively recent construction on the Dingle Peninsula. The stones presumably performed the function of a kind of ancient scaffolding, which one could climb either as the hut was a-building or as a means of reaching the top to effect necessary repairs – or both.

Grellan D. Rourke, of the Office of Public Works, who has been studying the buildings in conjunction with the Californian research team of Professor Walter Horn and Jenny White Marshall, has worked out a relative chronology for the construction of the beehive huts, without it being possible to establish the interval in time between each one, for the huts are not datable in themselves, as they are built of drystone without mortar. Another member of the Californian team, Professor Rainer Berger, has been able to establish a possible date for the rectangular church in front of the beehive huts. By extracting carbon from the mortar used in the older part of the church, he obtained a radiocarbon date of around the middle of the 9th century, roughly the same period as the first annalistic reference to the island, when Eitgall was carried off by the Norsemen. This date suggests that the works needed to create the perilous platform on which the church stands must have been constructed before that date, though how long before we cannot say. This church was presumably the central place of worship for whatever monastery may have been established on the island at that period, and there must have been something worth plundering on the island for the Vikings to have visited it on their forays.

Although the historical sources do not refer to a monastery, they twice mention the existence of an abbot. The island, isolated by bad weather from the mainland throughout many parts of the year, is unlikely to have provided much food for a monastic community other than vegetables or birds' eggs, and it seems improbable that the community would have been large at any one time. This raises the unanswerable question as to whether the beehive huts were built to house a permanent community of monks or for the shelter of pilgrims who came to be stranded on the island waiting for a favourable wind to get them away. Though the former is the normally accepted solution, the latter must also be kept in mind as a possibility. Perhaps we should envisage the beehive huts as having served both purposes.

The church was not the only place for praying on the island. Close by is an oratory of the Gallarus type, whilst outside the enclosure is yet another, even smaller example which stands on a man-made terrace, which had to have massive 'surgery' done to it by the Office of Public Works in 1987 to prevent it from sliding down a precipitous slope into the sea. Because other pilgrimage sites, notably Clonmacnois, had a church for women outside the main monastic enclosure, we may well ask if this small oratory was originally reserved for women pilgrims on Skellig Michael. In modern times, women were involved on the Skelligs in an interesting and unexpected way. According to Munster tradition, the holy season of Lent began on the Skelligs later than on the mainland, and couples were allegedly able to marry on the island during the fasting period when it would have been impossible on the mainland. It is likely that it was the 'courting, dancing and drinking' of these happy young people on the island which was responsible for the Catholic Church bringing this age-old pilgrimage to an end, so that nothing remains of it today.

If the voyage to the island were not a sufficiently ascetic exercise for any pilgrims to endure in the days before steam or motor boats, there was one other awaiting them on the island which required the strongest of nerves. This involved climbing up through a hole in the rock known as the Eye of the Needle, to the western summit of the island, 714 feet high. There the pilgrim was expected to clamber out on a narrow spit to kiss a carving (no longer extant) on the end of the spit; in 1839 one man actually walked out along the spit – quite a feat when the terrifying drop to the sea below is contemplated as an alternative. This exercise seems to have been the most difficult of the stations on the island, the others presumably having involved visits to the church and oratories as well as to the various crosses dotted around the island.

It is interesting to note that close to the spit there is a small and narrow platform on which there was a further small corbelled oratory of uncertain date. It smacks of a place where a solitary hermit could cut himself off from anyone else on the island – surely one of the eeriest hermitages known to man. It also raises the question as to whether the Skellig started off as a hermitage – used by St Finan – and later developed into the small monastery which would presumably have been responsible for undertaking the considerable site works involved in the construction of the platform or terrace on which huts, church and oratory stand. It was only through these terracings that it would have been possible to accommodate those innumerable pilgrims who must have visited the island down the centuries – and the tourists who visit the island in such numbers in our own time that one fears for the safety and future of the complex.

'ARAN OF THE SAINTS', GALWAY

The three Aran islands – Inishmore, Inishmaan and Inisheer (the large, middle and eastern islands respectively) – are like three jewels decorating the entrance to Galway Bay. Geologically, they are a continuation of the karst limestone of the Burren area in northern County Clare. Though now belonging to County Galway, in later medieval times they were the subject of bitter disputes between the O Briens of Clare and the O Flahertys of Galway; as early as 1587 they passed effectively into English control under Elizabeth I. The history, and prehistory, of the islands can be read through their numerous monuments, which have survived so remarkably well because they were built of stone, a material available there in abundance and which now divides up the land with a network of beautiful stone walls. Though perhaps best known for their great stone forts, of which Dun Aengus is the most famous, the islands are of great interest for our present purposes because of the considerable remains of the Early Christian period surviving on all three islands, which have for long been associated with pilgrimage. Indeed, a 9th-century poem on St Colmcille's goodbye to Aran quoted by John O'Donovan calls the islands *Ara Róimh na n-ailithreach*, 'Aran, the Rome of pilgrims'.

The islands' earliest known Christian inhabitant was St Enda who, having trained in Candida Casa in Galloway, settled on Inishmore, where his foundation became the nursery for a whole generation of great monastic founders, including St Ciarán of Clonmacnois, to whom a church and a holy well on the island are dedicated. A small stone church·– *Teaghlach Éinne*, St Enda's House or Household – housing fragments of not one but two high crosses (as Frank Mitchell has pointed out), .marks the site of St Enda's monastery, which he must have started in the closing years of the 5th century. This was a momentous event, which encouraged the development of those early monasteries throughout Ireland which were to become such great fosterers of learning and the arts in the first centuries of Irish Christianity. It is significant that in the *Navigatio Brendani* St Brendan is said to have visited St Enda before he set out on his wondrous voyage. This suggests that the Aran Islands were connected with that maritime pilgrimage traffic which was presumably mirrored in the *Navigatio*. And the 12th-century Welsh chronicler Giraldus Cambrensis, in stating that a Western island was 'consecrated' by St Brendan, may have been referring to Aran. A millennium after St Brendan, Aran of the Saints was one of the places visited by Heneas MacNichaill in around 1543.

On a slope above the church where, according to tradition, 120 of the islands' saints are said to slumber, there is the stump of a round tower, the top of which, when complete, would probably have reached higher than the stone ridge behind it to the south, thus providing for pilgrims coming by sea an indication of where the site lay. On top of that ridge is one of the smallest of the old Irish stone oratories – Teampull Benén - which, exposed on its commanding position, must also have been visible as a landmark by those approaching the island by boat. The dedicatee is the same saint around whose 'bed' pilgrims make a station on the climb up Croagh Patrick. He was, it seems, a disciple of St Patrick, and his main church is at Kilbennan (the church of Benén) on the mainland, where there is also a fragmentary round tower. It is not known whether he ever visited the Aran Islands. The same can also be said of a number of other saints to whom churches on the islands were dedicated: MacDuagh, whose main foundation was at Kilmacduagh (see pages 124-5) near the Clare border in south Galway, St Soorney, whose name is connected with Drumacoo on the south-eastern shore of Galway Bay, and St Gobnait, patroness of beekeepers, whose foundation still survives at Ballyvourney as a centre of pilgrimage in north-west Cork (pages 133-6).

The most important modern pilgrimage on the islands is not to St Enda's grave but to that of St Caomhán who, perhaps unjustifiedly in the light of history, was described by John O'Donovan in 1839 as 'by far the most celebrated of all the saints of the Aran Islands'. Surprisingly little is known about him, tradition saying that he was a brother of St Kevin (Irish: *Coemgen*) of Glendalough; his name is similar to that of the saint of Glendalough (where the existence of a brother to St Kevin on the Aran Islands is apparently unknown), suggesting that the two saints could be identical, but their feast-days are not the same. Close to St Caomhán's grave on the smallest island, Inisheer, there is a nave and chancel church, which is well below present ground level because it is smothered by blown sand. This is heaped out once a year to allow a pilgrimage to take place there (Fig. 31) on the saint's day, 14 June. Writing in 1683 Roderick O'Flaherty named a different day:

Fig. 31 *Pilgrims praying at the church of St Caomhán, Inisheer, Aran Islands, on the Saint's feast-day, 14 June, for which the sand is cleared from the church*

He [St Coemhan] lies buried in the island on the north side of the church dedicated to his name, where he is worshipped the 3rd of November. There is a marble stone over his tomb with a square wall built about it on a plain green field in prospect of the sea; where sick people used to lie overnight and recover health of God for his [Coemhan's] sake. I have seen one grievously tormented by a thorn thrust into his eye, who by lyeing so in St Coemhan's burying place, had it miraculously taken out without the least feeling of the patient, the mark whereof remains to this day in the corner of his eye.

In addition to St Enda and St Caomhán, and groupings of saints venerated on the island – the Four Comely Saints (Fursa, Brendan of Birr, Conall and Bearchan), and an unidentified king's seven sons and seven daughters – there is a third saint whose burial place on Inishmore has played an important role in pilgrimage on the Aran Islands. This is St Brecán about whom, like St Caomhán, we know little, though he may be identified with the saint of Kilbreckan in County Clare. A 14th- or 15th-century poem published by Anne O'Sullivan suggests that he was of the Clare sept of the Dál Cais, and a contemporary of St Patrick. Having given up the life of a soldier, his first mission was allegedly to Aran, where he destroyed a reigning idol, Brecán, whose name he adopted in preference to his own (Bresal), and converted the pagan sanctuary into a *dísert*, or hermitage, suggesting continuity from a pagan cult. One stanza of the poem runs as follows:

Fig. 32 *Temple Brecán on Inishmore, Aran Islands,
showing the church and the secular buildings*

*I got seven requests: God was satisfied with my offerings, not least of them was that on an
enclosed piece of land He created a sanctuary for pilgrims.*

St Brecán's Clare origins may well explain his oblivion today, since the Clare
O'Briens lost possession of the islands in around the 15th or 16th century. But the
existence of several later medieval buildings (Fig. 32) on the site argues for
considerable activity there at that period, probably of a pilgrimage nature.

The main church, dedicated to the saint, was rectangular in shape, had *antae* –
projections of the north and south walls beyond the east and west gables – and is
likely to have had an entrance doorway in the south wall, a feature which suggests a
date no earlier than the 12th century. The church was subsequently enlarged around
the 13th century. In the original west wall is a stone bearing the inscription *Or ar II
canoin* ('a prayer for two canons'), but what these canons' relationship to the church
may have been we cannot say. Another church, known as Teampull an Phoill
(?Church of the Hollows) located some 125 feet (43 metres) to the north-east, is
likely to be no earlier than the 13th century, and may well be later.

The whole complex, known as *Temple Brecán*, or St Brecán's Church, is
popularly called the Seven Churches. There are, in fact, only two churches
surviving within the surrounding wall, and the popular but misconceived

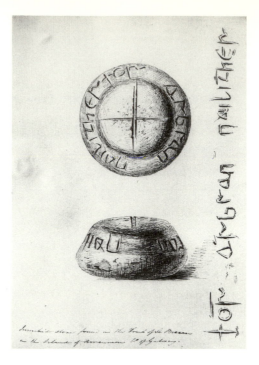

Fig. 33 *George Petrie's sketch of a cresset lamp inscribed in Irish 'Pray for Bran the pilgrim', found in the tomb of St Brecán at Temple Brecán, Inishmore*

nomenclature comes about because of a number of other buildings on the site which are, in fact, domestic structures dating from the later medieval period. They total seven, which would bring the number of buildings to nine, but not all have been well preserved. These stone buildings are simple rectangles in shape, and John Waddell – who has done a valuable survey of the site – has noted the similarity in design of many of them to the traditional thatched houses of the west and north of Ireland. We may presume that they were indeed roofed with thatch, but what purpose did they serve? Because some of the few medieval secular buildings to have survived outside towns in Ireland are found on pilgrimage sites such as Kilmalkedar, Kilmacduagh and Banagher in County Derry (see page 183), we may presume that they served some function connected with pilgrimage. Perhaps one was inhabited by an administrator of the pilgrimage, and others may have served as hostels for pilgrims.

Between the two churches is the saint's *leaba*, which may be variously translated as his 'bed' or his 'grave', and this was no doubt the main centre of devotion on the site. In 1822, George Petrie, the father of Irish archaeology, dug under a cross-inscribed slab bearing the inscription *sci Bre . . ni*, normally taken to read 'Saint Brecán', which lay on the *leaba*. Under another, uninscribed, slab four feet below the surface he discovered a deep grave containing rounded beach pebbles and a stone (now in the National Museum in Dublin), which bears the inscription *Or ar Bran n-ailither*, 'a prayer for Bran the pilgrim', the best evidence we have for Temple

Brecán having been a place of pilgrimage (Fig. 33). Macalister, who took the stone to be a cresset lamp, thought the name Bran was an abbreviated form of the saint's name Brecán, but this identification is not convincing, though the stone may have lain in what was the saint's grave. The lamp is more likely to have been placed in position by an otherwise unknown pilgrim named Bran at some undetermined period, for the study of Irish script is not sufficiently far advanced for us to be able to date the inscription through the shape of its letters.

Of the other cross-inscribed slabs known from Temple Brecán, none is more tantalising than that with the inscription 'VII ROMANI' (Fig. 9). Macalister took the 'Seven Romans' to honour the seven martyred sons of Symphorosa, and assumed that they were the object of special devotion in Ireland. But the inscription can be interpreted in other ways. The word *Romani* was used in early medieval Latin sources to mean those who were spiritually dependent upon Rome, and in the 7th century it denoted those who favoured the new method of calculating the date of Easter. The *Romani* of the Temple Brecán stone can, however, simply be taken to mean seven Romans who had visited the site, or seven Irish pilgrims who had made the pilgrimage to Rome. As the seven are unlikely to have died at the same time and been buried beside the slab, it is more likely to mean seven people who had come on pilgrimage to Temple Brecán, and who possibly commissioned the stone to commemorate the event. The Irish Litany of Pilgrim Saints, written perhaps around 800, opens with an invocation to 'Thrice fifty coracles of Roman pilgrims', and as Kathleen Hughes thinks that it is more likely that these were Irish pilgrims to Rome rather than Romans visiting Ireland, it would not be unreasonable to assume that this Aran Islands stone is an instance of Irish pilgrims to Rome who, in this instance, also visited Temple Brecán. But whichever meaning we take from the inscription, it is interesting to note that seven people who had visited Rome, or even came from there, thought it worthwhile to visit Temple Brecán. This underlines Temple Brecán as an important pilgrimage site at the time when the stone was erected, perhaps some time between the 8th and the 10th century, though it is as difficult to date the stone precisely as it is in the case of the cresset lamp mentioned above.

A dozen or more other cross-decorated slabs are known from Temple Brecán, all equally undatable. But we are on a surer footing with the remains of three high crosses on the site, all of which are in a fragmentary condition brought about, some have suggested on undocumented grounds, because of the iconoclastic proclivities of the Cromwellians who are known to have inhabited the island. The decoration on all of these crosses points to a date in the 12th century, and the same is equally true of the cross fragments at Teaghlach Éinne, also on Inishmore. The churches on the three Aran islands may be difficult to date accurately, but there is little to indicate that they are earlier than the 12th century. Even though none of them shows the Romanesque ornament so typical of churches built in 12th-century Ireland, this is the century to which many are most likely to belong, and Rainer Berger's recently-achieved datings of the radiocarbon content of mortar samples taken from some of them suggest dates in the 11th or 12th century. This dating of the churches, and the fact that all the Aran Island crosses, dating also from the 12th century, are found on two of the three main sites of pilgrimage, Temple Brecán and Teaghlach Éinne, would suggest that pilgrimage to the Aran Islands was at its height in the 12th century, though – as noted above – the buildings at Temple

Brecán support a continued use of that site into the Norman period of the 13th century and even later.

For a comparatively small area, the Aran Islands preserve the largest collection of beehive huts outside the Dingle Peninsula. The huts do not occur in groups as they do in Kerry – most of them are single – but they are found close to some of the churches, such as Teaghlach Éinne, and on the ridge near Teampull Benén, as well as at Temple Gobnait on Inisheer, where two bullauns are also present. One of the tall, thin pillar-stones at Mainistir Chiaráin on Inishmore may have served as a sundial as there is a large hole near the top of it, and at Kilcholan there is a fragment of a slab shrine described by John Waddell.

One further point calls for comment. This is the much greater abundance of high crosses and cross-decorated slabs at Temple Brecán than at any other site on the three islands, suggesting that it may represent the most important pilgrimage site. This is certainly surprising in view of the relative obscurity of the saint after whom the site is named. Why was his grave considered more important than that of St Caomhán, so much honoured in modern times, or St Enda, who brought such lustre to Aran in the 6th century? He was not even born on Inishmore, and there seems no reason to believe in this instance that the Church imposed him on the island, as he was not a saint of any national significance. One reason for the popularity of the site may have been its location near the western extremity of Inishmore, the most westerly of the three Aran islands. It would have been most convenient for those pilgrims involved in a maritime pilgrimage up and down the west coast of Ireland, obviating any need to travel further eastwards. However, the presence of the round tower at Teaghlach Éinne could suggest that it acted as an identifying landmark not for those on maritime pilgrimage but for people who made the journey from the mainland from either County Clare or County Galway, perhaps from Roscam not far from Galway city, where there is also a round tower. The comparative proximity to the Clare coast of Teampull Caomhán on Inisheer might indicate that it was more popular with Clare pilgrims, even if there is no evidence to support such a contention.

St MacDara's Island, Galway

In some parts of the English-speaking world today, the word 'hooker' has a perjorative meaning. On the west coast of Ireland, however, where good old-fashioned values are stoutly maintained, it would immediately be taken to mean a solid wooden sailing craft formerly used to ferry turf from the mainland to the Aran Islands. But it also has traditional associations with another, much smaller island off the coast of Connemara: St MacDara's Island, not far from Carna. When passing between this island and Mason Head, it was the custom for these sailing craft to dip their sails three times in honour of the saint; other saints were venerated in a similar fashion at Caher Island and Inishglora off the Mayo coast, at Scattery Island in the Shannon estuary, and also opposite St Gregory's Tomb on the Aran island of Inishmore. Ancient tales spoke of terrible things happening when the custom was not observed at St MacDara's Island, such as when a man of the Galway garrison was so beset by storms in 1672 that he failed to do obeisance to the saint: though he vowed that he would never pass that way again without paying due reverence to the holy man, he was lost at sea shortly afterwards. These hookers still ferry passengers out to the island on the day of the saint's pilgrimage, 16 July, and stand

PLATE IX *Pilgrims on St MacDara's Island, 1990*

PLATE X *Beehive huts on Skellig Michael, County Kerry*

Plate XI *The* caiseal *was the centre of the pilgrimage on Inishmurray, County Sligo, and contains St Molaise's House*

PLATE XII Opposite: *The holed Ogham stone stands in front of the Romanesque church at Kilmalkedar, County Kerry*

P<small>LATE</small> XIII *Doing the Stations on the Glencolmcille pilgrimage, St Columba's Day*

off with their sails dipped during the pilgrimage Mass. To ferry out the pilgrims, who in 1990 numbered well over 200, all the boatmen from the surrounding area with sail or motor boats foregather at points along the mainland shoreline and bring the passengers out on the ten to fifteen minute run to the island free, gratis and for nothing. On returning to harbour from the pilgrimage, I asked my boatman if he would be insulted if I were to offer him something towards his fuel costs, to which his reply was that, yes, he would indeed be insulted – but that I could offer him a drink next time we met in a pub!

It is curious that the saint is nearly always referred to as 'the son of Dara' but rarely given what was apparently his proper name Sionnach, 'the Fox'. It is difficult to know if this has anything to do with the superstition recorded by John O'Donovan in the Ordnance Survey letters of 1838 that no Connemara man would venture out to fish in the morning if he saw a fox, hare or rabbit or even heard the name of one of them even mentioned. We know little or nothing about the saint other than his name, not even the approximate century in which he lived. Yet his island is famous throughout Connemara and even beyond – on my way to the harbour I met a young man who was driving from Tuam, about forty miles away, to take part in the pilgrimage, and another man I met had arranged his holidays home to Connemara from his workplace in London so that he could participate. According to Roderick O'Flaherty, writing in 1683, the island was an inviolable sanctuary, and he also records that there was a stone on the island where women used to gather *duileasg* (a kind of seaweed) at low water, in the belief that any friend in captivity would soon get succour from the saint.

There is only one building on the island, a noteworthy stone church with *antae* continuing right up to the top of the gable (Fig. 34). Its roof is entirely of stone (the

Fig. 34 *The church on St MacDara's Island, County Galway*

Fig. 35 *Pilgrims doing the Stations on St MacDara's Island, County Galway, around 1943*

upper parts restored by the Office of Public Works in 1975). Seen in oblique light, some of the roof stones can be seen to have squares carved upon them in such a way that it is imposible to avoid the conclusion that these squares imitate the shingles of the wooden roof of an earlier church – so we may take the church to be a skeumorph, a stone church which copied the details of an earlier wooden church on the site. The church has Cyclopean masonry, large stones hammered smooth and fitted carefully into the spaces left by the stones beneath them. The doorway slopes gently inwards, and on the exterior top of the west window there is an arched moulding suggesting a 12th-century date. This date is supported by the dating of a sample of the mortar taken from the church. The former gable finial, replaced by Fergus O'Farrell's modern replica in 1975, had geometrical roundels with interlace carved on it, together with a head with high cheekbones, which would also argue for a 12th-century date, the same period to which most of the Aran Islands churches belong, suggesting that on St MacDara's Island, too, pilgrimage was at its height in the 12th century. The American photographer Paul Caponigro, who visited the church in 1988, described it as 'this solitary entity of myth' and said of it:

> *Saint MacDara's church appeared as a timeless edifice; a monument which dismissed the walls and veils of everyday structured events. What pulses forth from this gift of timeless thought is not the 'why', but the 'how' of the existence of this exquisitely proportioned building. It disarmed me. In the presence of this archetype in stone, the rational mind faltered and the heart dismissed all questions. The 'how' was held in stone and proportion, and the hand of man shaped herewith the force of an intangible ideal: heart and hand combined were offered as the tools to manifest the solid structure.*

The only ancient furnishing within the church was a wooden statue of the saint, but Roderick O'Flaherty tells us that Malachy O'Cadhla, Archbishop of Tuam, had it buried underground 'for special weighty reasons' probably around the 1640s.

Photographs (e.g. Fig. 35) in the archival material of the Irish Tourist Board show that in 1943 rounds were made at the stations on the island – mounds of stone surmounted by a cross – but today little remains of the custom, or of the stations. The modern pilgrimage, a rather joyful and colourful affair (Plate IX), consists of a Mass said at around 1 pm on a makeshift altar at the eastern end of the church, recited in Irish, as is the homily, by the parish priest of Carna. During Mass, another priest sits a little distance apart on the Saint's 'bed', hearing confessions. As soon as Mass is over, a musician strikes up some music on an accordion, giving a festive character to the occasion. If the wind is right, the hookers foregathered offshore sail around the island in an afternoon regatta, by which time most of the pilgrims have been ferried back to the mainland. St MacDara's pilgrimage is one of the last pilgrimages along the west coast of Ireland which is still able to attract hundreds from the surrounding countryside and further afield – one of the last surviving links, surely, of a tradition which brings us back many centuries to the early days of Christianity in Ireland – if not before.

INISHMURRAY, SLIGO

Like many of the other smaller islands along the west coast of Ireland north of St MacDara's Island, one notable island is not mentioned in any of the early historic documents as a place of pilgrimage. Yet it has many of the trappings of such a place, and is known in more recent times as the site of an important local pilgrimage. This is Inishmurray, a low island no more than a mile long, located about four miles off the Sligo coast, Streedagh being the nearest landfall.

It is named after an individual named Murray or, in Irish, Muiredach, about whom nothing is known for certain, though Wakeman – who provided us with an invaluable and detailed account of the antiquities of the island a century ago – suggests that he may have been the bishop of Killala of that name who lived at the time of St Patrick. Despite the island's name, its patron saint is generally taken to be St Molaise, whom some take to be identical with the patron of the island of Devenish in Lower Lough Erne. Yet there is even some confusion about his name, for the 17th-century *Martyrology of Donegal*, doubtless using earlier sources, says under 12 August: 'Molaisse, i.e. Laisrén, son of Deglan of Inis Muiredaich in the north [of Connacht]; he it was who, at the cross of Ath-Imlaisi, pronounced sentence of banishment on St Columba.' The much earlier *Martyrology of Oengus*, composed in around 800, states for the same feast day simply: 'the calling of Laisrén of the Island of Muredach, great, magnified'. There seems to be some confusion here. Presumably the earliest saint – if saint he was – associated with the island was Muiredach, after whom the island was called. But were Molaise and Laisrén one and the same person? The *Martyrology of Oengus* records Laisrén without mentioning the name of Molaise. One could imagine that Molaise – if he were to be identified with the saint of Devenish – could represent yet another case of the Church imposing a better-known saint upon a place of pilgrimage long associated with a lesser-known local saint (in this case Laisrén), but the fact that the feast day of St Molaise of Devenish is 12 September, whereas that of the Molaise of Inishmurray is 12 August, would seem to negate such a suggestion. Yet the differing feast days could create a niggling question in the mind as to whether an imposed Molaise may have taken on the feast day on which the cult of Laisrén was normally celebrated.

Other than the death of an abbot of Inishmurray in 747 – which implies the presence of a monastery there in the 8th century – and that of a learned man of the island in 798, the only historical reference to the island before the 17th century is to its burning by the Vikings in 807. This was one of the earliest attacks on an Irish monastery, suggesting that there was something worth burning there. Even in the 17th century, the island is only mentioned with reference to the death of someone who was buried there in 1612. Gwynn and Hadcock noted that the monastery moved to the mainland, perhaps after the Norse raid but certainly by the 13th century; an Augustinian foundation at Aughris continued to use the name Insula Mury until the 15th century. We have to wait until 1779 before we hear of the island again, when Gabriel Beranger visited it to do some sketches.

Beranger's sketches are the first illustrations we have of the island's rich collection of antiquities. Both John O'Donovan and W. F. Wakeman visited the island before the Board of Works carried out a number of repairs there in 1880 which, being unrecorded, make it difficult for us to know exactly what the various structures looked like before their restoration. Nevertheless, five of the plates in the Earl of Dunraven's *Notes on Irish Architecture* of 1875 give us an idea of the state of the ruins at the time.

The centre of the ecclesiastical remains on the island is the Caiseal (Plate XI), a great stone wall enclosing a roughly oval-shaped area. It is of drystone masonry, so there is no mortar in the wall which could help in providing us with a date. There is a considerable variance of opinion about the period of construction of the Caiseal. On the one hand, Dr Paddy Heraughty, an islander himself, who has given us the latest, informative book on Inishmurray and its people, believes that it may have been built after the Viking invasion of 807 in order to protect the inhabitants of the monastery from further attack. On the other hand, Jenny White Marshall of California has, after considerable study, come to the conclusion that the Caiseal is earlier than the structures within it, and that the monastery was therefore founded within a pre-existing stone enclosure. There is, frankly, in the present state of our knowledge, no way of knowing for certain which came first, the monastery or the egg-shaped enclosure.

The Caiseal is approximately one-third of an acre in extent, and is subdivided by a number of low stone walls. The purpose of these subdivisions is not immediately clear. The largest area, which could also be

Fig. 36 *W. F. Wakeman's sketch of* Teach Molaise *on Inishmurray, 1887*

described as unenclosed, contains the two churches Teach Molaise, literally 'Molaise's house', and Teampull na bhFear, the 'Men's Church'. Teach Molaise, with its stone roof, looks to be the older of the two, being almost square in shape (8 feet 10 inches by 7 feet 10 inches), with a small rounded east window and a low doorway (4 feet 11 inches high), the lintel of which is carved with an equal-armed cross. The entrance is extremely low and, with the cross above it, Teach Molaise stands out as being an example of a tomb-shrine of the patron saint. If he were buried within, this would support the contention of Dr Reeves that the Molaise of Inishmurray was not identical with the Molaise of Devenish, who was presumably buried on the Fermanagh island. Inside the church (Fig. 36), a wooden statue of around the 13th century was kept, which the inhabitants identified as that of St Molaise. Fortunately, it did not suffer the same fate as the statue of St MacDara in being buried underground, and is now preserved in the National Museum in Dublin.

Professor Rainer Berger, of the University of California, ably assisted by Aighleann O'Shaughnessy and Grellan D. Rourke of the Office of Public Works in Dublin, recently analysed a sample of the mortar from the oldest part of Teach Molaise (some of the upper parts look secondary), and this provided a calibrated radiocarbon date of AD 700-900, which suggests that the building is not only early in the history of mortared stone buildings in Ireland, but is probably the earliest surviving ecclesiastical structure on the island.

In the centre of the main enclosure is Teampull na bhFear, the Men's Church, which is a rectangular edifice originally probably roofed with thatch or wood. It was used for the burial of men, and an old tradition is recorded to the effect that if any woman were to be interred here, her body would be removed the following night. The church has usually been interpreted as the main church of the monastery. If so, it would add credence to the continued existence of the monastery after the Viking invasion, as Professor Berger's examination of the radiocarbon content of the mortar provided a calibrated date of 800-1150 for this church.

The enclosure in the western portion of the Caiseal is occupied by two structures, one of which is known as Teampull or Teach na Teine (Church or House of the Fire). Its internal measurements are 17 feet 4 inches by 11 feet 4 inches; it has a low gable which makes it look to be amongst the most recent buildings within the Caiseal. A cross decorates the soffit, or underside, of the lintel stone which, in all probability, belonged to an earlier church and was re-used here. The considerable amount of reconstruction done to the southwestern gable in the last century does not hide the probability that this was a late medieval structure which, because it has an entrance in both the long sides, can scarcely be regarded as ever having been a church. Its name derives from the fact that there was a square hearth in the centre. This was orientated differently to the building and, according to tradition, had a fire which never went out, its smouldering embers always providing the inhabitants with a light if necessary. It has been suggested that this fire may well be the successor of an old pagan fire that was never extinguished, like that at Kildare, which may have been Christianised to harmonise with the cult of St Brigid. If the cross-carved lintel derived from an earlier church of which there is now no trace, it may well be that a church formerly stood on the site, and, to judge by the style of its masonry, was replaced by the fire house probably long after the monastery moved to the mainland. The fire house may therefore have had nothing

Fig. 37 *The Big Station with the* Clocha Breacha
('Cursing Stones') inside the Caiseal *on Inishmurray,
County Sligo, with* Teampull na bhFear *in the
background*

to do with a pagan fire retained into the Christian period, and could have functioned
as a dwelling-house with central hearth built for some exalted personage involved
in supervising the pilgrimage and the religious life of the islanders during the later
medieval period. It may thus provide an analogy with St Brendan's House at
Kilmalkedar, or the late medieval houses at Temple Brecán on the Aran Islands.

Within the Caiseal there are further interesting antiquities. These include what
seem like three beehive huts. Those known as Trahaun na gCaoirais ('Lenten
Retreat') and Toory Bhrenell ('Wake of the Virgin' or 'of St Brendan') or,
alternatively, the Schoolhouse (from its 19th-century usage) appear to be genuine
beehive huts, though they differ from those in Kerry by having the door jambs built
of single large stones. The third is known as Teach-an-alais, or 'Sweat-house',
a name deriving from a type of building used in Ireland around the 17th century
and later as a kind of Turkish bath (or *römisch-irische Bäder* as they were termed
in the Germanic lands). The building is more horseshoe-shaped than round, and
is smaller than the two genuine beehive huts. A sweat-house was usually built
close to a stream or well, and as this building stands close to St Molaise's well, the
name given to it by the islanders may genuinely reflect its use within the last
three centuries.

In the south-western corner of the main enclosure within the Caiseal is the Big
Station (Fig. 37), an altar having a pillar and a number of rounded stones on it.
These latter are called the Clocha Breacha, which is translated literally as 'speckled

stones' but more usually as 'cursing stones'. Some of these stones are decorated with crosses; the total number of stones is said to be uncountable. They are one of the most celebrated features of the island, on account of the use to which they were put in the past. If an islander wanted to wreak vengeance on an enemy, he would undertake a nine-day ritual, fasting completely on the first three days, taking only one meal a day on the second three and returning to his normal diet on the final three days. Then he would go around the altar or station widdershins, against the course of the sun, turning the stones three times and unleashing his curse at each turn. But if the curse was unjustified, then it would recoil on the curser himself! How effective the stones may have been is reflected in the local story that during the Second World War the stones were turned against Hitler – and we know what happened to him. The islanders called the stones simply 'speckled stones' because they were sensitive about the translation as 'cursing stones', arguing that as five of the stones bore crosses, and were therefore Christian, they were unlikely to be cursing stones, which smacks too much of paganism. But there is perhaps some justification for the connection with pagan religion, as the ancient tale *The Burial of King Cormac*, a mythical pre-Christian monarch, records a similar incident, which Sir Samuel Ferguson rendered thus:

> *They loosed their curse against the king,*
> *They cursed him in his flesh and bones;*
> *And daily in their mystic ring*
> *They turn'd the maledictive stones.*

In addition to the Big Station with its maledictive stones there are two others within the Caiseal, one of which, the Altóir Beag, the Small Altar or Station (Fig. 15), has a fine cross-decorated pillar. It is only one of a number of finely carved stele which are preserved within the Caiseal, though not always in their original position. One, now in Dublin, (Fig. 38) bears an inscription saying that 'Muredach hú Chomocain sleeps

Fig. 38 *'Muredach sleeps here', says the Latin inscription from Inishmurray, County Sligo*

here'. Another, upright example bears holes that go through the corners of the stone. It was apparently the custom for expectant mothers on the island to put their fingers through the openings in the hope of a successful childbirth. There is another holed stone located close to Teampull na mBan. This is the Women's Church, which stands close to the shore in a walled enclosure some 100 metres southeast of the Caiseal, the line of the old path between the two being unexpectedly interrupted by a 19th-century house standing about halfway between the two. Much if not all of this high-walled church dates from around the 15th century.

A station close to the Women's Church formed the start of the pilgrimage round of the island, which took place on the Feast of the Immaculate Conception, 15 August, which is sufficiently close to St Laisrén's feast day of 12 August for one to wonder if the date of the pilgrimage may have been altered slightly at some stage. The islanders were usually joined by people from the mainland for the mid-August pilgrimage, though they sometimes did it themselves at other times of the year in the hope of obtaining a favour, or in thanksgiving for one granted. Pilgrims fasted from the previous night, and did the round of the stations barefoot, reciting five Our Fathers, five Hail Marys and the Creed at each of the stations (with only few exceptions). Dr Paddy Heraughty, who grew up on the island and lived there from 1912 until 1935, has given us the only detailed description we have of the pilgrimage. From his account, it would appear that Teach Molaise formed the start; the usual set of prescribed prayers were recited there before the pilgrim proceeded to the southwestern section of the wall of the Caiseal, where he or she knelt and recited the same prayers. The pilgrim then climbed to the top of the wall and made a circuit of it before kneeling and praying again. On leaving the Caiseal the pilgrim headed for the first of the stations around the island; he or she then visited all in turn in a clockwise direction, doing two circuits of each station (once inside the surrounding wall and once outside), praying whilst walking the circuit, and kneeling to say the requisite prayers both before and after each circuit. The stations around the island may be summarised as follows:

> Leachta (bed of) Cholmcille, near the Women's Church. St Colmcille (or Columba) is traditionally said to have visited Inishmurray, though there is no historical evidence for this.
> Roilig Odhráin, the island cemetery dedicated to St Odrán, who is also venerated at Colmcille's famous monastery on Iona.
> Ulla Mhuire, Mary's Altar, close to Classeymore, the usual landing place on the island.
> Trahan O'Riain, O'Ryan's Cell, on the westernmost point of the island, probably a beehive hut.
> Cros Mhór, the Great Cross, which today only has a small cross-inscribed pillar.
> Trahán Aodh, Hugh's Cell, and Tobar na Corach, a holy well.
> Leachta Phádraig, St Patrick's Bed, a mound of stones on the cliff edge.
> Trionóid Mhór, Big Station of the Trinity
> Trionóid Bheag, Small Station of the Trinity. Both these stations were near the central house of the island.

After completion of the island circuit, the pilgrim reached the Women's Church near which the island round had begun; there he or she went around the outside of the enclosing wall and then inside, around the church. Finally, the path led back to the Caiseal, where circuits were duly made around the Altóir Beag, then to another nameless altar to the east of the Men's Church, followed by the altar with the

Clocha Breacha and then finally – as the last station – back to the very start at Teach Molaise; the necessary prayers were said at each station, and the circuit culminated with further prayers within Teach Molaise. The full pilgrimage round or Big Station, as it was known, took four hours to complete. For those who did not feel up to the full circuit, there was a reduced version. This description of the pilgrimage was presumably gathered by Paddy Heraughty from his own experience and also from the memories of those who remembered making the pilgrimage before the island was deserted in 1948; sadly, this pilgrimage – which must go back many hundreds of years – is no more.

It is worth noting that the island has a number of bullauns as well as two holy wells. One of these wells, dedicated to St Molaise, lies – curiously – just outside the wall of the Caiseal. The other, known as Tobar na Corach and mentioned above, is on the other side of the island, and when the weather was so bad that communications with the mainland were interrupted, the islanders are said to have occasionally drained the well and poured its contents into the sea in the hope of calming the Atlantic waters.

GLENCOLMCILLE, DONEGAL

Glencolmcille, or Glencolumbkille, is a magical place, a broad glen on the western extremity of County Donegal, which until the construction of modern roads was largely cut off from the surrounding hinterland by a ridge of hills, and which sweeps generously down to the Atlantic Ocean. For its size, it has one of the finest collections of Early Christian pillar-stones anywhere in Ireland. These are spread over a wide area of the valley floor, and are located at the thirteen stations on the

Fig. 39 *The cross-decorated stone at the second station of the Glencolmcille pilgrimage, County Donegal, near where the pilgrimage round begins and ends*

turas, or pilgrimage, which takes place on 9 June, the feast day of St Colmcille or Columba, from whom the valley gets its name. The pilgrimage can also be done on other days: I was told by Seán Ó hÉinne that to do the pilgrimage, fasting, on three successive Fridays was regarded locally as the equivalent of doing the Lough Derg pilgrimage.

The Glencolmcille pilgrimage was done, ideally, at midnight, in the dark preceding the dawn on the saint's day, but this old practice has only very recently been discontinued. In 1990, only two people set out in the dark, at 3 o'clock in the morning, but the official 10 o'clock start saw about twenty taking part, a number – including children – from the glen, along with outsiders from Ireland, Scotland and Canada. It is one of the few pattern days still rigorously observed, and has the air of being very ancient, doubtless going back at least to the time when the pillar-stones were erected, in around the 8th/9th century. In style, it resembles the Lough Derg and Inishmurray pilgrimages in that the pilgrims do the rounds barefoot and say a set number of Our Fathers, Hail Marys and Glorias at the various stations. But, in contrast to Lough Derg, it is confined to a single day, during which, however, the pilgrim walks about three miles on a barefoot tour which can take four hours or more to complete. Participation is an uplifting experience, bringing one back into the atmosphere of the old Irish pilgrimage as practised a thousand years ago.

The pilgrimage starts traditionally at the Protestant chapel (Fig. 39) built in the 19th century. The very first station, outside the western wall of the churchyard, gives a hint that the *turas* may go back to some prehistoric practice in that it is located at what seems to be a megalithic tomb erected some 5000 years ago. All kneel and pray, the prayers being said throughout in Irish, which today is still very much a living language in the valley – one of the few areas in the country where this is still the case. It is a moving experience to hear all the children reciting the prayers in the same beautiful Donegal Irish which has been used on the valley pilgrimage for many centuries, and I felt very much as an outsider doing my bit in English, which seemed so out of place.

The second station is at a rock only a hundred metres further west (Fig. 39); prominently sited on the outcrop is one of the finest of all the pillars, decorated on both sides, around which the pilgrims walk three times before kneeling and repeating the usual prayers. The third station, Áit na nGlún, the 'place of the knees', has a small cairn of stones close to which is a hollow where the pilgrim kneels – hence the name. One of the customs practised at the cairn of stones has a very ancient ring about it. The pilgrim picks up a rounded stone, blesses him or herself with it, then passes it to the back of the body and around to the front again, and then repeats the same movement again twice over. This is presumably to help cure any part of the body touched by the stone, which is a rounded boulder.

The pilgrims then proceed along a modern tarred road to a prominent hillock at Beefan a quarter of a mile away, where there is another cairn with a cross-decorated stone within a circular wall. Close by is the next station, St Colmcille's Chapel, a rectangular structure orientated north-south, which suggests that it was not

Fig. 40 *Pilgrims at the ninth station of the Glencolmcille pilgrimage* (OPPOSITE) *in June, 1990*

originally a church; in addition, unlike a church, it has its entrance in the east wall. In the northeastern corner is a long flagstone, St Colmcille's Bed, where the pilgrim lies and turns over three times in a recumbent position – quite a strenuous task for the more portly. Before getting up, the pilgrim puts his left hand down to take some earth from underneath the bed as a protection against fire, and as a cure for headaches and other ailments. Clay is also taken from under a large stone a few yards or metres down the slope to the east, which bears an encircled cross on its flat top. This boulder is called Leach na mBonn, the 'flat stone of the requests', which is said to fulfil wishes if the pilgrim jumps from its highest point and walks around it three times, saying the necessary prayers the while.

Then pilgrims go up and down a small hill nearly to the bottom of another hill, where three stones should be collected to place later on the cairn beside St Colmcille's well. Before reaching the well, the pilgrim sits in the hollow of an upright stone, from which the saint is said to have surveyed the valley. The well itself is on one side of a long and slightly curved mound of stones, doubtless formed by the pilgrims who down the years have collected three stones at the foot of the hill and added them to the cairn. The well has good water, which is drunk by the pilgrims and filled into bottles for bringing home with them.

Beefan is the most westerly part of the *turas*, and from here the pilgrim starts the return journey eastwards down a steep hill named Mullach na Cainnte, the 'slope of conversation', the only part of the pilgrimage where the pilgrims may talk. Otherwise, the rest of the pilgrimage is meant to be conducted in silence, a stricture nowadays more honoured in the breach than in the observance. While going down the slope, I fell into conversation with two elderly cousins named Seán, one the aforementioned Ó hÉinne and the other a MacNelis, and shortly afterwards we passed the house where Seán MacNelis's grandfather's grandfather had lived – members of a family who were the erenaghs of St Colmcille, the traditional lay inheritors of the Columban tradition in the glen. In Garraí na Turas, the pilgrimage field, we passed a group of three cairns, at one of which a flat stone must be raised to just below the chin, to cure throat ailments. The pilgrim then passes further along the northern foot of the valley to a large stone with a concave upper surface which, not surprisingly, bears the name of St Colmcille's Boat. The water near it is said to cure warts, and the pilgrim washes his or her feet there, a rather pointless exercise, it would seem, as the next part of the pilgrimage goes circuitously through three-quarters of a mile of squelchy, marshy land full of reeds and yellow lilies, which can be inundated when there is a flood tide in the valley. At the start of this marsh there is a zig-zagging setting of pavement stones of uncertain age, which could have formed part of an ancient pilgrimage road.

At the far end of the marshy terrain, at Farranmacbride, there is another station, the ninth, where the decorated stone has a hole at the centre of the cross near the top (Fig. 40). Traditionally, engaged couples, one person on each side, would put their fingers through the hole, touching and entwining them. Pilgrims look through the hole, and it is said that those in a state of grace may be able to obtain there a vision of heaven; walking around the stone three times, they renounce the world, the flesh and the devil.

At Drumroe, a quarter of a mile to the southeast, at the most easterly point of the pilgrimage and not far from a church dedicated to St Kevin, is a further set of stations, one at the roadside having no cross-decorated stone. But on the opposite side of the road is another stone which has decoration obviously imitating metalwork of around the 8th or 9th century. Station thirteen is next to the garda barracks where the broken cross-decorated pillar (now in the Folk Village) has been replaced by a clever modern imitation. The pilgrim then continues via another station back to the Protestant church where another fragmentary – but original – cross-decorated stone marks the end of the pilgrimage, though final prayers are said by returning to the first station outside the west wall of the churchyard.

The Glencolmcille area also had two less important pilgrimages, one (no longer practised) in honour of St Fanad, after whom the townland Kiland – Cill Fhanaid – is named, and where the Folk Village is located. The second is outside the parish and is dedicated to another local saint, Conall. Yet a further place of pilgrimage in the locality was on the island of Rathlin O'Birne where there are more cross-inscribed stones. It lies not far from Malin Beg, just to the south of Glencolmcille, and within sight of Slieve League, the holy mountain we have already encountered in association with St Brendan.

The glen gets its name from St Colmcille, and the pilgrimage is done in his honour. Perhaps better known by his Latin name, Columba, the saint was born at Gartan about forty miles to the northeast in the year 521. At the age of forty-two, he went across the sea to found the great monastery on the Hebridean island of Iona, where he died in 597. From there he started evangelising the Picts, and he was the first of the many Irish monks who went into exile, voluntary or otherwise, to spread the gospels to the heathen. When Iona was plundered by the Vikings twice within the first decade of the 9th century, some of the monks moved to Kells in County Meath, where greater security was provided for both the monks and their treasures, which included the Book of Kells, which is now the greatest jewel in the collection of the library at Trinity College, Dublin.

Curiously, none of the early historical sources brings St Columba into contact with Glencolmcille. The place is not even mentioned by Adomnan, whose biography of Colmcille is one of the most detailed and accurate works of early Irish hagiography we possess. We have to wait for any historical source linking the saint with the valley until the 17th century, when Manus O'Donnell's *Life of Saint Columba* records a tradition that St Columba fought with devils in the glen. The cross-decorated stones at the pilgrimage stations bring us back to the period around 800. There is, however, no trace of any monastic foundation in the valley connected with the saint, either at the Protestant church where the pilgrimage begins and ends or anywhere else in the valley. The decorated stone at the second station (Fig. 39) has an interesting resemblance to a finger and, given the metalwork inspiration for some of the designs on the Glencolmcille stones, one could speculate whether this particular stone could imitate a metal reliquary containing St Colmcille's – or any other saint's – finger, which may have been brought to the valley in the 9th century or thereabouts, perhaps when Iona was dispersing some of its monastic relics in the wake of the Viking invasions.

One is faced, then, with the question as to what St Colmcille's connection with the glen really was – if any? Liam Price, who published the most exhaustive account of the stones and the pilgrimage, expressed the opinion that St Colmcille was not originally associated with the valley, but that his pilgrimage may have replaced an earlier cult – perhaps that of the lesser saint Fanad. Price's suggestion, along with the date of the stones, could lead to the hypothesis that St Fanad may have been the original saint of the glen, perhaps a hermit who sought solace and solitude there away from the temptation of the world, and that his cult was overlain by that of St Colmcille, whose relics may have been brought to the valley for safety some time in the first half of the 9th century. It is interesting, also, to find a church – though in its present state dating from the late medieval period – dedicated to another saint much beloved by pilgrims, St Kevin of Glendalough. It was, perhaps, the presence of his cult here that brought Liam Price to the site, as otherwise County Wicklow was his main area of study. Near St Kevin's church there is, incidentally, a stone bearing a cross of arcs.

Whatever the period when the cult of St Colmcille was introduced, it was almost certainly introduced by sea. Even the very much earlier megalithic monuments, which dot the valley and the area just around the corner from it at Malin Beg, only make sense when understood as having been built by people who came to the valley from the sea, since the ring of hills surrounding the glen cut it off very much from the surrounding hinterland. In the days when travel by sea up and down the west coast of Ireland was more widely practised than it is today, Glencolmcille would have been an easy landfall, offering protection and safety to the seafarer, and it is my contention that the cult of St Colmcille was introduced to the valley by people who arrived there by boat, rather than over the hills as most visitors come nowadays. Because of the motor car, we tend to see too many things from a purely land-based perspective; the understandable lack of any public maritime transport along the west coast of Ireland today makes us blind to the interesting prospect of looking at land sites from the sea.

CHAPTER 9

INLAND PILGRIMAGE PLACES

CLONMACNOIS, OFFALY

MANY OF THE PLACES ALONG OR NEAR THE WESTERN SEABOARD THAT WE looked at in Chapter 8 have managed to keep the tradition of pilgrimage alive and vivid. Historic sites in the midlands and east of the country have been less fortunate, though one site that does still cultivate an annual pilgrimage is Clonmacnois on the Shannon, about ten miles south of Athlone (Fig. 41). Clonmacnois has a longer history of pilgrimage than any other place in Ireland: the first pilgrim recorded there was noted in the annals as having died in 606. For centuries it remained one of the foremost places of pilgrimage in Ireland, and there is still an important Church of Ireland celebration annually which formerly took place on the feast day of the founder, St Ciarán, on 9 September, but is now held on the first Sunday in September.

Clonmacnois is a magnetic place. Its peaceful location, and the sanctity of the spot, can draw one back again and again – I have long since ceased to record the number of times I have visited Clonmacnois. Its geographical position as a central point in Ireland doubtless helped its rise to fame, for it is located close to where a glacial esker known as the Eiscir Riada, the most important east-west thoroughfare in early medieval Ireland, crosses the river Shannon, which was the main north-south traffic artery, thus making Clonmacnois the crossroads of Ireland. Its significance as a ford across the Shannon must have continued until the Normans made Athlone the main crossing-point on the middle reaches of the Shannon below Lough Ree, though they also secured the ford at Clonmacnois by building a mighty castle to the south of the monastery.

St Ciarán founded his monastery there around 545 having, as it were, served his apprenticeship with St Enda on the Aran island of Inishmore where a church was dedicated to St Ciarán. The saint only lived about seven months to enjoy his foundation before his untimely death at the age of 33. His *Life* records that, during his lifetime, some Gaulish merchants came upriver to sell wine to the saint. The

Fig. 41 *The Round Towers and churches of Clonmacnois, with the Pilgrims' road in the distance*

fame of his foundation is unlikely to have spread as far as the Bordeaux region within seven months, and this could be taken to imply that the saint had chosen the site of his monastery at or close to some previous settlement for which the wine may have been intended. One wonders indeed if some pagan sanctuary had not existed on the site previously, for a beautiful gold torc, or neckring, of eastern French or Rhenish origin dating from around 300 BC was found at Clonmacnois, and the question may at least be posed if it was not brought here and deposited as an offering to some deity of the pagan period.

St Ciarán was a Connacht man and, unlike many other monastic founders, his successors as abbot did not come from his own family but were drawn from many parts of the country (usually excluding Munster). Not all of these subsequent abbots came from the upper echelons of early Irish society; a number came from insignificant population groups, and must have been chosen for their personal qualities rather than for any important family ties. This had the effect that Clonmacnois was in no way a provincial monastery, but instead had – and retained – national significance, as Revd John Ryan made clear; it must have been the integrity and character of its abbots that built Clonmacnois up to be one of the most important centres of learning, writing and art in early Christian Ireland.

Fig. 42 *The east face of the 9th-century Cross of the Scriptures* (OPPOSITE) *at Clonmacnois*

One of its most important contributions to Irish art are the high crosses that still remain on the site. The most famous of these is the Cross of the Scriptures (Fig. 41), which a new reading of its much-damaged inscriptions suggests was erected by the High King Flann Sinna, perhaps some time after 879, though my own preference is for a slighly earlier date. As its name implies, this high cross is decorated with scenes from the Scriptures, from both Old and New Testaments. One of the panels has frequently been interpreted as the foundation of the monastery by St Ciarán and King Diarmait Mac Cerrbél, or the setting up of the cross by an abbot Colman and the High King, Flann Sinna. But the panel is more likely to have a biblical connotation, as befits the cross's traditional name, and is more likely to represent the Old Testament figure of Joseph interpreting the dream of Pharaoh's butler. Above this panel is another, which may be interpreted as the butler handing the biblical cup – represented here as a drinking horn – to Pharaoh, thus fulfilling Joseph's prophecy that he would be reinstated in his job after three days. Back to back with the lower panel on the other face of the cross is a representation of the moment of Christ's Resurrection, which he himself had foretold as happening three days after his death, and most of the other panels on the cross, and on its base, can be seen to focus on events surrounding the Passion, death and Resurrection of Christ.

Near this cross is another, the South Cross, also dating from the 9th century. The only biblical scene on its shaft is an interesting representation of the

Fig. 43 *St Ciarán's Church, Clonmacnois – the tomb-shrine of the founder who died in 545*

Crucifixion, showing the blood spurting from Christ's side into the eyes of Longinus, who had created the wound and who according to an old tradition was cured of his blindness by the blood of the Saviour. There are other cross fragments on the site, and others are now in the National Museum in Dublin.

What strikes the modern visitor approaching either from the river or by road is the number of churches at Clonmacnois. These now amount to seven if we include the Nuns' Church some distance away, and we know of others which have disappeared. The most important of the surviving churches is the cathedral, part of which may possibly belong to a church recorded as having been founded in around 908. Its west doorway is almost certainly a later insertion, being decorated in the Romanesque style of the 12th century. The north doorway is an addition of 1461, exactly one thousand years after the death of St Patrick who – surely by more than mere coincidence – is one of the three saints carved in stone above the doorway. Less than a century later, in 1552, the monastery was pillaged by an English force from Athlone, and the place has remained a romantic ruin ever since, and one which benefited greatly in 1955 from the laying flat of many of the tombstones around the churches by the Office of Public Works, which now owns the site.

Next to the largest church, the cathedral, is the smallest of all the ecclesiastical structures on the site, St Ciarán's Church (Teampull Chiaráin, Fig. 43). This measures internally only 12 feet 6 inches by 8 feet (about 4 by 3 metres), and has *antae*, those projections of the side walls out beyond the gable which are so characteristic of early Irish stone churches. St Ciarán's Church gives the impression of being lop-sided, the result of many repairs down the centuries, which become understandable when it is realised that this small building, as the place which housed the tomb of the founding saint, was the focal point of all the pilgrimage traffic to Clonmacnois. It remained roofed until around 1800; Bishop Dopping, who visited the site in 1684, remarked that St Ciarán's hand – and presumably the reliquary that housed it – was kept there. Two centuries ago, some impious digging in the church revealed the presence of 'a hollow ball of brass, which opened and a chalice and wine vessel' and, as the greatest treasure of all, the so-called Crozier of the Abbots of Clonmacnois (Fig. 64), dating from around 1100 and now preserved in the National Museum in Dublin. Whether the wood inside it was a crozier, let alone that of St Ciarán, is unknown. This small oratory is not a church in the normal sense but the tomb-shrine of St Ciarán, and a small area in the northeastern corner is hallowed as the saint's grave. Caesar Otway, who visited the church in the 1830s, noted:

Beside it was a sort of cavity or hollow in the ground, as if some persons had lately been rooting to extract a badger or a fox: but here it was that the people, supposing St Kieran to be deposited, have rooted diligently for any particle of clay that could be found, in order to carry home that holy earth, steep it in water, and drink it; and happy is the votary who is now able amongst the bones and stones to pick up what has the semblance of soil, in order to commit it to his stomach, as a means of grace, or as a sovereign remedy against diseases of all sorts.

In listing the objects found in St Ciarán's Tomb in the last century, R. A. S. Macalister pointed to the finding of a 'gold crown' and collar, apparently in around 1861. This gave rise to a story which circulated in newspapers at the time about the discovery of a cave, 'the retreat of the Irish kings' (which sounds like a not entirely unexpected souterrain or underground chamber) with stones 'covered with Ogham writing'. We are on somewhat surer ground with bronze finds from Clonmacnois – a beautiful Crucifixion plaque probably of around 1100, a kite-shaped brooch of around the 10th century, and various pins, found mostly in the vicinity of the Nuns' Church, which was built in the 12th century about 300 metres from the main church, where a bullaun stone was found. Another pin is reported to have been found on the pilgrim's way which joins the Nuns' Church with the main complex of buildings.

The end of the old pilgrimage road can be seen in the form of flagstones laid in the earth on the slope leading up to St Ciarán's Church. Following it further, it can be seen as a long raised area proceeding through the modern cemetery extension. A visitor going through the stile of that extension and crossing the modern tarred road can see its continuation in the form of a long flat-topped mound running parallel with the tarred road and stretching almost to the Nuns' Church. Macalister was of the opinion that this mound was likely to have been a natural esker, but it seems too straight and symmetrical. It is almost certainly not without significance that the view westwards back along it from the Nuns' Church towards the monastic complex leads the eye above the modern trees to the round tower, which may have acted as a kind of beacon, showing the pilgrims where the end of their road lay. The round tower, located at the northwestern corner of the monastic enclosure, is about 62 feet (almost 20 metres) high and is called O'Rourke's Tower because it is said to have been started by Fergal Ua Ruairc in 964. It was certainly finished in 1124, and the present top is likely to have been constructed after the tower had been struck by lightning eleven years later. Not far away is another, more perfect round tower, forming the junction of the nave and chancel of the Romanesque St Finghin's

Fig. 44 *Bartlett's engraving of* c.1840 *shows the Cross of the Scriptures to be the centre of pilgrims' prayers at Clonmacnois*

116

Church, which is instantly recognisable in any aerial view because it stands close to the round helicopter pad on which Pope John Paul II landed during his visit to Ireland in 1979.

The artistry of the Clonmacnois stonemasons found fruitful outlet in the production of slabs decorated with crosses of one kind or another and frequently bearing an inscription (Fig. 85), of which Clonmacnois has by far the richest collection in the country. Hundreds survive, but the fragmentary condition of many has made them a safety risk. So the Office of Public Works has wisely decided to take them all inside, and to display the important and representative samples in the modern buildings on site.

As mentioned earlier, the pilgrimage to Clonmacnois is no longer made on 9 September, the feast day which commemorates the death of St Ciarán on that date in the year 545, but on the first Sunday in September. The only good modern account of the pilgrimage round was compiled by Dr Patrick Logan in his book *The Holy Wells of Ireland*, and it seems most appropriate to round off this section on Clonmacnois with his own summary of the pilgrimage:

Pilgrims now do what is called 'the Short Station' and there was no rule about how this should be done; but some people still do 'the Long Station' and this was usually done by barefoot pilgrims. 'The Long Station' begins at St Ciarán's Well which is a few hundred yards from the ancient graveyard, and as the pilgrim comes to it, he kneels and says some prayers – usually a decade of the rosary. He then makes a circuit of the well and of the whitethorn tree beside it and may hang a votive offering on the tree or throw one into the holy well. The tree is a very special one: it has no thorns. It is commonly said that the water of the well cannot be boiled. By leaving the votive offering the pilgrim leaves his disease behind him.

From the well he moves on to a stone cross close by where he again kneels and says another decade of the rosary before going around the cross. He then moves on to a flat stone called 'the slab' where the ritual is repeated. There is still another stone to be visited, one on which a face has been carved. Here, in addition to the usual prayers etc., the pilgrim kisses the face. This circuit of well, cross, slab, and face, is carried out three times and each time the pilgrim crosses the little stream which flows from St Ciarán's Well. This ends the first part of 'the Long Station'.

The pilgrim then moves on towards the High Cross in the graveyard and as he goes says five decades of the rosary. First he kneels at the High Cross and says the usual decade. Then round the cross and on to the little mound beside 'the Protestant Church', where the ritual is repeated. Next, he moves to St Finian's Church, where it is again repeated and from there he moves around the perimeter of the graveyard, as always, in a clockwise direction, and back to the High Cross. This circuit is carried out three times and when he has completed the third circuit, he goes on his hands and knees from the High Cross to the site of the high altar in the ruined cathedral, where he says five Paters and the Creed.

The next circuit begins at the Little Cross with the usual prayers and circuit. From there he moves to the Cathedral and repeats the process. The other praying stations on this circuit are St Ciarán's Little Church, 'Cartland's Church', 'Claffey's Church' and back to the Little Cross. This circuit is completed three times and at the end of it the pilgrim recites the complete rosary, fifteen decades.

Next, the pilgrim goes to the Nun's Church, where he again kneels and prays. There are three small mounds near this church and he goes round each of them three times. He then goes round the church three times and then goes inside and kneeling at the high altar says fifteen Paters.

He then goes to St Finian's Well saying the rosary as he goes, and kneeling at the well says fifteen Paters. It is not necessary to walk around this well: it may be covered by the water of the River Shannon or, in very dry weather, there may be no water in it. This is the end of 'the Long Station'. My informant, Mr Jack Claffey, a man aged about sixty, told me that he had done this pilgrimage every year for forty years, but added, rather apologetically, that the last time, he had not done it barefoot – his rheumatism was troubling him. I have calculated that it would take at least four hours to complete this routine.

GLENDALOUGH, WICKLOW

Glendalough, the Valley of the Two Lakes, is one of the most romantically sited of all the ancient Irish pilgrimage sites, located in a beautiful, steep-sided glen, sometimes of almost melancholic aspect, deep in the Wicklow Hills some 30 miles (50 kilometres) south of Dublin (Plate VII). Few except the mountain walker would visit it today were it not for the historical importance of this picturesque place and its fascinating collection of monuments.

Glendalough is not only a valley of two lakes; it is also a valley of two saints, who lived half a millennium apart. The first, and best known, of these is St Kevin (in Irish, *Coemgen*), who is said to have died in around 618 at the biblical age of 120. He was of the Dal Messe Corb, royal stock who ruled parts of Wicklow in the saint's childhood. The six known lives of the saint, three in Latin and three in Irish, give us many stories about him which are attractive, but need to be taken with numerous grains of salt. One tells of how a maiden tempted him in his youth, but his desire for chastity broke down her persistence to such a degree that he convinced her to become a nun. A picture is created of him as being a hermit who performed heroic acts of asceticism. One of these involved him standing in the frigid waters of a brook and stretching out his arms in the pose of a cross: he stood there long enough for a bird to make a nest in his hand. Being a man who loved animals, he allowed the bird to hatch out and rear its young before he lowered his arms. We can imagine him in his hermitage, surrounded by his beloved birds and poring over a copy of the sacred Scriptures – like the anonymous hermit in a 9th-century poem of a St Gall manuscript who wrote:

Over me green branches hang   *The cuckoo pipes a clear call*
A blackbird leads the loud song;   *Its dun cloak hid in deep dell:*
Above my pen-lined booklet   *Praise to God for this goodness*
I hear a fluting bird-throng   *That in woodland I write well.*

[TRANSLATION BY MÁIRE MACNEILL]

It has often been presumed that St Kevin came to Glendalough as a hermit in search of a place of retreat where he could say his prayers in peace and commune with his Maker. But the lives of the saint make it clear that he came to the valley with the intention of founding a monastery, though its exact location within the valley is the subject of scholarly dispute. Some say that it was near the upper lake, others that it was close to the lower lake. The claim for the upper lake rests on the location of two churches, a beehive hut of sorts called St Kevin's Cell and a chamber cut into the cliff face above the lake, resembling the rock-cut tombs of the Bronze Age in Mediterranean lands. One of the churches, Temple na Skellig, perches on a ledge above the lake. The other, Reefert church (Fig. 16), is more accessible, located in idyllic, sylvan surroundings overlooking the lake. It was in this region that St Kevin is considered to have spent a number of years as a hermit. This he may well have done as a means of achieving solitude away from his monks, but it seems unlikely that the upper lake was the focus of the original monastery. Much the more probable location is the cluster of buildings on a natural hillock further downstream from the lower of the two lakes. There we find a well-preserved round tower, the cap of which was replaced with its original stones in 1876. Not far away is the cathedral, a multi-period structure finished in the 12th century with the addition of a chancel, accessible through a Romanesque chancel arch which is no longer complete. The date of the various stages of the building of the original part of the church (now the nave) is uncertain, and it seems to use stones of an earlier building. However, there is no strong evidence to suggest that the cathedral – or indeed any of the other churches in Glendalough – can be much earlier than about the 11th century.

On slightly lower ground to the south, past a monolithic granite-ringed cross, is the valley's most famous church – St Kevin's. This was originally a rectangular building to which a chancel, now ruined, was subsequently added. It is one of the few surviving Irish churches to have a stone roof, above which rises a miniature round tower, so chimney-like that it gave the church its colloquial name, St Kevin's Kitchen. This church is unlikely to be earlier than the 12th century. On the other side of a nearby wall is the church of St Ciarán, but only a few feet of its walls have been preserved. Beyond a

bridge over an adjoining stream is the Deer Stone, a bullaun into which a deer daily gave her milk to save two children of St Kevin's mason who had lost their mother, or so the legend goes.

Between St Kevin's Church and the round tower, but closer to the former, is the smallest, but also probably the most significant of all the buildings at Glendalough. This is now known as the Priest's House (Fig. 45), from a priest who was buried there in the 18th century. Its internal dimensions are 14 feet 8 inches by 7 feet 9 inches (around 4.30 metres by 2.35 metres). Its unique feature is a Romanesque arch facing outwards at the eastern end and almost closed off by a wall within the arch, which is the result of Board of Works reconstruction in the 1870s. Lennox Barrow pointed out that Beranger's plan of 1779 shows the wall to have been wrongly reconstructed, and that it originally stretched across the whole interior of the building, being built up against the east wall. Nevertheless, a narrow, upright slit in the wall may well reflect an original feature. Sir William Wilde, polymath and father of Oscar, first suggested what was probably the original purpose of this building – to hold the remains of the monastic founder. If his grave were inside, the myriad of pilgrims who came to Glendalough would have focused their attention on this building, as the shrine containing the mortal relics of the saint. But too many

Fig. 45 *'The Priest's House', Glendalough, built in the 12th century, is presumably the tomb-shrine of the monastic founder, St Kevin, who died in 618*

pilgrims would have created difficulties within such a tiny building, and if each wanted to touch a relic, or bring a piece of earth away with him or her, in a very short time there would be neither relic nor earth left. The purpose of the window-like slit was probably to allow pilgrims to gaze inside, or even to reach in a piece of cloth which could then touch the earth in which the saint was buried, yet prevent them from actually entering the building.

There is, however, a narrow doorway in the south wall, through which access could have been permitted to special pilgrims. It is capped by a now incomplete lintel, which originally would have had a gabled top. The upper part of the stone is now missing, but Beranger, who in 1779 discovered the stone lying face down nearby, made a drawing (Fig. 46) of what it may originally have looked like. Lennox Barrow has suggested that Beranger may never have seen the part now missing, and may have reconstructed the upper portion as he thought it might have looked. His drawing is interesting as it shows features that were altered in the better-known illustration of it in Petrie's *Round Towers* of 1845. It shows a large figure seated in the centre, with hands covered in a muff-like garment and seemingly wearing a long robe. He is flanked by two bowing figures, that on the left bearing an incurving staff of a kind used on the Continent, and that on the right a bell. Petrie's drawing suggests that the central figure wore a crown, but Beranger's suggests a tonsure-like head-dress. The most likely interpretation of this scene is that St Kevin is seated in the centre, flanked on either side by a pilgrim, one with a staff and the other with a bell. Such a scene would be a suitable theme above the door of the tomb-shrine of St Kevin. The stone was only placed in its present position by the Board of Works, but it seems to be the most obvious original

Fig. 46 *Beranger's 1779 drawing of the lintel of 'The Priest's House' at Glendalough, County Wicklow*

location for it. The tomb-shrine now stands within a scarcely perceptible quadrangular enclosure, which had one corner beside the cathedral and its entrance probably marked by the tall granite cross to the east of the Priest's House. The enclosure is regarded as marking the boundary of the ancient cemetery surrounding the building, but it may also have delineated the area of sanctuary around the saint's tomb.

There are three other churches outside the main group of monastic buildings just described. To the west is St Mary's Church, before whose doorway Sir Walter Scott stood in wonderment when he visited Glendalough in 1825. It has an equal-armed cross decorating the soffit, or underside, of the lintel, and a chancel that may be a later addition. Trinity Church is located beside the approach road to Glendalough, about a quarter of a mile northeast of the cathedral. It has a coeval nave and chancel, and the square room to the west once formed the base of a round tower, which fell in a storm in 1818. The third church lies about three-quarters of a mile down the valley, to the east of the cathedral. It, too, was a nave and chancel structure with fine Romanesque carving on the chancel arch and east window, the latter poorly reconstructed in the 1870s. The style of carving suggests a date around the middle third of the 12th century. Other buildings attached to it suggest that it was monastic.

This third church, known as St Saviour's, introduces us to Glendalough's second major saint, Laurence O'Toole (1123-80), scion of a local ruling family. He is alleged to have become abbot of Glendalough in 1153, only to be called nine years later to take over the archbishopric of Dublin. On his way back from Rome, he died at Eu in Normandy, where he lies buried; in 1226 he became the second of Ireland's three formally canonised saints. He is the most likely person to have built St Saviour's Priory, and it is not improbable that the Priest's House in its Romanesque form may have been built by him. Glendalough continued to function as a monastery until around 1500, after which it was abandoned to become the beautiful complex of ruins which we see today.

But abandonment did not mean that it was not visited. On the contrary, it seems to have been a pilgrim's goal for centuries. A Latin Life of St Kevin, dating from no earlier than the later medieval period, was probably not being particularly biased when it claimed that Glendalough was one of the four chief places of pilgrimage in Ireland; it also stated that seven pilgrimages to Glendalough gave the equivalent in indulgences and profit as a pilgrimage to Rome. Glendalough remained the haunt of pilgrims until the second half of the 19th century. This is vividly brought home to us by a painting of Glendalough in 1813, executed by Joseph Peacock and now housed in the Ulster Museum in Belfast (Plate VIII) It shows that pilgrimage then was not the purely ascetic exercise we might imagine it to have been in the early Christian period. Instead, it had become a kind of carnival performance, with 'pilgrims' dressed up for the day in all their finery, various games being played, and items of food and drink being offered for sale. It had, to all intents and purposes, become a summer fair, and it came to be accompanied by rowdiness and drunkenness (discreetly omitted from the painting), and faction fights, which Sir William Wilde stayed on in the darkness to watch. It was this irreligious aspect of such mass expressions of popular piety that led the Catholic Church to suppress the Glendalough pilgrimage in 1862. Items associated with the pilgrimage began to lose the respect that pilgrims had paid to them, as instanced by a yew tree near the cathedral which was said to have been planted by none other than St Kevin himself. Writing in 1887, Wakeman described how it had 'slowly vanished, its very roots being utilised by the manufacturers of paper folders, snuff-boxes, cigar cases and other trifles'.

Pilgrims came from far and wide to visit St Kevin's Tomb, and Glendalough is one of the few ancient pilgrimage sites in Ireland which preserves a well-defined pilgrimage road (Figs 53-5). It came from the west Wicklow area over the Wicklow Gap, starting probably around Hollywood. Close by, in Lockstown, a great granite boulder decorated with a labyrinth (Fig. 47) stood close to the old pilgrimage road; it was removed for display to the National Museum of Ireland in Dublin. The labyrinth design has been interpreted as having been carved in pagan times, but the proximity of the stone's original position to the pilgrims' road argues much more strongly in favour of its connection with the pilgrimage to Glendalough.

Doctors Michael Ryan and Pat Wallace of the National Museum excavated a part of the road in 1972: the two fenced-in sections (Fig. 53) located close to the road over the Wicklow Gap on either side of the new road leading up to the Electricity Supply Board's water generating station at Turlough Hill. Their excavations revealed a stone pavement covering much of the flattened top of the ten-feet wide road, which is partially raised above the level of boggy terrain surrounding it on either side.

The course of St Kevin's Road (Fig. 54) was charted more than fifty years ago by Liam Price; he pointed out the former existence of two cross-decorated stones along its route, before the road descends into the valley. Numerous other cross-

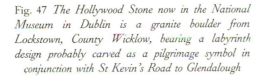

Fig. 47 *The Hollywood Stone now in the National Museum in Dublin is a granite boulder from Lockstown, County Wicklow, bearing a labyrinth design probably carved as a pilgrimage symbol in conjunction with St Kevin's Road to Glendalough*

decorated stones, many of them now gathered together in the Board of Works' fine new Interpretative Centre at Glendalough (which also houses a model of the main monastic complex), may possibly have connections with the pilgrimage. This was certainly the case with a number of rude stone crosses located at sites along the valley floor, the most obvious one being at the junction where the road to Glendalough branches off from the road leading from Laragh to the Wicklow Gap. This stone may well have marked the confluence where pilgrims coming up the valley from the east would have joined those coming over the Wicklow Gap from the west, before they proceeded together to the main monastic enclosure. This, to judge by Peacock's painting, they would have reached by a series of stepping-stones (now replaced by the modern bridge), and entered through the unique archway (Fig. 75), which welcomes the pilgrims with a cross carved on a large boulder just inside the inner arch. Corbels on the inside walls of this gateway were designed to bear heavy wooden beams supporting an upper floor, which presumably provided accommodation, perhaps for someone to supervise those entering the sacred place of pilgrimage through the archway below. Arched entrance buildings at Mellifont, County Louth, and Athassel, County Tipperary, probably served a similar function, and the tower shape may be mirrored in a structure at Banagher, County Derry (see page 183).

There are also some stations in the flat area between the upper lake and the nearby car-park. These stations are marked by mounds of stone, some surmounted by a simple, unadorned stone cross. Close by is what has usually been described as a ring-fort, an almost circular wall of stone, now much tidied up, around an empty enclosure. Rather than being a secular ring-fort, this stone-walled enclosure, being located so close to the stations, would make eminent sense as having offered some kind of roofed shelter to pilgrims who might otherwise have been drenched by a shower of rain, or it may even have provided them with overnight accommodation.

KILMACDUAGH, GALWAY

Only 2 miles from Gort, and with the hills of the Burren providing a scenic backdrop, Kilmacduagh has been called the Glendalough of the West, a title appreciated by the all too few who go slightly off the beaten track to visit it.

The site is visible from a distance because of its excellently preserved round tower, which leans out of the perpendicular by at least 2 feet (60 centimetres) (though Petrie considered it to be more than twice that). Although it is many centuries older than its more famous counterpart at Pisa, one cannot claim with any justification that the Irish taught the Italians how to build leaning towers. Close by is the cathedral, an early building with blocked-up trabeate doorway, which was later extended considerably in the Gothic style. John O'Donovan's plan of 1839 shows the site of a now vanished church, dedicated to St MacDuagh, between the round tower and the southwestern corner of the cathedral, and near – if not actually on – the site of Leaba Mhic Dhuaigh, the bed of the founding saint, which is now marked by the 1852 grave of Bishop Trench. To the southwest of the round tower, outside the graveyard enclosure, are the remains of a church described by O'Donovan as St MacDuagh's small church.

Also outside the present churchyard are three further churches; one, to the east and on the other side of the road, is St Mary's Church, with a cross-inscribed stone of Clonmacnois type built into the interior north wall. The second is to the north of the cathedral, and is a building of uncertain age known variously as the church of St John the Baptist or of St Francis. Down a laneway a few hundred metres to the northwest of the cathedral is the third church, known as O'Heyne's Church, of around 1200, showing fine masonry and carving in the style of the School of the West, and with the remains of a small cloister garth to the south. This makes a total of six churches formerly or still in existence at Kilmacduagh, which in itself is a likely sign that this was a place of pilgrimage. Further to the north of St John's Church is an interesting two-storey building called by John O'Donovan Seanchloch, or the House of the Clergy. Recently restored by the Office of Public Works, it is sometimes referred to as the Abbot's House or the Glebe.

The monastery's founder was St Colman MacDuagh, who lived in the first half of the 7th century and was related to King Guaire Aidhne, a man famed for his hospitality. Until the 19th century, a reliquary containing the saint's belt was preserved by its family of hereditary keepers, the O'Shaughnessys. John Colgan and his 17th-century contemporary Geoffrey Keating, author of *The History of Ireland*, tell the story of how the saint was saved from starvation by divine intervention. He lived for just over seven years in a hermitage at the foot of the Burren some miles from Kilmacduagh, and as the food for himself and his servant ran out at the end of the lenten season, all the servant was able to offer his master was a bird he had caught in a wood. At the same moment, the saint's cousin, King Guaire, was celebrating Easter Sunday with a great feast at Durlus (probably near Kinvara) and expressed the wish that the viands of the feast would be with some more needy servants of Christ 'who are many'. Thereupon, the dishes with the victuals of boar and stag were taken up into the air and borne away from them, Guaire and his men following in hot pursuit to find out what would happen to them. When the contents of the feast reached St Colman and his servant in their woody retreat, the two rejoiced, but the saint refused to eat anything until he found out where they came from. An angel appeared at the appropriate moment and told him that they were due to the liberality of his cousin, Guaire. Right on cue, Guaire then appeared and asked who the hermit was, only to discover that they were cousins. The king thereupon offered the spiritual care of his life to St Colman and offered to build a church, which was thenceforth known as the Church of MacDuagh, or Kilmacduagh as we know it today.

The hermitage where St Colman lived for seven years is at Keelhilla, at the foot of Slieve Carran, visible from a distance by virtue of a large modern cross, and indicated on the ground by a small stone church, an active well and a penitential station, suggesting that it was a place of pilgrimage too. Weatherings in the limestone exposures in the area in front of the hermitage are still pointed out as the Road of the Dishes, and one may well ask if this old name does not indicate the course of an old pilgrimage road to the hermitage, possibly from Kilmacduagh itself. In describing Keelhilla, Lord Killanin and Michael Duignan wrote in the first edition of *The Shell Guide to Ireland*: 'Keelhilla in its isolation well exemplifies the character of the ancient Irish hermitages. The view from the Saint's Bed is inspiring, and helps to explain the contribution of the hermits to early Irish nature poetry'.

INISHCEALTRA, CLARE

Pilgrimages favoured islands not only in the ocean but also on inland lakes. One of the finest examples is Inishcealtra in the lower reaches of the river Shannon. Though it is not apparently mentioned as a pilgrimage site until the 17th century, it has features which make it probable that it was a very ancient pilgrimage site.

It is situated in Lough Derg – not the Lough Derg of St Patrick's Purgatory in Donegal, but the last of the large lakes the Shannon flows through before its final, slow descent into the 'Atlantical Ocean'. Formerly part of County Galway, Inishcealtra now belongs to County Clare. It lies less than a mile offshore near the charming village of Mountshannon, and at the entrance to a small bay leading to Tuamgraney, which has the oldest church in Ireland still used for divine service.

The earliest saint associated with the island was Mac Creiche, whose name is also attached to some seaside locations on the Atlantic coast of Clare. Mac Creiche was already an old man when he was visited by St Colm of Terryglass in the first half of the 6th century; the *Life* of St Colm records that on that occasion an angel told Mac Creiche to go and seek a hermitage elsewhere. St Colm found on the island a tree that distilled juice tasting of honey and with the headiness of wine. The fabulous nature of Mac Creiche, and the previous existence of what sounds like a

Fig. 48 *'The Confessional' on Inishcealtra, County Clare, probably the tomb-shrine of a founding saint*

sacred tree, together with the angel's injunction that Mac Creiche should move elsewhere, smacks of Christianity taking over a pagan sanctuary on the island. It is perhaps no coincidence, therefore, as Westropp claimed, that 'St' Mac Creiche's feast day was Garland Sunday, the pagan festival of the Celtic god Lug, though there is no ancient testimony to confirm this. But St Colm may not have been a hermit, because later abbots claimed abbatial descent from him, and he may well have founded a monastic community on the island.

Yet a third saint associated with Inishcealtra is St Caimin, said to have been a half-brother of King Guaire Aidhne whom we encountered at Kilmacduagh. Caimin is said to have died in 652, and he is the saint after whom the major church on the island is named. It may have been built by the great local king Brian Boru in around 1000, but it had a doorway inserted in the Romanesque style of the 12th century, rebuilt in 1879 and again exactly one hundred years later. Traditions recorded centuries after the death of St Colm tell of his relics being moved from his burial place at Terryglass on the eastern shore of the lake to the island of Inishcealtra, before being finally brought back to Terryglass as their final resting place, the surface of the lake being illuminated for three days and three nights at each successful translation. It is difficult to know, therefore, if it was the relics of St Colm or of St Caimin that may have helped to give the place its alternative name of Holy Island, but some revered relics were certainly honoured there. Not far from St Caimin's Church there is a small rectangular building in which two massive stones incline towards one another at an angle; these are almost certainly a slab shrine of the kind found on other sites covering the tomb of a local saint. This building, known as the Confessional (Fig. 48), was probably the focal point for the pilgrims who came here for many centuries. Liam de Paor, who conducted excavations on the site, discovered that the Confessional had been reconstructed many times, and had been preceded by a timber structure which, he suggests, may once have been the centre of a pagan shrine. He also discovered a mud-walled oratory, of 7th- or 8th-century origin, and some large huts with internal subdivisions which, he thinks, may have belonged to the Christian community possibly set up to tend the shrine.

To anyone looking at the island from the lakeshore, the most obvious monument is the round tower, 79 feet (24 metres) high, which lacks a top storey and the usual conical roof, which may never have been built. Even from a distance, it can be seen to be accompanied by a number of churches in addition to St Caimin's. Thomas Dyneley, writing in 1680-1, tells of the remains of 'Seven Churches called ye Seven Churches of Asia'! Some of these seven, of course, may have disappeared in the intervening three centuries; at present there are only five, of which St Caimin's is the largest. Roughly contemporary with it is the small Baptism Church, or St Brigid's, which seems to have been replaced in its probable function as a parish church by the featureless St Mary's Church some time around 1300. Others include Teampull na bhFear nGonta ('Church of the Wounded Men') and a diminutive structure known as St Michael's.

The island also houses a number of very interesting small antiquities which deserve mention. Prime among these are the high crosses, though they may not be as spectacular as the better-known examples at places like Clonmacnois, Kells and Monasterboice. The base of one 9th-century cross is located outside St Caimin's Church, and its head is preserved within the church. In the interior of the church are two further crosses, one of which was erected to commemorate Cathasach 'the arch-senior of Ireland' who died in 1111. In his excavations, Liam de Paor discovered a beautifully carved head (now in the National Museum in Dublin) which he believes to be the head of Christ from a 12th-century cross, the other parts of which have not yet been discovered. There are also some cross bases on the island with no crosses in them; perhaps they supported crosses of wood that have long since disintegrated.

Within St Caimin's Church and in an enclosure close by known as the Saints' Graveyard are preserved a number of cross-decorated slabs which – after Clonmacnois – form one of the finest collections in the country. Only a few achieve the high quality of design and execution found at Clonmacnois; the majority bear Latin crosses of various types with the curious characteristic that the inscriptions (where present) are carved upside down, so as to be read from the end bearing the top of the cross. One of the slabs with this feature is that inscribed *Cosgrach Laighnech* (Fig. 49). What makes this slab of interest here is the presence of two shoes – not feet – inscribed on the stone, suggesting that Cosgrach came on pilgrimage here from Leinster, the province indicated by the adjective *Laighnech*. But in view of the remarks made below about the Clonmacnois slabs (page 202), it must remain an open question whether Cosgrach was actually buried under the slab.

Other interesting smaller antiquities known from the island, if not still preserved there, include two sundials, the origin of at least one of which is probably earlier than the 13th century, and a gable finial that may have belonged to a stone shrine of

Fig. 49 *A cross-slab on Inishcealtra, inscribed with the
name of Cosgrach 'the Leinsterman', and bearing the
imprint of his pilgrim's shoes*

some sort, as well as a total of five bullauns located in various positions on the
island.

One unusual feature on the island are the earthworks, low mounds of earth
enclosing areas of different sizes and shapes, and allowing space for paths between
them. They are concentrated in the area around the churches and leading up to the

highest point of the island. Liam de Paor's excavations showed these to belong to the period after the decline of the island's monastery in around 1200. One of the enclosures at the top of the island, known as St Michael's Garden (which encloses St Michael's Church), is traditionally said to have been an infants' burial ground, and is considered to have been used as such since the 15th century. These earthworks are probably to be understood in conjunction with the pilgrimages which took place here at Whitsuntide from at least the later medieval period, though doubtless also many centuries before that too. Sir Arthur Chichester, in a letter written to the Privy Council in 1609, talks of 15,000 people foregathered on the island on that day 'and some say there were many more'.

T. O'Conor, working for the Ordnance Survey in 1838, gives us a most valuable account of the pilgrimage, which also provides us with a graphic illustration of why the Church felt constrained from the late 18th century onwards to bring to an end pilgrimages such as this. O'Conor's account, which is contained in the third volume of the Ordnance Survey letters for County Galway, is as follows:

Lady Well is situated near the shore to the N. east end (corner) of the large church called St Mary's. A patron used to be held here annually 4 days, Friday and Saturday before Whitsunday, on which day and on the following Monday it was continued. No assemblage of persons was allowed here those years past on this occasion, in consequence of the outrageous conduct of some illbehaved young rascals, who were wont to seize the opportunity of providing for themselves, fresh consorts for the ensuing year, by carrying off by open force from the island, young girls, in spite of all their friends and relations.

Three brothers of a family of the O'Briens, who resided in the county of Clare, within view of the island, used to frequent the patron at which they conducted themselves, it is said, in a most disgraceful manner. On one occasion, one of them carried off a young girl by force from it; whom he afterwards detained till he had three children by her. The neighbours state that no law corrected such detestable conduct at the time.

The station was commenced at Lady Well; and the performers went round the extremity of the island, 1 mile in circuit, 7 times, equal 7 miles. The short rounds were commenced at a station monument (a little mound of earth and stones) lying 35 yards to the west of the round tower.

They went round this monument 7 times, and proceeded through the door on the west gable of St Caimin's church and as far as the altar in St Columb's chapel. They went this length seven times from the monument just mentioned, and at the commencement of every seven times of these; they went round the monument itself seven times. They went round St Caimin's church 14 times; the tower and all the churches around it being included in the rounds. They went round a station monument at the end of St Caimin's church; either the one (a little mound of earth) immediately at the S.W. corner or the one (also a little mound of earth) within a few yards of the N. west corner of it. They also went 7 times round Gáraidh Mhicheáil, St Michael's garden; and 7 times round the bank of earth about S. Michael's garden, and 7 times round the church itself, and 7 times round a large flag stone lying at it, on which stone they finally (i.e. after having gone round it the 7 times) impressed kisses. They went 7 times round St Mary's church, and 7 times round the baptism church. They finished at the well and drank of its water.

This is the most accurate description I could get of the mode in which the station on the island was performed. I could not get a minute description which would detail the number of prayers repeated during the process of the rounds. Nor am I certain that the description I have given here, affords a correct view of the order of the process. I introduced it here merely to show what station monuments were made use of.

INCHCLERAUN (INIS CLOTHRANN), LONGFORD

Where the Shannon escapes from those islands.
. . . .
I shall first visit Inis Clothran,
Which exceeds all the others far in beauty.
It was on this isle of grass and beauty
That Meava of Croghan, Queen of Connacht,
Fell by the son of the king of Uladh.
In time of war and bloody murders,
The clanna Rory, and the sons of Uisneach,
Mighty men of strength and courage,
Rose up to war and emulation,
For one fair damsel ycleped Deirdre,
Five hundred years after the Saviour
Had suffered for the sins of mankind.
The holy Diarmid here erected
Seven churches and a steeple;
He also placed on Inis Clothran,
That beauteous, fertile, airy island,
Two convents, of which the ruins
Are to be seen still on the island.

Francis Joseph Bigger quotes this portion of John O'Donovan's 1838 translation of an Irish poem of 1320 which the latter had come across in the papers of Mr Hardiman, author of the famous *History of Galway*. The reference in the poem to Queen Maeve reflects an old tradition that this famous Queen of Connacht (who is more likely to have been a Celtic goddess of drunkenness!) was killed while bathing on the shore of the island of Inis Clothrann, by the sling-stone of an Ulsterman fired a mile away from the County Longford shore. Inis Clothrann, or Inchcleraun as it is called today, is an island in Lough Ree which forms a part of the modern county of Longford, and which allegedly gets its name from Queen Maeve's sister Clothran. Local residents believed that a fort near the highest point of the island was the legendary Queen's residence. But no matter how little we may believe of this story about the lady who instigated the Cattle Raid of Cooley, the subject of the most famous epic of Celtic Ireland, it may echo the pagan background to a sanctuary which in Christian times was dedicated to St Diarmid, who lived on the island in the 6th century. According to the 14th-century poem quoted above, he erected 'seven churches and a steeple', seven churches being a frequent feature of a place of pilgrimage, which we know the island to have been even before 1200. O'Donovan made the number of churches seven because the old inhabitants of the parish in his day (following the 14th-century poem) called the island *oileán na seacht dtempull*, 'the island of the seven churches', though no more than five are visible today (a sixth recorded church seems to have disappeared).

The smallest, and probably the oldest, ecclesiastical structure on the island is known as Teampull Dhiarmida, St Diarmid's Church. In a manner so typical of early Irish churches, it has *antae* projecting from each side of the gable; a doorway with inclining jambs leads into the interior, which measures a mere 8 feet by 7 feet (2.40 metres by 2.1 metres) inside. It is the smallest church with *antae* to survive. As was the case with the almost equally small Teampull Chiaráin at Clonmacnois, we must have here the tomb-shrine of the saint himself – though probably erected in stone some centuries after his death, and it is this building and the relics it housed that must have been the focus of pilgrimage to the island in centuries past.

All the other churches on the island have a different orientation as can easily be seen when comparing the orientation of Teampull Dhiarmida to that of Teampull Mór, the Big Church, which stands a mere 12 feet (4 metres) away. This, the largest church on the island, was monastic, not the direct continuation of the ancient foundation going back to St Diarmid's day but rather a foundation of the order of Saint Augustine, an order which, as with the Donegal Lough Derg, frequently gave new life to the old Irish monasteries it took over. Attached to the church are the remains of some buildings – a sacristy and chapter house – which were placed around a small cloister garth, and probably subdivided at some stage. The church and the existing cloistral buildings were probably built around 1200, though some of the windows were added later. Of the other surviving churches, the most unusual is the Belfry Church, known as the Clogas, built on the highest point of the island. It is a mono-cellular church unique in Ireland in having a square tower at the western end, which was reached from the interior of the church by a set of steps, some of which have survived. The western wall of the tower was denuded of much of its masonry in the early 19th century by a Quaker, Mr Fairbrother, who rented the island and gave it its alternative name, Quaker Island. The tower was considered by O'Donovan and Petrie to be as old as the Irish round towers, but the church and tower are unlikely to be much earlier than about 1200.

One of the churches – it is not certain which – was identified in 1837 as Templemurray, or Our Lady's Church, by O'Donovan, who relates a belief on the island – most unexpected, given the name of the church – that no woman could enter it without dying instantly; but one lady put an end to the superstition by entering the church and living on to die at a ripe old age.

The island possessed at least four cross-decorated stones, some of which conformed to types known from Clonmacnois. One had disappeared before 1900, when another was discovered by Bigger; the last one to survive on the island was stolen in 1989, but was fortunately recovered in America two years later.

MONAINCHA, TIPPERARY

Few of the Romanesque churches of Ireland seem more beautifully sited than that at Monaincha, only about two miles from the town of Roscrea in County Tipperary. It is located on what is now a mound held in place by a low wall, and the surrounding low land is interspersed with grassed earthworks which do not appear to make very much sense. But even 200 years ago, the place looked very different. What is now the walled-in mound was an island in a bog, rather like the one in the same county where the now famous Derrynaflan chalice and paten were found in 1980. When Ledwich drew his plan of the place almost exactly two hundred years ago, the island housed not only the existing Romanesque church but also another smaller one, probably belonging to the later medieval period. To the east of the island he marked some old fish ponds, now completely dried up, as is the surrounding bog, which must have been drained not long after Ledwich's day. Further west of the fish ponds was a piece of slightly raised ground, which connected the island to another smaller one, on which there was a stone building which Ledwich described as the 'abbot's apartments'.

Fig. 50 *Monaincha, County Tipperary, one of the four
great places of pilgrimage in medieval Ireland*

The Romanesque church on the main island is one of the most delightful gems of 12th-century architecture in Ireland, beautifully shaded in the summer months by the leaves of some fine trees which grow beside it, giving it a small and compact, not to say homely, appearance. What makes it such a distinguished example of its genre – leading to its description as the thirty-first Wonder of the World in the 14th-century Book of Ballymote – is the quality of the carving on its doorway and on the arch which separates nave and chancel, resting on columns with scalloped capitals that indicate a date in the second half of the 12th century. The sandstone used in both the doorway and the chancel arch seems to have a tighter consistency than many of its peers carved at around the same time, and this has allowed the details – particularly of the chancel arch – to retain a great amount of their original sharpness. Attached to the church is a late medieval two-storey building, the ground floor of which was probably a sacristy, whilst the upper floor provided accommodation, presumably for a priest. Preserved on the ground floor are the sad remains of a cross-inscribed slab of Clonmacnois type (with what is almost a cross of arcs in the centre) which, when compared to its condition in a rubbing published in 1911, shows it to have suffered much more than the architectural carving of the church. Outside the church stands the head of a 12th-century high cross supported by an incongruous modern shaft of cement embedded in a base which, despite suggestions of an earlier date, may belong to the same period as the head of the cross.

For a site so small, it is remarkable that Monaincha was, according to the (?)late medieval *Life* of St Kevin of Glendalough, one of the four chief places of pilgrimage in Ireland. Originally called the island of Loch Cré, it seems to have started life as a hermitage, inhabited by holy men such as St Canice of Aghaboe and Cronán of Roscrea in the 7th century. Later, through another hermit and scribe named Hilary (died 807), it became associated with the ascetic reform movement known as the Culdees (Servants of God).

The Romanesque church and cross would suggest that the pilgrimage was at its height in the 12th century. The church was built perhaps by the Augustinian canons who took over the island around the time of the Norman invasion in 1169-70, and the whole island was described by the Anglo-Norman chronicler Giraldus Cambrensis as the 'Island of the Living' where no one could die – except women, who would die instantly on entering. Unlike Inchcleraun, apparently no one here dared to prove the superstition wrong. The island pilgrimage must have experienced a considerable revival when Pope Paul V granted a plenary indulgence to pilgrims in around 1607; the same Lord Deputy Chichester who recorded 15,000 or more pilgrims at Inishcealtra in 1609 gives a similar number as resorting to Monaincha in 1611. George Cunningham, Roscrea's modern historian, quotes a letter written by David Rothe, Bishop of Ossory, in the same year, which gives a grim picture of women pilgrims being molested by the soldiers of a local English garrison:

> *The spectacle of these women being molested, the noise and din of the soldiers attacking, would upset you deeply, and be more offensive to you than the total laceration of your feet and limbs, than the cold and constant perspiration which you remember from last year when you undertook that penitential pilgrimage and almost collapsed from the kneeling, and certainly all those who visited the island itself are fully aware how painful this kneeling can be in these holy places where the ground is sandy and rough, especially when it is done barefoot every day and in many different forms.*

Although the pilgrimage was revived in the mid-1970s, this ancient monastic and pilgrimage site no longer resounds to the low murmur of prayers uttered as late as the 1840s by those who did the pilgrimage rounds here; nothing now disturbs that ancient place except the sound of birdsong and the occasional mooing of the cattle who graze in what was once the boggy terrain surrounding the beautiful island church.

BALLYVOURNEY, CORK

One of the most hallowed places in Cork is Ballyvourney in the barony of Muskerry. It owes its fame to one of the few celebrated women of Early Christian Ireland, St Gobnait, a patron saint of beekeepers, who is likely to have lived in the 6th century. In 1951, the well-known Cork sculptor Seámus Murphy carved her statue, resting on a base of bees and a beehive, and it was erected close to a round beehive hut known as St Gobnait's House which, on excavation by Professor Michael J. O'Kelly, provided evidence of iron-working within.

This hut is the first station on the pilgrimage in the saint's honour, which takes place annually on her feast day, 11 February, though there used also to be a more boisterous pilgrimage on Whit Sunday. The remainder of the stations are all in or

Fig. 51 *The jaunty figure of a pilgrim seems to be on top of the world at Ballyvourney, County Cork*

close to the churchyard only a little distance away on the other side of the road. Close to the 19th-century Protestant church there is a later medieval church with added chancel, and over the exterior of a south window is one of those primitive naked female figures known as a sheela-na-gig which pilgrims touch as part of the station by reaching up their hands and rubbing it while they are standing *inside* the window. The only other piece of sculpture in the church is a head projecting from the western side of the wall above the chancel arch; it probably formed the *voussoir* or keystone of the arch of a Romanesque church which stood on the site earlier. One of the stations is a mound of stones outside and to the west of the church, with a bullaun on top of it; and this mound is supposed to mark the saint's last resting place. The final pilgrimage station is a holy well some distance away, where water is taken, and a series of Paters, Aves and Glorias are said, as at each of the preceding stations. About a mile away to the east is an interesting stone (Fig. 51) with an encircled cross of arcs on each face, and with a charming figure striding along the top of the circle on what is now the east face. The stone was removed some years ago, but later returned, after which it was enclosed by an incongruous circular wall.

Associated with the pilgrimage is a wooden statue of St Gobnait dating from around the 13th century, now kept by the local parish priest, Fr Michael Williams. It is exhibited to the public twice a year, on the saint's feast day and on Whit Sunday, when pilgrims buy locally a blue ribbon or thread known as 'St Gobnait's Measure' and place it first lengthwise and then across the statue, before taking it home to protect them from illness. The Protestant John Richardson describes in 1727 how the statue was set up on the wall of the old church, and pilgrims went around it three times saying prayers, then kissing it and making an offering. He went on:

> The image is kept by one of the O Herlihy's, and when anyone is sick of the small-pox, they send for it and sacrifice a sheep to it, and wrap the skin about the sick person, and the family eat the sheep. But this Idol hath now much lost its Reputation, because two of the O Herlihys died lately of the Small Pox. The Lord Bishop of Cloyne was pleased to favour me with the narrative of this rank idolatry, to suppress which he hath taken very proper and effectual methods.

The pilgrimage to Ballyvourney is not mentioned in any of the old historical sources, and the wooden statue is probably the best surviving link we have with the pilgrimage of earlier centuries, so it is no longer possible to estimate how old the pilgrimage really is. It is certainly vigorously practised today, particularly by women of the surrounding communities, and not just on the saint's feast day, but on almost every day of the year; pilgrims can be seen doing the rounds in all weathers.

In the 19th century, Ballyvourney was the centre for a school for *bacachs*, that curious community of beggars who were frequently to be found at the various locations where pilgrimage patterns and fairs took place. In an article on *bacachs* written in 1861, William Hackett of Cork, who compared them in true 19th-century style to the fakirs of India, wrote of Ballyvourney:

> Ardmore, Gougane Barra, Lough Dearg, Shruel, Croagh Patrick, and other places of pilgrimage, are the resorts of the Bacach tribe; but Ballyvourney would appear to have been their 'Fakeerabad.' There dwelt the professors. What the precise course of studies might have been, is easier to imagine than to ascertain: they might have comprised instructions as to habits, rules of conduct, and secresy; but there was one qualification which the ordinary observer could not fail to perceive, and which appears to have been the leading performance of their lives, this was the crónawn or beggar's chaunt. As the traveller passed through the village of Ballyvourney, he heard from the interior of many houses various repetitions of this strange Oriental-sounding appeal. When the aspirant had acquired a proficiency in all the requisite qualifications, he received his diploma in the shape of a goodly black thorn stick, at the upper end of which were conspicuous a certain number of brass nails: to a thorough proficient, the highest number of nails was given, which was seven; and the great virtue of these nails lay in the supposed fact that each nail indicated the efficacy of the prayers of the professor, which was increased in such ratio, that one prayer of the Bacach with a seven-nailed staff was as efficacious as sixty four prayers from one of the single nail. Their mode of ascertaining whether the pupil was entitled to a full diploma was quite practical and by no means equivocal. It is told of the once well known Cormaceen-a-Dèirc (Little Cormac of the alms), that when his studies were nearly completed, he felt perfect confidence in his own powers, but his instructor, doubtful of his competency, determined on applying the usual test. Accordingly, the next coming 'pattern' was fixed upon for the trial. Cormaceen was stationed at one end of the village, and the professor, 'Bacach na Barrlin,' (the Bacach of the sheet), so called from his dress, occupied the bridge, each being provided with a seven-nailed staff. In the evening, on comparing their receipts, Cormaceen produced a considerable surplus, and thus proved himself qualified to depart on his vocation. There might have been in other parts of the country, similar colleges, but in the south of Ireland, Ballyvourney was the only one of any celebrity; so much so, that in describing one of the fraternity, he was always stated to be 'Bacach o Ballyvourney,' or 'Cleire Gobnaiti,' (Gobnat's clergy). St Gobnate was the patron saint of the place, her name like that of St Bridget having probably had its prototype in that of some ancient Irish goddess.

Together with St Ita of Killeedy, St Gobnait was the most revered female saint of the south of Ireland, and her cult spread from the Aran Islands to the Dingle Peninsula and as far east as Dungarvan in County Waterford, where patterns were held in her honour at churches or holy wells where she was venerated. One tradition recorded in Kerry tells that St Gobnait was the daughter of a sea-robber, and that when his ship was anchored in Ventry harbour, she escaped ashore and took refuge in a wood where an angel told her not to return to her father's ship and that she would find her resurrection at the place where she would find nine white deer. It was at Ballyvourney that she finally discovered them.

Her name is linked in Ballyvourney to that of another local saint, Abbán, who is credited with having given her the site for her nunnery. His grave is located about three-quarters of a mile away from St Gobnait's House, hidden away in a magical spot in the woods, marked by a mound of stones surmounted by a bullaun and flanked by three Ogham stones (Fig. 10).

ARDMORE, WATERFORD

Ardmore stands sentinel over a fine sandy bay on the southeast coast of Ireland (Plate V). Near the shore is a large boulder called St Declan's Stone, which is believed to have floated from Rome in the wake of St Declan's ship, bearing a bell which the saint had forgotten to bring with him. It was claimed that anyone who could creep under the stone would be cured of rheumatic pains.

Ardmore prides itself on having one of the finest, but also one of the latest, round towers in Ireland, 98 feet 7 inches (just under 30 metres) high, its carved ornament at the top indicating a 12th-century date. Nearby is St Declan's Cathedral, built in various stages in around 1200, with carvings probably from an earlier church built into its west gable. Within the church is preserved an Ogham stone (Fig. 87); with inscriptions carved on three of the four corners of the stone. Not far away is St Declan's House, a small building which was the tomb-shrine of the saint, who is one of those said to have brought Christianity to Ireland before St Patrick. The Saint's House was an important station on the annual pilgrimage on 24 July, and a flagstone which covered the saint's grave within has long since vanished, a prey to centuries of relic-collecting. A few hundred metres away, to the east of the modern village and close to a ruined church, is St Declan's Holy Well. There are, surprisingly, no early references to the pilgrimage here, but it had become popular by mid-19th century. A great influx of pilgrims from various parts of the country was reported in 1832, after the *bacachs* from the Ballyvourney school had put about tales of recent cures at Ardmore.

FORE, WESTMEATH

Fore is one of those places of pilgrimage to which Pope Paul V granted an indulgence in around 1607, though the pilgrimage is probably much older. The most important structure on the site of the monastery, founded by St Feichín in the 7th century, is St Feichín's Church; it has a massive west doorway, with an encircled cross carved on both the interior and the exterior of the lintel. The church had a chancel added to it in around 1200, and in this chancel are preserved some slabs with simple crosses carved in relief. To the east of the church is a plain ringed cross. Below the church, on the other side of the road, is the well (see page 229).

PART THREE

PILGRIMAGE THINGS

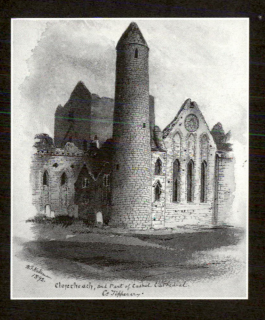

Fig. 52 *W.F. Wakeman's 1892 watercolour of the*
Round Tower and Cathedral on the Rock of Cashel,
County Tipperary

CHAPTER 10

PILGRIMAGE ROADS

WE MUST NOW TURN TO CERTAIN FEATURES FOUND AT THE IRISH
pilgrimage sites that may have been associated with pilgrimage.
Proof of an association is lacking in many cases, so that some of
what follows in this section of the book is pure hypothesis on my
part. But I hope that a study of what hints may be available – evidence is too strong
a word – may help to harden the hypothesis, and give us a greater understanding of
these features where they are seen in a pilgrimage context. The first item I shall
discuss is also the one that can most clearly be identified as having formed a part of
the pilgrimage process, and that is the pilgrimage road.

TÓCHAR PHÁDRAIG, MAYO
The longest of all the surviving old Irish pilgrimage roads is known as the Tóchar
Phádraig, St Patrick's Road, which leads to Croagh Patrick. Its traditional starting
point is the Abbey of Ballintubber, 'the settlement of St Patrick's well', founded in
1216 by Cathal Crovderg, king of Connacht, for the Canons Regular of St
Augustine and dedicated to St Patrick, Mary and St John the Apostle. Refurbished in
the 1960s, Ballintubber is one of the finest examples of that late flowering of the
Romanesque style of architecture christened by H. G. Leask 'the School of the
West'. But it has been surmised that the road from here to Croagh Patrick goes
back to pagan times, and was originally a road that led to 'the Reek', as the
mountain is known locally, from Cruachan, seat of the prehistoric kings of
Connacht. One possible indication of a pre-Christian origin for the road is the
presence on it, at Boheh, of a large boulder called St Patrick's Chair, which is

Fig. 53 *Fences at the Wicklow Gap* (OPPOSITE) *enclose
excavated flagstones of St Kevin's Road, which brought
pilgrims eastwards over the hills to Glendalough*

139

decorated with small circular hollows in the stone known as cup-marks, which are generally considered to date from the Bronze Age. The road from Ballintubber has recently been cleaned up by local effort and initiative, which has also provided a number of stiles to facilitate movement on the ancient route. In the course of the clearance, a number of stone flags came to light which must have belonged to the Tóchar Phádraig.

One of the most remarkable places along the road is Aghagower, visible from some distance away because of its round tower. Beside it is a medieval church, the bell from which, according to local folklore, lies buried in a nearby bog. At a crossroads in the centre of the village is Dabhach Phádraig, a circular 'bath' surrounded by a stone wall. Beside it is an ancient tree, the clay at the base of which is said to have curative powers. Modern repairs to it and to the nearby Deacon's Well make it difficult to know what either of them looked like originally. Stations used to be performed at both of these places, as well as at St Patrick's Bed nearby. Out in the middle of the Mayo countryside, and also situated along the Tóchar, is Lankill. Here we find a raised stone altar with a small cross-inscribed stone on top of it, as well as a curious pillar-stone with concentric circles (of the Bronze Age?) and a cross inscribed. The authenticity of the markings has been called into question, but the cross would seem to be a genuine Early Christian monument. Not far away is a holy well dedicated to St Brendan.

THE SAINT'S ROAD ON THE DINGLE PENINSULA

Mention of St Brendan brings us to the second extensive pilgrimage road, for he is the saint to whom the Saint's Road on the Dingle Peninsula refers. Considerable traces of this road remain but parts of it have to be followed on the old Ordnance Survey maps and, to some extent, reconstructed with the eye of faith. Its course has been indicated in Fig. 21. Though its original starting point may have been close to Ventry harbour, its present visible start lies just to the north of Kilcolman, a round enclosure in a field located in the townland of Maumanorig, which contains the cross-decorated boulder with an Ogham inscription (Fig. 23) asking for a prayer for Colman the pilgrim. The first traces of the Saint's Road can be picked up just south of a saddle in the ridge of Lateevemore to the north of Kilcolman, where a narrow, sunken way is flanked on either side by an earthen bank and an occasional standing stone. From this ridge a fine view can be had of the three main land falls for those who went on the maritime pilgrimage to Mount Brandon: the harbours of Dingle, Ventry and Smerwick. Maumanorig is unusual in that, while it is entirely surrounded by the modern parish of Ventry to the south of the Lateevemore ridge, it is an enclave belonging to the parish of Marhin, which lies largely to the north of the ridge. This creates an unexpected yet understandable link between Kilcolman and the area to the northeast of the ridge inland from Smerwick harbour, where the main course of the pilgrimage road can be followed (after an interruption on the northern slope of the ridge) on its way to Mount Brandon. Its path near the edge of the plain can clearly be seen in panorama from the top of the ridge as it skirts along near the northern foot of Lateevemore, its broad sweep outlined in relief by its border of fuchsia hedges (Plate III).

Beside the road in Lateevemore itself is a standing stone decorated with a fine cross of arcs, now scarcely visible because the stone leans perilously towards a disfiguring metal water-tank. The Saint's Road merges with the modern

Ballyferriter-Dingle road for a while, rising to a point near the crossroads at Ballynana. There it once more becomes an independent, untarred road, off which an old path led down to Gallarus oratory, which lies less than 300 metres from the Saint's Road. Passing the ruins of the (?)17th-century Chancellor's House (not to be confused with the two-storey building sometimes called by the same name) the road reaches Kilmalkedar church and holy well. From there, the road is difficult to trace as it climbs over Reenconnell hill down to Currauly, where there is a broken cross-inscribed stone. It then disappears completely (probably under the modern road) as it crosses the valley of the Feohanagh river, only to reappear again at the small village of Ballybrack, where it begins the final ascent to Mount Brandon. After about a half a mile, on the far side of a bridge, the line of the road gradually peters out in the boggy terrain over which the pilgrims must have trudged before the final steep climb to the summit. The modern pilgrim should only attempt the walk when the mountain is clear of cloud, for it is easy to lose one's way in the mist which can very quickly envelop the summit, only 20 feet east of which a rock face drops precipitously about 2000 feet.

The Ordnance Survey six- and one-inch maps often precede the marking of the Saint's Road with the words 'site of', simply because it is often not visible nowadays and is not indicated by any flat stone flags, which is sometimes the case elsewhere. It is frequently no more than an untarred path 12 or more feet (4 metres) wide. It should be noted that a fine road about 20 feet (6-7 metres) broad leads up the mountainside from Tiduff (Black House) towards, but not as far as, the cross-inscribed stone at Arraglen (Fig. 28), which lies at a height of about 2000 feet (650 metres) in a saddle to the south of Masatiompán. Local wisdom suggests that this road, which is raised some feet above the bog, is a military road made almost two centuries ago to facilitate access to a look-out tower on the mountainside. But as it veers off towards Mount Brandon before petering out, one may well ask if it was not built over some earlier road which may have provided pilgrims with an alternative route to the summit.

St Kevin's Road, Glendalough

The last of the longer pilgrimage roads to be discussed here is St Kevin's Road (Fig. 54), which brought pilgrims eastwards over the Wicklow Gap to Glendalough. Its course was monitored more than fifty years ago by the late Liam Price, a district justice and the greatest expert on Wicklow field antiquities. He pointed to the fact that the road is not marked on the Ordnance Survey maps west of the Wicklow Gap but, as he puts it:

> . . . if one looks down on the bog from the steep hill on the south side, a straight green line can be seen across it over a mile long; this, no doubt, represents the track of the road, for it ran, according to local tradition, straight down to where the Glashaboy brook joins the Kings river, and from there on to a church, the ruin of which still stands in the townland of Ballinagee.

At Ballinagee (known locally as Tampleteenawn), the road, as such, ended. But Liam Price argued that other stone monuments further west may have indicated to pilgrims the way to Glendalough. One is a roadside boulder marked with an equal-armed cross at a place known as The Wooden Cross at Togher (a name derived

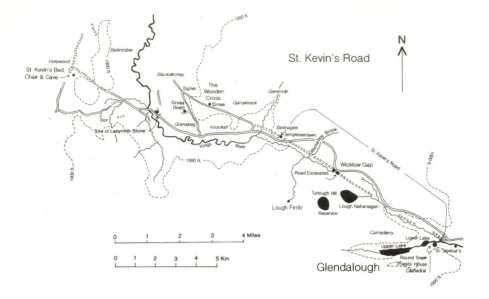

Fig. 54 *Map of the area around St Kevin's Road to*
Glendalough (after Liam Price)

from the Irish for 'trackway'), another is a cross-marked stone formerly at Granabeg (and now unlocatable). Finally there is the famous labyrinth stone. This is a large granite boulder commonly called the Hollywood Stone (Fig. 47), though originally it was located at Lockstown, about 4 miles (6.5 kilometres) southeast of Hollywood, from whence it was removed in the 1920s to the National Museum in Dublin, where it is now on display. The labyrinth carved on it was called the Walls of Troy by the locals, who must have heard the name from some visiting antiquary many years ago. Some scholars have proposed a prehistoric date for this stone, but Liam Price – in my view rightly – argued for a Christian significance for the design. The labyrinth is known from the floors of medieval French cathedrals, such as Chartres, where penitents used to walk on their knees upon it as the equivalent of a pilgrimage to the holy places; it was called, among other things, the Jerusalem Mile. The only other example of a labyrinth in Ireland is on a stone of uncertain (but not earlier than later medieval) date at Rathmore, County Meath. As regards the Hollywood Stone, obviously its origins cannot be decided conclusively, but its local context would suggest that it had some connection with the pilgrimage road to Glendalough. What may be a small, subsidiary pilgrims' path at Hollywood itself may lead from near the village to St Kevin's Bed, an undefined 'cave' at the foot of a cliff face, now topped by a modern statue of the saint.

In the area around the Wicklow Gap, traces of the Saint's Road can be seen in the face of a turf bank; on either side the road was straight, whereas the modern road tends to curve, fitting in to the local contours. Today, the ancient paving of the pilgrimage road can be seen within two wooden enclosures (Fig. 53) flanking the

Fig. 55 *St Kevin's pilgrimage road descends from the Wicklow Gap towards its goal at Glendalough*

entrance to the Electricity Supply Board's generating station at Turlough Hill. The areas within these enclosures were excavated by Drs Michael Ryan and Pat Wallace of the National Museum in 1972. Although somewhat overgrown since then, the features they uncovered can still be made out. The excavations showed that the road was raised somewhat above the adjacent boggy terrain; it was about 10 feet (3 metres) wide and was covered by large stone flags. Sadly, no finds were made that would help indicate the period at which the road was built.

From the Wicklow Gap, it drops down the valley (Fig. 55); it meets the modern road into Glendalough close to Trinity Church, near the junction marked with a stone bearing a Latin cross like the lost example from Granabeg mentioned above. Writing in 1870, Dr Colles pointed out that the road extended also from Reefert church northwards across the valley near the Upper Lake to the river that connects the two lakes, bordered by the cairns and station crosses in the open field to the south of the Upper Lake, but that the southern half of the road had been destroyed.

The Pilgrim's Way, Clonmacnois

Prime among the surviving shorter pilgrimage roads is the Pilgrim's Way at Clonmacnois. In the field to the west of the Nuns' Church, there is a long flat-topped mound a few hundred metres long. Macalister pointed out that this could be a natural esker, on the top of which ancient but also modern roads could run. But even if this Clonmacnois mound, which runs parallel to the modern tarred roadway leading from the monastic enclosure to the Nuns' Church, was an esker originally, it is very likely that it was also used as part of the pilgrimage road to Clonmacnois. It certainly faces towards the centre of the monastery, the round tower and St Ciarán's Church, which marks the burial place of the founding saint. At the foot of the mound, a stone is sunk level with the surface of the ground; the stone has two deep conical hollows in it, which local tradition states were made by St Ciarán's cow when it stumbled. The mound may be identical with 'the pavement from the place in Clonvicknois called the Abbess her Garden to the heape of stones at the three crosses' which was made by Breassall Conealagh in 1026, according to Connell Mageoghagan's surviving 1627 translation of the Annals of Clonmacnoise, the Irish original of which is now lost.

If the mound does represent a man-made construction forming the road from 'the Abbess her Garden' (probably now the Nuns' Church), or the culmination of the pilgrimage road, it was either never finished or was used as a quarry after completion, for it stops abruptly about 100 metres to the east of the roadside gate of the modern cemetery extension to the main monastic complex. Within this extension there is a raised path partially covered with stone flags, which undoubtedly formed part of the old pilgrimage road, leading the pilgrim up his last few steps to the saint's tomb. This may be the 'Saint's Walk' where a ring-headed pin, perhaps of the 9th or 10th century, was found in 1917. Other ring-pins probably of roughly the same date in the National Museum in Dublin are recorded as having come from Clonmacnois, and Mrs Heather King showed me further examples which she excavated in 1990 within the cemetery extension. The site was about 30 metres from the Pilgrim's Way, and within a few feet of where an Ogham stone was discovered in the making of a grave in the same year. The concentration of these pins close to the Pilgrim's Way may suggest that they were worn by pilgrims.

Lemanaghan, Offaly

Ten miles (16 kilometres) east-southeast of Clonmacnois is Lemanaghan, where there would appear to be another short pilgrim road. The site is best known as the place of origin of St Manchán's Shrine, a 12th-century reliquary (Fig. 56) now preserved in the Catholic church at Boher a few miles away. Little or nothing is known of St Manchán, but his relics must have been important to have merited such

Fig. 56 *The National Museum's copy of the 12th-century gabled shrine of St Manchán, which is decorated with an equal-armed cross on each face. The original came from Lemanaghan in County Offaly, and is now preserved in the Catholic church at Boher some miles away*

a wonderful shrine, and were presumably the goal of pilgrims, who would probably have included a visit to them on their way to or from Clonmacnois. Few of the decorative details of the church at Lemanaghan are much earlier than 1200, though parts of the masonry may well be earlier, and the church appears to have been reconstructed in the later medieval period. Near its north-western corner is a rectangular building that may well have enclosed the saint's tomb-shrine. A number of cross-decorated slabs are known from Lemanaghan, some of which are said to have come from the Saint's Well to the south-east of the church. This well is close to the commencement of a well-preserved, raised trackway some 300 metres long leading to an old church some hundreds of metres away from the main church and traditionally said to have been the church of the saint's mother. Legend has it that mother and son used to meet daily on the trackway, 280 metres from the well at a now recumbent but originally upright stone, where they sat back to back without saying a word to one another, the saint having vowed never to speak to a woman. The trackway, which is now about 10-12 feet (up to 4 metres) wide, can be seen to preserve a number of stone flags. One of these, not very far from the well, has a number of depressions in it caused, it is said locally, by the saint's cow when it was abducted backwards by some thieves; it was recovered later through discovery of the holes its hooves had left in the stone. In the last century, tradition averred that a

145

draught of milk was provided gratis to wayfarers by the farmer's wife, as cow's milk was not to be sold there. This hospitable tradition may not be honoured much nowadays, but it is interesting to find that the Lemanaghan road shares a cow tale with the Pilgrim's Way at Clonmacnois.

OTHER SMALL PILGRIMAGE ROADS

Other pilgrimage roads may be mentioned briefly. The island of Inishcealtra in Lough Derg on the lower Shannon (see pages 125-9) was said in 1838 to have had a pilgrimage road leading from the landing place to the main cluster of monuments on the island; it was even suggested that, in summer, one could walk upon its continuation to the mainland. The other Lough Derg, in County Donegal, had a pilgrimage road leading from Pettigo to the lake, and beside it, at Drumawark, was a round enclosure like a ring-fort with a cross formerly within, suggesting that the enclosure may have been associated with the pilgrimage traffic. Another island that may have had a small pilgrimage road is Inchagaoill in Lough Corrib, County Galway, where in 1867 Sir William Wilde mentions 'an ancient flagged way leading up to the west doorway [of the Romanesque church], and one of the flags has a cross with fish-tail terminations'. An old trackway on Caher Island off the west Mayo coast was known as Bóthar na Naomh, 'the saint's road', in 1839, and was said to have been the head of a causeway running under the waves in the direction of the Reek, that is, Croagh Patrick. Petrie reported in 1820 that there was a 220-yard-long artificial stone path or causeway along the western side of the lake on High Island (Ardoileán) off the Galway coast, and that it led to an oval stone cell or house. A further, more extensive, road is reported from Ardmore in County Waterford, where it is largely co-terminous with the modern road network. The story of the Road of the Dishes (page 125) leading to St MacDuagh's Hermitage may reflect an ancient pilgrimage road to the spot. There is no obvious pilgrimage road on the Aran Islands, but probably it ran the same course as the existing roads and paths on the islands. Finally, at Glencolmcille (page 108), there are the remnants of what may once have been a more extensive pilgrimage road through boggy terrain traversed after the eighth station.

Chapter 11

Tomb-shrines

AS A GENERAL RULE, THE MAIN GOAL OF MOST PILGRIMS IN EARLY HISTORIC Ireland would probably have been the grave of the founding monastic saint. Clearly, there were exceptions. The mountain-tops of Croagh Patrick or Mount Brandon are unlikely to have been the permanent custodians of relics of Saints Patrick and Brendan respectively, and not even Armagh could offer the grave of St Patrick, much as it would have liked to have done. But in most of the other sites discussed in some detail in previous chapters, it is almost certainly true that the saint's grave was the light that attracted the moth. This can be inferred from the care and attention that was devoted to the area around the saint's grave, and the buildings that were erected as shrines over it.

A number of these still survive, though they show considerable signs of repair down the years. The clearest example is known as Teampull Chiaráin, or St Ciaran's Church, at Clonmacnois (Fig. 43), which is dwarfed by the cathedral that lies close to it. On the Continent, a saint's tomb usually had a large cathedral built over it, which was the pilgrim's ultimate goal. These Continental buildings were large enough to house many hundreds, if not indeed thousands, of visitors on special occasions such as the saint's feast day. In Ireland, however, the main churches, such as the cathedrals at Clonmacnois or Glendalough, were constructed on a much smaller scale. When the Irish saw St Malachy of Armagh building Ireland's first really large-scale church along Continental lines at Bangor, County Down, in around 1140, they shook their heads in disbelief and asked why it was necessary to build such a large church. 'We are Irish, not Gauls', was their comment. The story serves to demonstrate the conservatism of Irish building tradition, and when the Irish began to translate their wooden churches into stone, they retained the size and proportions of the earlier wooden structures, obviously feeling that what was good enough for St Patrick was good enough for them.

But the smallness of the cathedrals at Clonmacnois and Glendalough cannot have been entirely the reason why they were not built over the saint's tomb. In

147

many Continental churches, the saint's tomb was in a crypt well below ground level, but the early Irish churches did not have crypts (with one possible exception to be mentioned below), and this may have been a contributory reason why even the largest of the Irish pre-Norman cathedrals did not house the saint's grave, though it is possible that St Brendan may have been buried within the walls of Clonfert cathedral (Fig. 1). Perhaps the desire not to have too many pilgrims milling around the saint's tomb in the altar area was one of the main reasons for building the largest church or cathedral close to – but not over – the saint's tomb, and usually, though not always, to the south of it. Clonmacnois is a good example. The cathedral is built 40 feet (13 metres) to the south-west of Teampull Chiaráin, and is not even orientated in the same direction. This small church (Fig. 43), which is better described as a tomb-shrine, shows at both gables the extensions of the north and south walls beyond them, known as *antae*, after the word used for this feature in classical Greek architecture. *Antae* have been taken to be translations into stone of the stout corner posts of the wooden churches that acted as models for the early stone churches. Clonmacnois is known to have had a wooden church as late as the 12th century, but the building of stone churches, whilst recorded historically as

Fig. 57 *The west gable of Killinaboy church, County Clare, bears a double-armed cross, possibly imitating a reliquary of the True Cross once housed inside*

early as the 8th century, is unlikely to have become common until the 9th/10th centuries; perhaps the popularity of stone buildings increased because of the vulnerability of wooden churches to being set on fire, particularly by the Viking marauders. *Antae* continued to be used in the construction of Irish churches until the 12th century, as evidenced by the Romanesque church at Kilmalkedar (Plate XII), and possibly even as late as the 13th century, as exemplified by the church at Killinaboy, County Clare, with its double-armed cross, which may date from after 1200 (Fig. 57).

Professor Rainer Berger's recent research into dating mortar samples from early Irish churches on the basis of determining their radiocarbon content has provided a calibrated date of 8th-9th centuries for a mortar sample taken from behind a large stone set in the exterior wall to the left of the doorway of the Clonmacnois tomb-shrine of St Ciarán; this gives us the likely period when the shrine was constructed. The upper part of the doorway shows obvious signs of secondary repairs, and no wonder, as hundreds of thousands of pilgrims down the centuries must have entered through the portal to reach the saint's grave, which is pointed out in the north-eastern corner. It was in this building that a relic of St Ciarán's hand was kept when Bishop Dopping made his visitation in 1684, and it was here too that a chalice and a wine vessel, as well as the splendid Crozier of the Abbots of Clonmacnois (Fig. 64) were unearthed within the last few centuries. The stone tomb-shrine was roofed until the 18th or 19th century, but that it was by no means the first structure over the saint's tomb is suggested by a story related in *The Annals of Clonmacnoise* under the year of St Ciarán's death. The King Diarmuit who reigned at the time of the saint's demise is said to have grieved so much for him that he became deaf. He turned to St Colmcille for advice, and was told that he should repair to Clonmacnois and put some earth from the saint's grave into his ears. As the abbot, Ciarán's successor, was absent when the king arrived, the parish priest of Clonmacnois (as he is described in Connell Mageoghagan's 1627 translation of the *Annals*), Loway by name, fasted and watched that night in the little church (probably of wood) where the saint was buried. The next morning the priest took a bell known as the White Bell and mingled in it part of the clay from St Ciarán's grave and some holy water, and put both the clay and the water into the king's ears. Thereupon, the king's hearing improved instantly 'and the whole sickness and trobles of his braines ceased at that instant'. The story, though probably late, is interesting as an early Irish example of the use of earth from the saint's grave to obtain cures, a custom widely practised in Europe and beyond in the early centuries of Christianity.

Rather similar in shape and in dimensions to Teampull Chiaráin at Clonmacnois is another island tomb-shrine further up the Shannon, that of St Diarmid on Inchcleraun. Within, it measures only 8 feet by 7 (2.40 by 2.1 metres), has *antae* and is only 12 feet (4 metres) south of the main church; like the tomb-shrine of Clonmacnois, it is orientated somewhat differently. The gable over the west doorway shows signs of having been secondarily repaired. It may originally have had a strong and heavy lintel, like that of another probable tomb-shrine at Labba Molaga in County Cork, which has a monumental look about it, and the doorway consists of only three stones – two jambs and a lintel. Inside the Labba Molaga church is a stone said to cover the grave of the saint, Molaga; to spend a night beneath it was said to cure you of rheumatism – though what colds or other ailments you might acquire in the process is not recorded. The small building known as St James's Chapel at St Mullins in County Carlow may originally have been St Mullin's tomb-shrine, again located outside the main church, as is another unrecorded example on Church Island in Lough Key, County Roscommon. Almost exactly the same size as the building at Labba Molaga is St Declan's House at Ardmore. This structure, re-roofed in modern times, is traditionally known as the saint's tomb, and the stone flags and the earth from the interior have fallen a constant prey to the relic-seekers down the years. It too is located some distance away from the cathedral.

What may have been a similar – and probably earlier – tomb-shrine of a different kind was discovered by Professor M. J. O'Kelly in his excavation near Carnsore Point, County Wexford, carried out as a preliminary step in the plans to create Ireland's first nuclear power station, which, as it turned out, was never built. The stone church of St Vogue still stands, therefore, and within its walls Professor O'Kelly uncovered post-holes which, when tentatively reconstructed, suggested a wooden structure about 6½ feet by 4½ feet (2.25 metres × 1.5 metres), giving a date most likely to have been within the 6th or 7th century. This wooden feature could well suit interpretation as an early wooden tomb-shrine, the only problem being that no body was found within it. But it may have been erected on this site at the extreme south-eastern corner of Ireland to contain some corporeal relic of the saint, thus acting as an attraction for pilgrims from Wales and Cornwall.

One further island building deserves mention here: Teach Molaise (St Molaise's House) on Inishmurray, off the Sligo coast (see page 101). This building, of exactly the same interior dimensions as St Diarmid's tomb-shrine on Inchleraun, inside has a small bench around two of its walls (Fig. 36); it was in this small building that the 13th-century wooden statue of St Molaise was preserved before it was brought to the National Museum in Dublin for safekeeping, and it is in all likelihood the tomb-shrine of the saint. It has massive masonry, whose mortar provided Professor Rainer Berger with a radiocarbon date which, when calibrated, turned out to be of the 8th-9th centuries, and thus roughly of the same period as St Ciarán's little church at Clonmacnois. It is interesting to note that these two dates are among the earliest for church buildings provided by Professor Berger's new dating technique. Others of a similar date range included the oldest part of St Michael's Church on Skellig Michael and St Columb's House at Kells, with its stone roof, though the date cannot necessarily be taken as indicating the date for the whole structure as it stands. Two buildings off the west coast – the church on Ardoileán, otherwise High Island, in County Galway, and the so-called Priest's House on Caher Island – provided a variety of dates, which vary too much among one another to be certain about the probable date of the buildings. But it is interesting to consider those which fall closely together in their uncalibrated form, all of which give calibrated dates in the 8th/9th century:

BUILDING	DATE BP (BEFORE THE PRESENT)	LABORATORY NUMBER
Clonmacnois, St Ciarán's Church	1245 ± 55	UCLA 2727B
Inishmurray, Teach Molaise	1215 ± 45	UCLA 2725D
Skellig Michael, St Michael's Church	1250 ± 25	UCLA 2738D
Kells, St Columb's House	1270 ± 125	UCLA 2714A

We can note that the first two are almost certainly tomb-shrines. The Skellig Michael and Kells buildings are somewhat larger, but one may well ask if St Columb's House at Kells is not a rather larger version of the Clonmacnois and Inishmurray tomb-shrines built to house the relics of St Colmcille brought to Kells by the monks of Iona after the Viking attacks on that Hebridean monastery in the early 9th century? The association of the name of St Michael with the island of Skellig Michael, as already pointed out, only appears in the annals after the year 1000, and as the name of the church, and its dedication to St Michael, may only have materialised at around that time, there is quite a possibility that when this Skellig church was built in the 8th/9th century it was dedicated to some local saint such as Fionán or Finan, whose name is traditionally associated with the island. It may even have been intended to house one of his relics, if he was not actually buried on the island. It would have been rather more difficult to obtain a relic of the Archangel Michael for the island!

These considerations lead further to the speculation that the first stone structures of an ecclesiastical nature in Ireland may have been those small buildings erected to house the grave or a relic of a particular saint, not only to give them special importance and status among the wooden buildings of a monastery, but perhaps also to protect the buildings from the firebrands of the Vikings, and the relics within from the preying hands of pilgrims. Furthermore, it may have been these small tomb-shrines that provided the Irish monks with the impetus, the necessary spark, to start translating their wooden churches into stone.

Two of these dated buildings share the traditional description 'House', as opposed to 'Church', setting them apart from the churches on the same site, giving the faithful the impression that they were the everlasting home of at least some of the saint's corporeal relics. The same description is applied to another notable small building, the Priest's House in Glendalough, the priest who gave it its name being, allegedly, an 18th-century priest who is said to have been buried there. But there can be little doubt that this building (Fig. 45) was the tomb-shrine of St Kevin, lying some 60 feet to the southwest of the cathedral. The Romanesque arch at the eastern end is unique in that it points outwards, and its decoration suggests a 12th-century date for the building in its present form, though it may, of course, replace – or even partially incorporate - an earlier stone structure on the same location. The wall that at present blocks the arch is a 19th-century reconstruction based on Beranger's drawing of 1779 in which, however, the wall is shown abutting on the interior east face of the building. It is therefore unlikely to have been an original wall, but it may have replaced an earlier wall which had become ruined. In Beranger's drawing of 1779, the upright slit in the middle of it is blocked by hay! But the slit is likely to have older roots, as the 12th-century shrine (and perhaps also an earlier predecessor) probably had a small slit that enabled pilgrims to gaze upon the tomb of the saint, and perhaps even to insert their *brandea* or rags on a piece of string so that the rags could fall and touch the earth in which the saint was buried, and be retrieved after they had done so. But the slit would have prevented access to the ordinary pilgrim, unlike the shrines at Clonmacnois and Ardmore where considerable amounts of earth must have been removed. Unlike St Ciarán's at Clonmacnois and Teach Molaise on Inishmurray, which have west doorways, St Declan's House at Ardmore and the Priest's House at Glendalough both have south doorways, suggesting a date no earlier than the 12th century for both of them, as no rectangular building with a south doorway is documented in Ireland before the 12th century. The south doorway leading into the crypt of St Columb's House at Kells is modern, but in view of the suggestion made above that St Columb's House may have been a shrine for the saint's relics, it may have borrowed the Continental idea of a crypt to house the relics of the saint.

One other remarkable 12th-century building, which has no west doorway but three others – the main one in the north wall, and subsidiary doors in the north tower and the south wall – is Cormac's Chapel in Cashel, a place where Heneas MacNichaill was sent on his pilgrimage rounds in the 16th century (see page 52). We have no early references to any saint or relic in relation to 'Cormac's Chapel', which in itself is a modern name based on the belief that the building may be equated in all probability with the church annalistically documented as having been built by Cormac MacCarthy in 1127-34. Liam de Paor has argued persuasively that Cormac's Chapel was probably the first Irish church to have been built in the Romanesque style. Could it have been built in conjunction with, or even to house, a relic of a very special nature – perhaps even a relic of the True Cross? There is, of course, not the slightest documentary evidence for such a suggestion, but since Turlough O Conor, king of Connacht, had obtained a relic of the True Cross and

Fig. 58 *One of the tent-shaped slab-shrines at Temple Cronan, County Clare, stands beside a larger – but nevertheless small – Romanesque church*

Fig. 59 *A cross-decorated stone leans towards the remains of a slab-shrine at Killabuonia, County Kerry, where a rubbed-in cross on the triangular closing-slab is evidence of continuing pilgrimage tradition down to our own day*

enshrined it in the cross of Cong (Fig. 65) less than a decade before work on the chapel began, dynastic rivalry could well have been the spur that goaded Cormac into building his masterpiece. Not far from Cashel is another of the stopping points on Heneas MacNichaill's journey that really did have a relic of the True Cross, and that is Holycross Abbey, which derives its name from a relic of the True Cross it must have been given some time during the 12th century.

The grave of a local saint was often traditionally marked by his *leaba* or bed of stones (such as the Leaba of St Brecán on the Aran island of Inishmore) and could be just a small, rectangular area slighly raised above the surrounding surface, and provided with some form of stone kerb. In other instances, a kind of roof was constructed over the saint's tomb, by the simple provision of large slabs which inclined towards one another to form an inverted V. This is probably the nature of what is known as the 'Confessional' or the 'Anchorite's Cell' at Inishcealtra (Fig. 48), which looks as if it were the tomb-shrine of one of the saints associated with the island and was placed, as elsewhere, at some distance from the main church dedicated to St Caimin. Other, somewhat similar shrines consisting of inwardly inclining slabs forming, as it were, a roof without supporting walls, were neatly described by Charles Thomas as resembling ridge tents; they were apparently known as a *cumdach*, or 'Bone box'. They are found predominantly on the west coast, the Hill of Slane in County Meath being the only obvious exception. They are seen to good advantage in two instances. The first is at Temple Cronan (Fig. 58) in the Burren area of County Clare, where there are two such shrines close to a

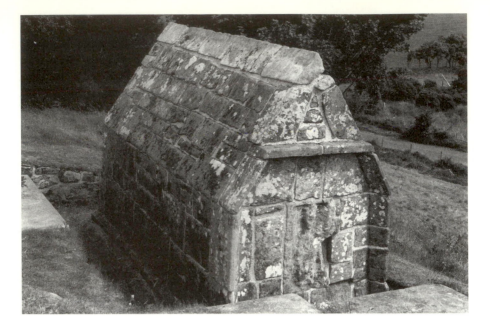

Fig. 60 *The 'mortuary house' at Banagher, County Derry, shows a 12th-century carving of a bishop, perhaps Muiredach O Heney, whose tomb it may cover*

rectangular church decorated with curious animal heads probably of the later 12th century. Only one shrine can be seen in Fig. 58, the other being on the far side of a modern boundary wall. The second example is at Killabuonia in the great semi-circular hills forming an arena overlooking the isolated St Finan's Bay in south-west Kerry. Here (Fig. 59) there is a closing triangular stone at the western end, with a hole at the bottom through which pilgrims doubtless stretched their arms to touch the earth in which the obscure local saint was buried. Standing guard over the tomb is a pillar decorated with crosses. On the same peninsula there are other examples at Illaunloughan, a very small, low island near Portmagee, and at a neglected site at Killoluaig, less than 5 miles (8 kilometres) north-east of Killabuonia. John Waddell has recently given a detailed description of a further shrine on the Aran island of Inishmore, at a place called Kilcholan, though nothing is known of the saint after whom the site is named.

In the north of Ireland, the tomb-shrines take on the appearance of houses (Dudley Waterman has aptly given them the generic name 'mortuary houses') each enshrining the body or relics of a saint. One, at Saul in County Down, where St Patrick is alleged to have died, is about 6 feet high and 5 feet long (1.80 metres by 1.50 metres), though the western end is no longer intact. Another, at Cooley in Donegal, known locally as the Skull House, is slightly shorter but almost 8 feet (2.50 metres) high, and has a small opening in the western end only large enough to allow a person to crawl through on hands and knees.

County Derry preserves three analogous monuments – at Bovevagh, Tamlaght and Banagher. Of these, that at Tamlaght is poorly preserved and lies adjacent to a

Fig. 61 *The 12th-century stone sarcophagus in the shadow of the Round Tower at Clones, County Monaghan probably imitates a wood and metal reliquary containing the relics of St Tighernach*

church. The other two are in a better state of preservation, that at Banagher (Fig. 60) bearing on the western end the figure of a bishop, perhaps St Muiredach O'Heney, whose grave the mortuary house is traditionally said to mark.

The style of carving suggests a 12th-century date, as does that on a further unique monument, the stone sarcophagus standing in the shadow of the round tower at Clones in County Monaghan (Fig. 61). Here, too, we find the figure of a bishop or abbot (St Tighernach, the local patron?) but, unlike the other mortuary houses, this is a solid stone 6 feet (1.80 metres) long and 2 feet 10 inches (0.85 metres) high; in this it is akin to the Hedda Stone in Peterborough Cathedral in England, and the two sarcophagi at St Andrews in Scotland. It can also be compared to the hogback stone (Fig. 62) with cross decoration from Castledermot, County Kildare. Each end of the ridge of the Clones sarcophagus is carved with a small finial, and the juncture of gable and wall on one side appears to bear stone copies of hinges, suggesting that this was the translation into stone of a sarcophagus with a wooden core and decorated with precious metals and gems. While the mortuary houses were presumably designed to stand in the open air, the Clones sarcophagus and the Castledermot hogback probably stood over a saint's tomb in a church now long disappeared, as the model on which the Clones sarcophagus was based must have stood inside a church.

Though probably 12th-century, it is reminiscent of two other well-known Irish sarcophagi that have also disappeared. These housed the bodies of St Brigid and St Conlaed in the vanished (probably wooden) 7th-century church of the double monastery at Kildare. We know of them only through the description given by St

Fig. 62 *The cross-decorated stone at Castledermot,*
County Kildare, resembles in shape the Viking-period
hogbacked stones of northern England

Brigid's 7th-century biographer, Cogitosus, who tells us that the sarcophagi lay to the right and left of a beautifully decorated altar, and that they themselves were richly ornamented with gold, silver and many-coloured gemstones, and bore pictorial representations both in beaten metals and in colours. How much richer the treasury of early Irish Christian art would be had they survived, but even the description is important in giving us the earliest known details of the enshrining of corporeal relics of Irish saints.

Chapter 12

Relics and Reliquaries

AS WE HAVE SEEN IN AN EARLIER CHAPTER, RELICS PLAYED AN IMPORTANT ROLE in the religious life of continental Europe from the 4th century onwards. Relics may have been introduced from there into England in the same century, but Ireland was probably somewhat more tardy. The reference in the Tripartite Life of St Patrick, of around 900, to Palladius having left a casket with the relics of Saints Paul and Peter in Cell Fine in Leinster in the early years of the 5th century may be interpreted with some scepticism, though the fact that Cell Fine was an obscure church in Leinster could lend credence to the tradition. The sarcophagi of the bodies of saints Brigid and Conlaed in the 7th century as described by Cogitosus may be taken as representing the beginnings of serious reverence of local saints' relics in Ireland. At the same period, in order to support the cult of local saints, the writing of saints' lives began to become common, as witnessed by Cogitosus, by Muirchú's *Life* of, and Tirechán's notes on, St Patrick, and also by Adomnan's *Life of St Columba*. Tirechán mentions that St Patrick gave to Bishop Sachellus of Baslick in County Roscommon 'a portion of the relics of SS. Peter and Paul, Stephen and Lawrence which were in Armagh', though this may not represent a genuine introduction of these relics in St Patrick's day, but the fact that they were in Armagh when Tirechán was writing in the 7th century might suggest that they were brought back by an Irish deputation that had visited Rome in connection with the Paschal controversy in 631-2. Charles Doherty has suggested that the use of the word Baslick (Basilica) in early Ireland, as in the Roscommon instance, may denote a church building that contained relics. Certainly, from the 7th century onwards, Armagh itself, because it did not possess the body of St Patrick, was sorely in need of relics such as those of the first martyrs in order to press its claims to supremacy within Ireland.

From around the same period, the custom arose of bringing the relics of the saints on tour. Already at the end of the 7th century, St Colmcille's relics were being brought on tour around the island of Iona at a time of great drought; this had the desired effect of creating rain. The relics of his biographer, Adomnan, abbot of Iona, were brought to Ireland in 727 to help promulgate his law to encourage the protection of clerics. In the 8th and 9th centuries in particular, but also in the 12th century, saints' relics, particularly those of St Patrick, were brought on tour within Ireland. The reasons for doing so were not just to prevent natural and pestilential disasters, and to promulgate laws, but also to act as insignia of abbatial authority and rank, and to collect tributes for the monasteries which possessed the relics. A relic was frequently used as a talisman in going into battle, the prime example being one of Ireland's earliest surviving manuscripts, the Cathach or 'Battler' of St Colmcille, written possibly by the hand of the saint himself; it now rests peacefully in the library of the Royal Irish Academy in Dublin. It should be noted that the early 9th-century Book of Kells, the great Gospel of Colmcille now in the library of Trinity College, Dublin, was described as 'the chief object [or relic] of the western world' when the account of its theft from the stone church at Kells was described in the *Annals of Ulster* in 1007. Though written at least two hundred years after St Colmcille's death, the manuscript was obviously regarded as a kind of associative relic of his. Relics of whatever kind were apparently as sacred as the Scriptures for the purpose of swearing oaths in medieval Ireland, and they also served as witnesses to solemn treaties between secular leaders.

The relics used in early Ireland were, as elsewhere, of two kinds: those that were secondarily associated with the saint or had come into contact with him, and those that were actually part of the saint's body. The historical sources lay particular emphasis on three kinds of associative relic – bells, belts and croziers, objects that were regarded as the standard equipment of any saint worth venerating; other items, such as the chasuble (*casula*) of St Enda of Aran, are also mentioned.

Bells of both iron and bronze survive in considerable numbers from a great variety of sites up and down Ireland. The lives of the saints show the bells to have been closely associated with particular saints, and that said to be of St Patrick was given a splendid shrine around 1100 (now in the National Museum in Dublin). We have already seen how earth and water were mixed in the White Bell of Clonmacnois to cure the deafness of King Diarmuit and, if we can believe his *Life*, St Colman mac Lúacháin succeeded in bringing one Onchu back to life by pouring three 'Waves' out of a bell.

The Black Bell of St Patrick was used as an integral part of the pilgrimage to Croagh Patrick, during which pilgrims were to kiss a cross engraved on the bell and move it three times sunwise around the body, as the modern pilgrims do with a stone at the third station on the Glencolmcille pilgrimage today. Bells were the most commonly recorded relics for cures, including those of the stomach, and it was thanks to St Samthann's bell that her prioress was able to make a tree fall in the right direction after it had already begun to tilt the wrong way.

In Ireland, the saint's belt played an important role as a relic, in contrast to its comparative rarity in the rest of Europe. The tale is told of St Colman of Kilmacduagh that he was prepared to build his monastery wherever his belt should fall to the ground, and thereafter it was adorned with gold and gems and preserved by the O'Shaughnessy family near Gort – doubtless a neat story invented to stress the importance of the relic, which was credited with many cures. This belt was also clever enough to be able to differentiate between those who had preserved their virginity and those who had lost it, by closing or refusing to close respectively.

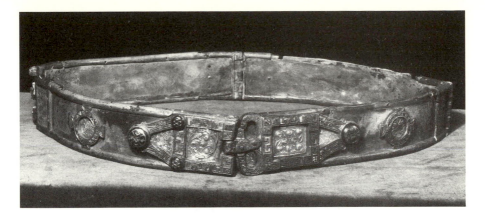

Fig. 63 *The belt-shrine found at Moylough, County Sligo, and now in the National Museum in Dublin, is the only one of its kind known to survive*

Only one saint's belt has been preserved for us. Who its owner was we have no way of knowing, but it was found enshrined in a wonderfully decorated reliquary of around the early 9th century which was discovered in a bog at Moylough, County Sligo, in 1945. Now in the National Museum in Dublin (Fig. 63), it shows considerable wear and tear around the hinges of its four separate segments, which sugested to M. J. O'Kelly that the belt must frequently have been extracted from the reliquary to help bring about a cure for some ailment or other.

Also used for cures, not only for humans but probably for animals as well, was a saint's *bachall* or crozier; these croziers may have been encased in tightly fitting bronze reliquaries preserving the same drop-head shape as the original wooden croziers or staffs. While Cormac Bourke is probably justified in doubting whether the wood contained in some of the croziers ever was part of the saint's staff, the saint's *bachall* was, in the words of A. T. Lucas, 'thought of as the principal vehicle of his power, a kind of spiritual electrode through which he conveyed the holy energy by which he wrought the innumerable miracles attributed to him'. The finest example of such a crozier is that of the Abbots of Clonmacnois (Fig. 64), so-called, which was found in the 18th century in the diminutive tomb-shrine of St Ciarán at Clonmacnois. But the most famous *bachall* of all was not one belonging to any local saint, but to the National Apostle himself. Known as the *Bachall Íosa* (of Jesus), it was reputed (page 56) to have been received directly from heaven by St Patrick, and it came to be closely associated with his most important foundation at Armagh. It turns up in a great variety of contexts in medieval Ireland before it was ignominiously burned by Reformation iconoclasts in Dublin in 1538.

Whatever the true origin of the Bachall Íosa, undoubtedly many non-Irish relics were preserved in early historic Ireland. Other than the relics of the early martyrs Peter, Paul, Stephen and Lawrence, which on dubious authority were said to have been brought from Rome in the 5th century, the earliest reliable information we have of imported relics are those brought by St Colman to his new foundation on

159

Fig. 64 *The 'Crozier of the Abbots of Clonmacnois' of c1100, now in the National Museum in Dublin, was found in the tomb-shrine of St Ciarán at Clonmacnois some time in the 18th century*

the island of Inishbofin off the west coast of Ireland four years after he had lost the argument at the Synod of Whitby in 664. The *Annals of Clonmacnoise* tell us that one of the relics stolen from the altar at Clonmacnois in 1129 was a model of Solomon's temple which, when compared to other Irish reliquaries that have survived, seems very non-Irish, and may have contained some relic imported from elsewhere.

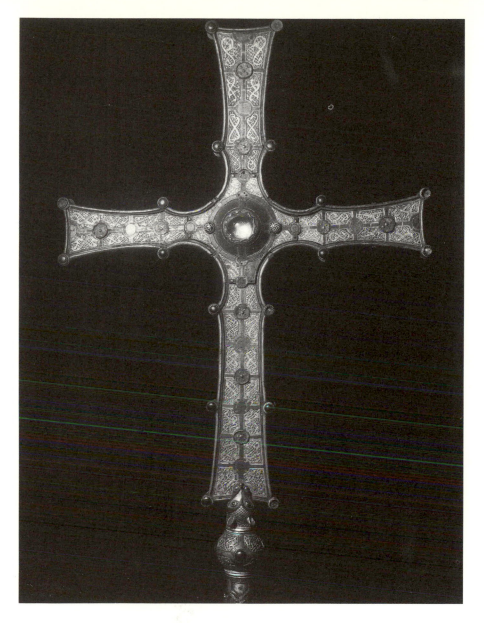

Fig. 65 *The Cross of Cong, now in the National Museum in Dublin, was created c1120 to enshrine a fragment of the True Cross*

Perhaps the most extraordinary collection of relics known from the early Christian centuries in these islands was that assembled by Adomnan. According to a 12th-century account, Adomnan treasured on Iona a relic of the Virgin's hair and a piece of her clothing, the girdle of St Paul and a piece of the tree upon which he was martyred, and possibly even a relic of the True Cross, though this last is by no means certain. The first relic of the True Cross in Ireland of which we have evidence is the piece that was enshrined in the magnificent Cross of Cong (Fig. 65) commissioned by Turlough O Conor, king of Connacht, in around the early 1120s. The Cistercian abbey of Holycross in County Tipperary gets its name from another fragment, which may have been presented to it in 1169. Further fragments are encountered in later medieval Ireland enshrined in reliquaries in the shape of a double-armed cross; this shape, though best known from the Cross of Lorraine, was a form used in Continental Europe for enshrining fragments of the True Cross. It recurs in very much magnified form in the west gable of the church at Killinaboy, County Clare (Fig. 57), near which is the stump of a round tower. Though the cross was probably re-assembled in its present form in around the 16th century, the capitals that decorate its extremities suggest a date around the first half of the 13th century, at which period a relic of the True Cross may have been displayed in the interior of the church. It might seem surprising that such a comparatively insignificant-seeming church as this should contain a relic of the True Cross, but it ought not to be forgotten that the Fourth Crusade brought many relics back to Europe, including fragments of the True Cross, from the disgraceful sacking of Constantinople in 1204.

Much more important than the associative relics of Irish saints were the relics of the saints' bodies themselves, which helped their possessors to greater power and material wealth, to such an extent that we find many references to the exhumation of saints' bones. One possibly fabricated reference was the case of St Colman mac Lúacháin who, when he lay on his deathbed, was begged by the monks of his community to allow his remains to be disinterred after his death so that 'they might be kept amongst them in an adorned shrine like every other great saint and chief apostle throughout Ireland'.

A saint's corporeal relics took various forms. One that could even be obtained during the saint's lifetime was his teeth; allegedly St Patrick's were bestowed on various churches as they fell out one by one! One of them was placed in a shrine made for the church at Killaspugbrone in County Sligo, and now preserved in the National Museum of Ireland in Dublin. The Ulster Museum in Belfast preserves a shrine of St Patrick's hand, and the Dublin Museum houses a fine shrine of St Lachtin's arm. That teeth were not the only part of a saint's body sought after during his lifetime is demonstrated by the strange story of the poet Onchu, a Connacht man who, like Adomnan, obviously took a delight in collecting relics. On a visit to Clonmore in County Carlow he asked the local saint Maedoc for a relic to add to his collection. Though the saint protested, saying that the request was too difficult, a portion of his finger fell to the ground and was avidly picked up by Onchu. But St Maedoc's obvious anguish led him to prophesy that Onchu's collection would remain at Clonmore, where he would be buried with it – and so things came to pass. Onchu's burial place beside an Ogham stone and the shaft of a high cross is still pointed out to this day.

The story of Onchu's relics was obviously designed to lend an importance to this now much-neglected site. Relics were of such importance to the economic vitality of a monastic establishment because of the pilgrims who would come to visit them that disputes broke out between rival monasteries for their possession. One recorded instance is that of St Abban, a south Leinster saint. His (8th/9th century?) *Life* tells of a struggle between the monks of Killabban, his Kildare birthplace, and those of his foundation at Maganey, for possession of his body. The former claimed it because they were his first followers, while the latter based their claim to it on the fact that the saint had lived and died amongst them. Divine Providence settled the matter satisfactorily by bestowing an identical body of the saint on each of the communities!

The value placed on possession of a saint's corporeal relics is reflected in the reliquaries created to house them. We often regard these shrines as fine museum objects displaying the intricacies of the early metalworker's craft, without realising sufficiently the awe in which these reliquaries must have been held in the years and centuries after their creation. In most cases, they have been preserved for us through the institution of hereditary family keepers of reliquaries, who kept them intact down to the 19th century, when they found their way into museums and private collections. Paradoxically, it was the monk-bashing and church-destroying Vikings to whom we should be thankful for the preservation of others. The case of the relics of St Comgall, which, according to the *Annals of Ulster*, were shaken out of their shrine by the Vikings when they raided Bangor in 824, is doubtless only one of many where the Vikings took monastic reliquaries as booty and brought them back to their homeland, where they served as jewel-caskets for the wives of successful raiders and were subsequently placed in their graves. Someone named Ranvaig carved the owner's name in runes on one of these caskets, which was probably found in Norway and is now in the Danish National Museum in Copenhagen. Other examples are preserved in Trondheim, near their finding places at Setnes and

Fig. 66 *The smaller shrine was contained within the larger one from Lough Erne in County Fermanagh*

Fig. 67 *The Emly Shrine, an Irish house-shaped shrine*
with silver grille of crosses of arcs, dating from 800, and
now in the Museum of Fine Arts in Boston

Melhus. The National Museum in Dublin houses other examples that escaped the Vikings' clutches, such as the Lough Erne shrine (Fig. 66), which contains one within another; a similar shrine, decorated with crosses of arcs on one face, is preserved in the Museum of Fine Arts in Boston (Fig. 67).

Sadly, we do not know which saint's relics were preserved in any of these shrines, as the tradition of their identity has not been preserved down to our own day, but we can be fairly sure that they were venerated Irish saints. But we ought to be less sure that this was the case with two reliquaries of Irish or perhaps Scottish origin, which recently came to light in Italy – one in the Abbadia San Salvatore in Tuscany and the other in the Museo Civico in Bologna, where it had long been regarded as Etruscan. Like many of the shrines mentioned above, these may be ascribed to the 8th or 9th century; they may well have been made in Ireland or Scotland, but carried empty to Italy in order to bring back relics from Rome, since this was just the period when Roman relics were finding their way across the Alps by the cart-load to be sold to monastic foundations in the heartland of the Carolingian empire.

Seeing a number of these reliquaries together, along with others such as the famous Monymusk reliquary now in the National Museums of Scotland in

Edinburgh, makes one realise just how small they were. The Emly shrine now in Boston is only 4 inches (10.5 centimetres) long and even less in height; the largest of them, the bigger of the two Lough Erne shrines, is only just over 7 inches (18.2 centimetres) long and a little over 6 inches (16 centimetres) high. So we can presume that they housed only very small relics. One feature that unites them all is that they are in the form of houses, which give them their generic title, house-shaped shrines.

The 8th- or 9th-century date suggested for these house-shaped shrines on art-historical grounds finds echoes in the historical sources, for we hear in the *Annals of Ulster* of 'the placing of the relics of Conlaed in a shrine of gold and silver' in the year 800, and of 'the placing of the relics of Ronán son of Berach [of Dromiskin, County Louth] in a gold and silver casket' in 801. Cogitosus's 7th-century *Life of St Brigid*, referred to above, tells us that the bodies of two Kildare saints, Bishop Conlaed and Brigid herself, lay enshrined on either side of the altar in the double church at Kildare; they must have lain in highly decorated metal sarcophagi similar in size to the stone sarcophagus at Clones (see page 155). If the two Conlaeds were one and the same person, then it could be argued that the enshrining of his relics in 800 implies that his bones must have been dismembered at that time in order to ensure a wider distribution of his relics in neighbouring churches, and that the shrines used were presumably smaller, and probably corresponding in size to that of the house-shaped shrines. As early as 553, the lost Book of Cuanu reported that relics of St Patrick – his goblet, the Angel's Gospel and his bell – were disinterred and enshrined, but this did not involve the saint's bones. Hagiographical literature mentions other instances of the enshrining of corporeal relics of Irish saints, but these sources are notoriously difficult to date. However, the annals do refer to the enshrining of various relics in the 12th century, and it is to this period that the gable-shaped reliquary of St Manchán (Fig. 56), now preserved in the Catholic church at Boher, County Offaly, belongs.

Some of the stone high crosses hitherto dated to the 10th century, but now ascribed by some to the 9th, have on top a feature which looks like a house. Perhaps the best example is that on the top of Muiredach's Cross at Monasterboice in County Louth (Fig. 68). It has an imitation of wooden shingles on its roof, and round mouldings at the corners may imitate the corner-posts of a shrine, a house or a church. The significance of these house-shaped capstones of high crosses has proved problematical. But in trying to ascertain their purpose, it is well to remember that many of the high crosses show signs of having been imitated from crosses in other materials and probably smaller in size. Furthermore, the top of Muiredach's Cross is formed of a separate stone, as also is the top of the cross at Tihilly in County Offaly, whose capstone is preserved in University College, Dublin. A further lost example is recorded from County Kildare, and on one or two crosses such as those at

Duleek and Cloonfad, the tenon at the top of the cross suggests the former presence of a house-shaped capstone. One might advance the hypothesis that on those crosses on which the stone high crosses were modelled, the house-shaped top could conceivably have been a house-shaped reliquary containing a relic of the founding saint, which could have been detached from the cross and shown to the public, or even brought on tour, as the occasion demanded. This feature would then have been copied on the stone cross where it would have made very little sense, though preserving for us the shapes of house-shaped shrines in wood and metal that have long since vanished. The shrines would probably have attracted pilgrims to the site, and the high crosses would have had the function of teaching them the Gospels and Church dogma through the biblical panels on the crosses.

The bottom, rather than on the top, of one high cross may show a house-shaped shrine carved in stone. This is on the west face of the so-called Doorty Cross at Kilfenora, County Clare, where the shingle-topped roof of the shrine is surmounted by a horseman. If he were to be understood as a pilgrim coming on horseback to the shrine, this would raise the question of whether the horsemen, and even the chariot processions, seen on a number of 9th- or 10th-century crosses, ought to be interpreted in a similar fashion? Fergus O'Farrell has made the interesting suggestion that the West Cross at Kilfenora may have had a saint's tomb-shrine abutting on to the bottom of its shaft, but if his suggestion be correct, the cross may have been moved subsequently to its present site from somewhere in or around the site of the present cathedral where the local saint, Fachnan, is likely to have been buried, as the West Cross now stands well outside the bounds of the present churchyard.

These two Kilfenora crosses are no earlier than the 12th century, and it can be shown that many of the 12th-century crosses are located on known sites of early pilgrimage, such as Glendalough, Tuam, Cong, the Aran Islands, Monaincha and Cashel. The staff- or crozier-bearing figures standing out in high relief on many of these 12th-century crosses may represent the local saints whose relics the pilgrims came to venerate, thus creating a further link between pilgrimage and 12th-century high crosses, a link which is more difficult to forge for crosses of earlier centuries.

When the wooden and bronze shrines were brought on tour, it would have been necessary to prevent them from suffering damage in the course of transport. One method of avoiding damage would have been to carry them in a leather satchel. One such satchel probably used to carry a shrine or book was excavated in a 10th-century layer in the Viking settlement at Fishamble Street in Dublin. It bears a cross with forked terminals of a kind that may well indicate the former presence within the satchel of some important relic – perhaps discarded by the Vikings when they took the leather container as booty from some unidentified Irish monastery.

Fig. 68 *The shingle-roofed capstone of Muiredach's Cross at Monasterboice, County Louth* (OPPOSITE), *may imitate a house-shaped shrine*

CHAPTER 13

ROUND TOWERS

THE MOST PROMINENT BUILDING ON MANY EARLY IRISH MONASTIC SITES IS undoubtedly the round tower, and George Petrie's essay on these towers, published in 1845, placed beyond all doubt their Christian context. It is not surprising that before his day, yet astonishing that after the publication of his work, the towers were associated with a bizarre variety of cultures and peoples – Druids and Danes, Phoenicians and Buddhists – and given a multiplicity of uses from fire temples to astronomical observatories, baptisteries and phallic symbols, as anchorites' perches for the Irish versions of St Simeon Stylites, in addition to more reasonable interpretations such as watch-towers or beacons. Petrie was the first to comb through the references to these towers in the early historic literature, and he came to the conclusion that, as their Old Irish name *cloigtheach* (literally 'bell house') implies, they served primarily as bell towers, but could also be used to store monastic treasures and to protect humans in times of danger. The danger was frequently conceived of as being the nasty Viking raiders, until Dr A. T. Lucas pointed out in 1967 that raids on Irish monasteries were carried out just as much by the nasty Irish as by the Vikings. Such was the thoroughness of the Petrie thesis that it was well over another century before any further comprehensive book on the subject saw the light of day. This was the late G. L. Barrow's *The Round Towers of Ireland* (Dublin, 1979) which provided us with the first detailed survey of the towers, though the book has been rightly criticised for its dating of the towers to around the 7th century. Since Petrie's time, both Margaret Stokes and Ann Hamlin have given us useful lists of the annalistic references to the

Fig. 69 *The stocky Round Tower at Timahoe, County Laois* (OPPOSITE), *has a Romanesque doorway well above ground level which dates it to the 12th century*

Irish round towers, which show that historically the towers are vouched for from 950 until 1238, but not before. A number of towers, such as Timahoe (Fig. 69), have Romanesque decoration, suggesting that at least some of them were built in the latter part of that date range.

The question has further arisen of the likely origin of these towers. Were they an almost entirely Irish invention, because outside Ireland there are only three such towers – two in Scotland and one in the Isle of Man? Or could they be derived from slightly earlier towers of the Carolingian period on the Continent, as represented by the towers at the western end of churches such as those in the plan of St Gall in Switzerland of around 820, or the roughly contemporary church of St Riquier/ Centula in northern France, or those carved on Carolingian ivories which can be seen at St Gall, in the Louvre in Paris and in Cleveland, Ohio. The word *cloigtheach* brings to mind the similarly derived *campanile* of Italy, best exemplified by the Leaning Tower of Pisa. But long-vanished Italian *campanile* of a much earlier date than Pisa may well have played a role in the development of the Irish round tower for, as Cormac Bourke pointed out to me, the term 'bell-house' may well have been introduced from abroad along with the tower it describes. One Italian tower of earlier date which does not survive was illustrated in frescoes or mosaics usually ascribed to Pope John VII (707-7), though Tronzo has recently suggested that they may be many centuries later.

We are fortunate that the papal archivist, Grimaldi, recorded many of these frescoes (and sometimes mosaics) before Old St Peter's was finally demolished in the early 17th century; his drawing of a Roman tower is preserved for us on fol. 89 recto of the manuscript *Barberini lat. 2733* in the Vatican Library in Rome (Fig. 70). In the lowermost register of Grimaldi's drawing we see a tall free-standing tower from which Simon Magus is seen to jump headlong in the presence of the named Emperor Nero and Saints Peter and Paul to the left, while on the right is a representation of the martyrdom of St Peter. In the middle register two other towers are shown illustrating the story of Saints Peter and Paul in dispute with Nero, which had led to the fall of Simon Magus on the bottom register. Here, however, the two towers are close to one another and could well represent towers in the city wall. More significant for us are the two towers in the top register, of which the free-standing example in the centre apparently belongs to Jerusalem (named 'Civitas Hierosolyma' beneath), while that on the right (possibly also part of a town wall?) is ascribed to the city of Antioch; St Peter is illustrated in conjunction with both of them. It is significant that these three great cities, Rome, Jerusalem and Antioch (whither the body of Simeon Stylites was removed after his death) are among the three greatest centres of pilgrimage in the early centuries of Christianity. From Grimaldi's drawing of the frescoes of Pope John VII (705-707) – or later – in Old St Peter's, we get a hint that round towers may have been present in major centres of Christian pilgrimage.

Although the two and a half centuries which may separate the Roman fresco from the first historically recorded round tower in Ireland are not otherwise filled out with surviving examples, the Carolingian towers referred to above may possibly have acted as a link. But could not some Irish pilgrims to Rome have seen a tower like that shown in the centre of the bottom register of Grimaldi's drawing of around 1634 and brought the idea back to Ireland to recreate a slightly altered version in their homeland? It is scarcely mere coincidence that the first recorded

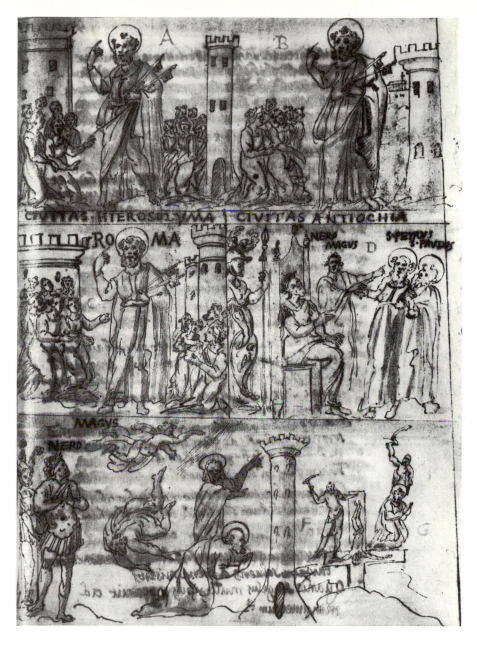

Fig. 70 *Round Towers at Jerusalem, Antioch and Rome were illustrated in a fresco or mosaic of Pope John VII (705-707) or later, in Old St Peter's Basilica in Rome, and recorded by Grimaldi around 1620*

Irish round tower, the vanished example at Slane burned by the Vikings around 950, comes at a time when there seems to have been a revival of pilgrimage activity in the country after the shockwaves of Viking invasions had receded (see pages 52-3). Lack of historical references to round towers much before 950 could imply their introduction to Ireland no earlier than the 10th century. Their absence before that may reflect lack of experience in stone-building on the part of Irish craftsmen who appear at that time to have been erecting less sophisticated structures such as the tomb-shrines discussed in an earlier chapter.

In one or two instances Irish round towers reach a height of 100 feet (30 metres); and their graceful form is usually topped by a conical roof which, in cases like that at Glendalough, is known to have been reconstructed in the last century. This roof type differs from the crenellated tops of the towers in Rome, Jerusalem and Antioch in Grimaldi's drawing, and has led Etienne Rynne to call for a closer look at the crenellated tops of a few Irish towers (such as those at Kildare and Castledermot) that are generally ascribed to the later medieval period.

One other feature in which the Irish towers differ radically from those in the Grimaldi drawing is the placing of the doorway: these are uniformly on the ground in the Roman picture, whereas in Ireland they are usually placed anything up to 12 feet (4 metres) above ground, except for the tower at Scattery Island in the Shannon estuary where the door is at ground level. It was the raised position of the doorway that led Petrie, and most authorities after him, to see refuge as one of the subsidiary uses for the Irish round towers. It was suggested that a ladder giving access to the doorway must have been capable of being hauled up after the refugees had retreated into the tower, in order to prevent attackers following them. But the numerous annalistic references to the burning of towers shows us that the towers must have been a most unsafe refuge. A burning arrow fired through the upper-floor windows could all too easily have caused the wooden floors and the ladders connecting them to be set alight, thus quickly turning the interiors into blazing infernos, fuelled by draughts through the openings.

In considering another, alternative reason for the raised position of the doorway, and thereby reducing the strength of the argument that sees the towers as having a secondary purpose as citadels, we must look at some annalistic references to the contents of the towers. The first of these is in the *Chronicum Scotorum* under the year 949, where we are told that the tower in Slane was burned with crozier and bell, along with a lector of the community. The same annals record under the year 1020 the burning of the tower in Armagh 'with its bells', and under 1097 the Monasterboice tower burned with books and treasures. Ann Hamlin has noted that the *Annals of the Four Masters* record that, in 1552, the English of Athlone removed the large bells from the round tower at Clonmacnois; she has also speculated on whether one of the lector's jobs was to retire into the round tower with the monastery's books and treasures whenever danger threatened.

But were these books and treasures only removed to the tower in times of danger? Or could it have been that the tower was their semi-permanent home? The specific objects listed by the annals as having been burned in towers comprise bells, croziers and books, but these were also some of the most important 'relics' of the monastery. We may speculate that

Fig. 71 *W.F. Wakeman's 1892 drawing showing the
Cathedral and vanished Round Tower at Downpatrick,
County Down, as they were about two centuries ago*

the towers may have been the treasury of the monastery's relics, and that the relics were not only preserved there, but may also have been displayed within for the public gaze.

Following up this line of thought, we may consider the possibility that the reason for placing the doors of towers well above the ground may have been to allow the relics to be viewed and venerated, but at a height sufficient to keep them beyond the reach of the pilgrims who had come to venerate them. This would be analogous to the use of the slit in the east gable of the Priest's House at Glendalough. The ladder up to the doorway of a round tower would have allowed monastic personnel to reach the relics and to bring them down to ground level for display on special occasions or to be used for ceremonial or other purposes, and would also have facilitated the opening and closing of the door, which may have been a daily occurrence. The books in the tower are unlikely to have been part of the monastery's reference library, which would have been out of place in an ill-lit tower; instead, we would expect them to have been in the main manuscripts old enough to have been respected as relics, like the Book of Kells. The fact that bells, rather than one bell only, are specifically mentioned as having been in the towers, would suggest that they were not necessarily all regarded as relics of the saints, but may have been rung in the tower, as the name *cloigtheach* would imply.

If the bell-bearing figure beside St Kevin on the lintel of the Priest's House at Glendalough (Fig. 46) is correctly interpreted above (page 120) as a pilgrim, then some of the bells in the towers could even have been pilgrims' bells donated to the monastery on completion of a pilgrimage.

If we look at the location of the towers, we can see that some are found on sites specifically mentioned in early historic sources as places of pilgrimage, or where pilgrims died, or which were visited by Heneas MacNichaill on his penitential pilgrimage in around 1543. Going from north to south, these include Downpatrick (Fig. 71), Clonmacnois, Killeany on the Aran Islands, Glendalough, Roscrea, Inishcealtra and Cashel. The Mayo group of Aghagower, Turlough, Meelick and Balla are probably related to the Croagh Patrick pilgrimage. Others are located at sites where relics of saints are known to have been preserved, such as Kells and Dysert O'Dea, and it was suggested above that Killinaboy may even have housed a relic of the True Cross. There are, of course, other sites that fit into none of these categories, but it may be only by the accident of history that we do not have references to pilgrims dying at these sites or to relics being preserved there. Other pilgrimage sites have no record of the former presence of a round tower, but of these, Croagh Patrick and Mount Brandon would have had no need, as they dominate the surrounding countryside, and may not have preserved valuable relics on their respective summits.

Croagh Patrick and Mount Brandon were visible from afar, but monasteries may have built round towers, among other reasons, to act as indicators to pilgrims of the location of the monastery; they would not have needed to be as tall as they are if they were simply repositories for monastic treasures, or were used for ringing bells. The first indication the modern visitor is given that he is approaching a site like Glendalough or Clonmacnois is the sight of the top of a round tower above the trees or a ridge of hills. The tower at Killeany, now a stump, may once have been tall enough to have reached above the level of the horizon, thus enabling a pilgrim setting out for Aran to point his boat in its direction, and the same is true to a lesser extent for the other island locations such as Devenish or Inishcealtra. Round towers may therefore have beckoned to the pilgrim from afar, and encouraged his flagging spirits in the last few miles before he reached his destination. The round tower at Clonmacnois is almost, though not exactly, in a direct line with the Pilgrim's Way as it approaches the tomb of St Ciarán.

CHAPTER 14

ROMANESQUE AND OTHER CHURCHES

N O MATTER WHETHER HE CAME FROM IRELAND, ENGLAND, THE LOW Countries, Germany or France, the medieval pilgrim to Santiago de Compostela encountered not only numerous hostels on his route, but also a considerable number of churches. As mentioned earlier, the great Burgundian monastery of Cluny was the prime mover in promoting the Santiago pilgrimage, and as Cluny was also influential in the dissemination of the Romanesque style of building, it is not surprising that many of the smaller churches built along the Pilgrims' Route were also built in the same style. The rounded arch as used by the ancient Romans gave this type of architecture its name, and most openings – doorways, windows and the divisions between nave and aisle or between nave and chancel, in addition to the cloister arcade – were spanned by a round arch. Usually these arches were richly decorated, often with figures and animals, which must originally have had a symbolic meaning now lost to us. St Bernard of Clairvaux found these carvings so distracting in saying prayers that he railed against them and ensured that his Cistercian churches were severely simple.

In the Romanesque churches, the carvings present a world full of wonderment and imagination, and the churches have a human scale which makes the visitor feel at home with the Deity, in contrast to the later Gothic churches, whose graceful lines and characteristically pointed arches strive heavenwards. The Romanesque style apparently developed in France during the 11th century, but came to its full flowering in the 12th, when it spread to many parts of Christianised Europe. Ireland was no exception, and the Romanesque churches of the 12th century are among the most charming to be found in the Irish countryside (e.g. Fig. 50). Romanesque brought out the best in the Irish mason's ingenuity and artistry, and 12th-century decoration is generally of a high standard. The love of beasts and fabulous monsters expressed on the Continental Romanesque churches obviously touched a receptive chord in Ireland where Germanic animal art had been warmly welcomed by Irish artists as early as the 7th century. The Vikings, after they had become less

175

Fig. 72 *The Gothic Cathedral in Killaloe preserves the finely-decorated doorway of its Romanesque predecessor*

aggressive and had integrated with the native Irish, contributed a new variant to Irish animal ornament, and this becomes a very dominant feature in Irish metalwork of the 11th and 12th centuries as represented, for instance, by the Cross of Cong and the shrine of St Manchán (Fig. 56). Variations of these Viking animals were also used by stonemasons, who built them into their designs on church doorways, such as that at Clonfert (Fig. 1) or on the Nuns' Church at Clonmacnois.

Just how many Romanesque churches were built in Ireland in the 12th century is difficult to estimate, as a number no longer stand and are only represented by the almost chance survival of small decorated fragments. The Romanesque style continued in Ireland (most noticeably in the West), after Gothic had already become firmly established in the Norman-occupied parts farther east. Only when the Normans added the western province of Connacht to their conquests in 1235 did Romanesque church-building in Ireland come to an end.

It is all too easy to think of church-building in 12th-century Ireland purely in terms of those churches built in the Romanesque style. But this century also saw the introduction of the Gothic style, encouraged by the arrival of the Normans as well as the new Continental monastic orders, in particular, the Cistercians. Moreover, a quarter of the century had probably passed before the Romanesque style was introduced, and a number of Irish churches may well belong to the 12th century, even though they show no trace of Romanesque decoration. Such may be the case with those on the Aran Islands, for instance. Trinity and Reefert churches at Glendalough, characterised by a contemporary nave and chancel, and undecorated granite arches, could also belong to the 12th century, though they could equally be a century earlier.

The 12th was certainly one of the most active centuries for church-building in Ireland, but it was also – as in the rest of Europe – one of the busiest for pilgrimage activity. We have seen in chapter 6 how the annalistic entries recording the deaths of pilgrims in the 12th century add a number of new locations to those known from earlier centuries, the first references to them being as follows: Aghaboe, Laois – 1100; Derry – 1122; Lismore, Waterford – 1123; Monaincha, Tipperary – 1138; Killaloe, Clare – 1142; Cong, Mayo – 1150; Tuam, Galway – 1170; Mellifont, Louth – 1186 and Inchcleraun, Longford - 1193. From this list, we can see that the 1120s seem to bring a new wave, and it is notable that all the places mentioned in the last three-quarters of the century, that is, from 1125 onwards, have Romanesque churches. This prompts me to correlate pilgrimage activity with the building of Romanesque churches. It has already been noted that Liam de Paor has made a convincing case for seeing Cormac's Chapel on the Rock of Cashel as the first of all the Irish Romanesque churches, and it is almost certain that it can be equated with the church that the annals record as having been built between 1127 and 1134. It is a structure with many unique features, such as the towers where one might expect transepts, and the multi-storeyed blind arcading on the exterior wall of the nave. It may also have been among the first of the Irish churches to have been built with a stone roof and without the customary west doorway. Both Liam de Paor and Roger Stalley have argued persuasively for seeing English, and particularly West Country, influence in Cormac's Chapel. It was so original that its features were little copied in Ireland, with the apparent exception of Kilmalkedar.

More typical of the Irish Romanesque churches are the smaller examples with the decorated west doorway (e.g. Fig. 72) and chancel arch. In one of these, Dysert O'Dea in County Clare, George Zarnecki and Françoise Henry saw strong influence from the Saintonge area of western France; the impetus for its decoration may have been when a pilgrim from County Clare saw the small intimate churches of the Pilgrim Road to Compostela and decided that a church with comparable detail should be built at his local place of pilgrimage, where the crozier of its founder, St Tola (now in the National Museum in Dublin) was originally venerated.

The doorway in the south wall of the church at Dysert O'Dea (detail, Fig. 73) is a hotch-potch of stones reassembled in their present location probably some time in the 17th century. Some of the stones, including the curious collection of human heads, probably came from the west doorway of the original church, but it is likely that not all the stones belong to one and the same doorway. Whoever was responsible for reassembling the doorway could have collected other Romanesque fragments from another church of similar style in the locality to provide enough stones for a full doorway. As it happens, there was another Romanesque church at Rath Blathmaic only two miles away, where the crozier of the local founder, St Blathmac (also preserved now in the National Museum in Dublin) was held in high esteem. In Ireland it is unusual to have Romanesque churches on two separate sites in such close proximity to one another, as most are well spread out in the countryside, each representing a main centre of local pilgrimage for a larger area. One feature common to these two Clare sites is a round tower, though that at Rath Blathmaic is only represented by a few recently discovered fragments. The unifying factor may have been pilgrimage: and we have seen in the previous chapter how round towers and pilgrimage sites frequently go hand in hand. Only half a dozen miles from Dysert O'Dea is a third round tower, that at Killinaboy, located close to the church with the double-armed cross on the gable (Fig. 57), perhaps indicating the former presence there of a relic of the True Cross, to which pilgrims would almost certainly have flocked. (The church at Killinaboy still preserves in the interior of its south doorway one stone which is carved in what looks like the late Romanesque style of the early 13th century.)

The correlation of Romanesque church and round tower shown in these three sites in Clare cannot consistently be sustained throughout the rest of the country. Slightly fewer than half the places where round towers stand or are known to have formerly stood have Romanesque churches or fragments, a cross, lintel or a sarcophagus of the 12th century. There are, however, many sites with a round tower but with no trace of a Romanesque church, and others with a Romanesque church or its surviving fragments but no round tower. This disparity may be partially explained by a number of the towers having been built before the arrival of the Romanesque style, but also perhaps by the existence of churches contemporary with those built in the Romanesque style but having none of their characteristic decoration. We need not expect, in any case, that churches and round towers would necessarily have been built at the same time. But there is a sufficiently high number of instances of round tower and Romanesque church on the same site – and the two are neatly integrated in St Finghin's Church at Clonmacnois – to permit the hypothesis that both may at the time have been linked in people's minds with pilgrimage activity. Some of the main pilgrimage sites – Clonmacnois, Glendalough, Inishcealtra and Monaincha, for instance – are sufficiently rich in Romanesque remains to add credence to the hypothesis.

Further support can be supplied by the veneration accorded to one particular saint who is associated with a number of sites. This is our old friend St Brendan the Navigator, who was born near Ardfert in County Kerry. There, the lower part of the west wall of the 13th-century cathedral preserves part of a fine Romanesque church (Fig. 11) which preceded it, and which, like the Romanesque church of St Canice in Kilkenny, probably stood for less than a century before being replaced by the larger Gothic edifice. Near it stood a round tower, until it fell in 1771. In

Fig. 73 *The jumble of human and animal heads on the south doorway at Dysert O'Dea, County Clare, shows that it was reassembled from two different portals of 12th-century date*

addition, Ardfert has another church nearby built in the Romanesque style of the 12th century. St Brendan is known to have died at Annaghdown in County Galway, where he had established a convent of nuns under his sister Briga. The site no longer has a Romanesque church, but it still preserves some very fine Romanesque fragments including parts of a pilaster, and capitals of a chancel arch, as well as a window carved by a mason who probably also worked at Rath Blathmaic. St Brendan's grave at the monastery he himself had founded at Clonfert near the banks of the Shannon is probably marked by the cathedral (Fig. 1) whose Romanesque doorway of around 1200 represents the apogee of the style in Ireland. The exuberance of its detail and the fascinating collection of human heads in the apex of its pointed hood make it one of the greatest feats of Romanesque decoration anywhere in the country. The strength of Romanesque presence at these three sites – Ardfert, Annaghdown and Clonfert – prompts the idea of the former existence of a network of 12th-century churches which, even if unrelated to one another in terms of their architectural decoration, may well have been the high points in a network of 12th-century pilgrimage in honour of the saint who must have been one of the principal patrons of the maritime pilgrimage along the west coast of Ireland.

Churches on an early monastic site were frequently named after the saint who originally founded the monastery. But where a number of churches survive on the same site, we occasionally find churches dedicated to other saints whose foundations were also sites of Irish pilgrimage. The Romanesque church with inbuilt round tower at Clonmacnois was dedicated to St Finghin or Finian, probably to be identified as the teacher of St Ciarán, and at whose foundation of Clonard in County Meath four pilgrims are recorded as having died during the 11th and 12th centuries. St Ciarán himself is the dedicatee of a church close to St Kevin's Church at Glendalough, and of another on the Aran island of Inishmore, where there is also a well dedicated to him. On the same island the small oratory, known as Teampull Benén, is dedicated to the same Benén after whom the station on Croagh Patrick is named, and whose presumed burial place at Kilbennan in County Galway, which has a round tower, may have acted as a stopping-off place on that pilgrimage. On the smaller Aran island of Inisheer, there is a church dedicated to St Gobnait of Ballyvourney, and another to a saint who may or may not (see page 91) be identical with St Kevin of Glendalough. The St Kevin to whom a medieval church is dedicated at Glencolmcille is almost certainly the saint of Glendalough. Churches dedicated to the Virgin and to internationally known saints (with the possible exception of John the Baptist) are probably no earlier than the 12th century, whereas those churches at old monastic sites dedicated to Irish saints are likely to be earlier. We can surmise that those sites with churches dedicated to a number of Irish saints formed part of a pilgrimage network, founded before the 12th century, that encompassed the burial places of all these saints. The same network idea may be applicable to the 'beds' in St Patrick's Purgatory in Lough Derg dedicated to such saints as Colmcille, Molaise (of Devenish or Inishmurray?) and Brendan; it is interesting to note also that a well was dedicated to St Brendan on the Tóchar Phádraig, the pilgrimage road to Croagh Patrick. A similar pattern of wells dedicated to Irish saints on the Dingle Peninsula (see page 86) may also fit in with the notion of a pilgrimage network.

The epithet 'of the Seven Churches' has been applied frequently to some well-known pilgrimage sites such as Clonmacnois, Glendalough and Inishcealtra. The number is not necessarily always correct – the first two of those places have eight churches surviving – but the nomenclature, of uncertain age, is probably a reflection of pilgrimage activity on the site, as the pilgrim to Rome normally visited seven churches during his visit to the Holy City.

Chapter 15

Beehive Huts and 'Chancellor's Houses'

'**B**EEHIVE HUT' IS THE NAME COMMONLY GIVEN TO THE STONE HUTS FOUND SO frequently in the Dingle Peninsula in County Kerry, where the locals call this kind of hut *clochán* or, in the plural, *clocháin*. The word *cloch* in Irish means a stone, and these huts are built of stone and nothing else, for the builders used no mortar in their construction. They are built on the corbel principle, which was already a fine art at Newgrange in the Stone Age. The technique was to lay down circles of flat stones one above the other in ever-decreasing size until the circle could be closed by a single stone at the top. The method was widely used in other European countries. In Italy, for instance, there are the well-known *trulli* of Alberobello in the heel of Italy, which are still used as permanent homes. Whether found in Apulia, Sardinia, southern France or in Dalmatia, the majority of these huts are usually intended for temporary habitation by shepherds as they move their flocks from one pasturage to another in a process known as transhumance. Because the method of corbel construction used in these huts is not only simple but also ageless, it is almost impossible to date these structures. But examples have been excavated in Ireland at various Kerry sites including Leacanabuaile, Reask, Loher and Dunbeg, and the last-named site provided a rough date of around the 9th or 10th century; and the other examples are likely to date from some time in the second half of the first millennium – it is impossible to be more precise.

In Ireland, the best-known examples of beehive huts are on the island of Skellig Michael (Fig. 30), off the coast of the Iveragh peninsula. Here, though the outside of the *clochán* is round, the interior is square. The largest hut has a series of stones projecting from the outside wall; the same feature recurs on a *clochán* built around the turn of the century on the Dingle Peninsula. I well remember the late Myles Dillon telling me how, when he went back one year on his annual visit to the peninsula, he remarked to his host that he did not remember having seen a particular *clochán* in the backyard the previous year. The reason for this, explained the host, was that he had built it as a henhouse during the winter. So we may take it

that the simple *clochán* has a history going back at least a thousand years in Ireland and probably many more. Brendan O'Flaherty found in his excavations at Loher, County Kerry, that underneath one of the *clocháin* there had lain a wooden structure of dried stakes – in other words, a *clochán* had been preceded by a round wooden structure.

By far the greatest concentration of these *clocháin* in Ireland is on the Dingle Peninsula, and almost all are found west of Mount Brandon. There are many more than are shown on the map (Fig. 21) which only marks those described specifically as *clocháin* in the *Archaeological Survey of the Dingle Peninsula* of 1986. As I have argued above (see page 76), the fact that these huts are found in such great numbers to the west of Brandon, yet are very much rarer in other parts of Kerry and elsewhere throughout the country, strongly suggests that these *clocháin* were the temporary habitations of pilgrims waiting for sufficiently clement weather to climb Mount Brandon. In a similar vein, one can explain those in the Glenfahan area, between Ventry and Slea Head, as temporary shelters for those awaiting the right wind to waft them to the Skelligs. If this explanation is correct, then the *clocháin* could truly be described as Ireland's first and oldest surviving bed and breakfast establishments.

Their curious density and distribution pattern is, in my view, consistent with their use as temporary habitations for those participating in the maritime pilgrimage which has to be 'reconstructed' along the west coast of Ireland in Early Christian times. In chapter 5 it was suggested that this seaborne pilgrimage was probably connected with the cult of St Brendan, among others, and its spread along the 'Atlantic face' of Europe. It is highly significant, therefore, that we find other beehive huts on islands (Fig. 74) off the west coast of Ireland, not only on the Aran Islands, which St Brendan is said to have visited, but also on Inishark, as well as on Inishglora off the northwest Mayo coast, where St Brendan was patron of the settlement. In Kilkenny, there is a stone church at Clonamery with a fine equal-armed cross over the doorway. In the field to the west of the church there are what two authorities accepted as being perhaps the only pair of *clocháin* from the interior of the country. The patron saint is given as Broondawn, and although the much-respected local historian Canon Carrigan would disagree, there is a considerable possibility that he is none other than our navigating saint from·Kerry. If so, it is surely more than mere coincidence that his church is accompanied not only by a holy well dedicated to St Brendan, where a pattern was held on St Brendan's Day, but also by two rare inland *clocháin*.

If the *clocháin* were virtually pilgrim hostels, then the oratories of Gallarus type, which use the same principle of corbel construction, should also be seen as being connected with pilgrimage traffic. They also share a similar distribution pattern: the oratories too are clustered mainly in the Dingle Peninsula, with a smaller scatter on the neighbouring Iveragh Peninsula to the south; though by-passing the Aran Islands, they follow the path of the beehive huts northwards to the islands of Inishglora and Duvillaun More off the Belmullet peninsula in County

Fig. 74 *Beehive hut on the Magharee Islands off the north coast of the Dingle Peninsula*

Mayo. But the beehive huts go further north via Inishmurray and Slieve League to Scotland, where a single and a double *clochán* survive at Eileach an Naoimh in Argyll, where St Colmcille's mother is said to be buried. If these Scottish *clocháin* too were used to provide overnighting facilities for seaborne pilgrims, is it possible that they could also have been the progenitors of the cleits on the outermost Hebridean island of St Kilda, where a long-vanished church was dedicated to St Brendan?

In addition to the ageless *clocháin*, some medieval Irish buildings designed to provide more permanent accommodation ought perhaps also to be associated in a particular way with pilgrimage traffic, as they are all on sites that have been shown to be associated with pilgrimage. Some are single-storey structures, such as those at Temple Brecán (Fig. 32) on the Aran Islands, or the (?17th-century) ruins known as the Chancellor's House at Kilmalkedar. But others are more grandiose two-storey buildings, such as the so-called St Brendan's House or the Priest's House also at Kilmalkedar (Plate IV), where it is also called the Chancellor's House, perhaps indicating that it was the late medieval predecessor of the similarly named ruins just mentioned. The most imposing structure of them all is the Abbot's House alias the Glebe at Kilmacduagh in County Galway. Looking more like a tower-house is the two-storey building at Banagher in County Derry, which prompts the question of whether the ruinous tower at Our Lady's Island in County Wexford, and also the tower-like entrance gateway at Glendalough (Fig. 75), which had an upper floor, may not originally have served the same function.

Fig. 75 *Could the two-storey gateway into the monastic enclosure at Glendalough have provided accommodation for the administrator of the Pilgrimage in honour of St Kevin?*

But what was that function? Given the fact that all of these buildings are located on sites that are known or – like Banagher - can be presumed to have been places of pilgrimage, it is not too far-fetched to suggest that they may have provided accommodation for priests who supervised and administered the pilgrimages to these places, and who may have borne the title of 'chancellor' preserved for us at Kilmalkedar. If special accommodation were provided for such supervisors, one could surmise that the vanished building at Monaincha which Ledwich called 'the Abbot's apartments', the two-storey building added to the Romanesque church on Inishbofin in Lough Ree, as well as the so-called Sacristy attached to the cathedral at Clonmacnois, may also have served a similar function.

CHAPTER 16

CASHELS AND FORTS

BUILT INTO THE PORCH OF THE CHURCH OF IRELAND CHURCH AT TERMONFECKIN in Louth is an Early Christian limestone slab (Fig. 76) bearing a small equal-armed cross followed by the inscription:

OROIT DO ULTAN ET DO DUBTHACH DO RIGNI IN CAISSEL
A prayer for Ultan and for Dubthach who made the cashel.

It marks the site of a monastery of St Féchín (*d.* 660), whose other foundations include Fore in County Westmeath and High Island (Ardoileán) off the west coast of Galway, where there is also a beehive hut and a stone oratory.

Nothing is otherwise known of Ultan and Dubthach, yet the fact that the word 'and' in the inscription is given in an abbreviated form of the Latin *et* would suggest that the inscription had something to do with the monastic foundation, where there is also a fine high cross of 9th- or perhaps 10th-century date, with which the slab must be roughly contemporary. The only claim to fame of Ultan and Dubthach is through this inscription, which gives them credit for the construction of the *caissel*, anglicised as 'cashel', a word derived from the Latin *castellum* denoting a round stone wall, sometimes of a fortificatory nature. The inscription, found on a monastic site and using a Latin formula expected of a monastery, is unlikely to record the construction of a cashel purely for the makers' own use or defence; rather it would have been one connected with the religious establishment, and possibly also used by the general public. But we will never find out, as nothing remains of the cashel which Ultan and Dubthach built.

This Termonfeckin cashel may have been similar to the one near the Upper Lake in Glendalough, which is normally described as a fort or ring-fort, implying its use as one of those numerous round enclosures surrounded by an earthen or stone wall which are the common domestic habitation of Early Christian Ireland. Yet the

185

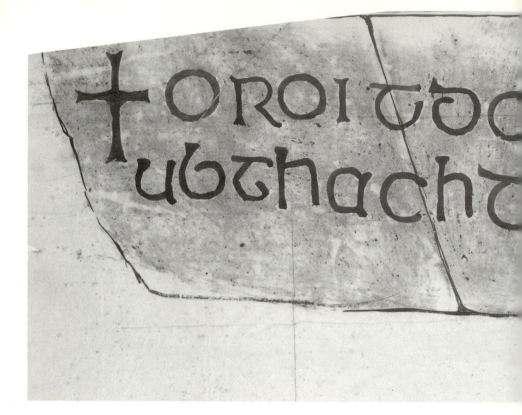

Fig. 76 *An inscribed stone in the porch of the Protestant church at Termonfeckin, County Louth, asks a prayer for Ultan and Dubthach who built the* caissel, *a stone-walled enclosure*

location of this neatly cleaned-up cashel close to some pilgrimage stations marked by stone crosses would place it much more in the context of the pilgrimage to this famous site, which the third Latin *Life* of St Kevin states to have been one of the four most important places of pilgrimage in Ireland. Rather than having served as a purely domestic habitation, its proximity to the stations would suggest that it may have been a meeting-place for pilgrims and its now empty interior may once have contained a wooden or stone building or buildings to provide shelter for pilgrims doing the rounds to the churches and stations of the Upper Lake. Such may also have been the context of the *caissel* which Ultan and Dubthach built at Termonfeckin for those on pilgrimage to the relics associated with St Féchín, who was probably buried not there, but at Fore.

Stone forts usually described as cashels are found in many of the stony areas of the country, as exemplified by the Burren region in north Clare or the geologically related Aran Islands. Some of these cashels, including those on the Aran Islands, might well be prehistoric in date, and the great Grianán of Aileach in County Donegal suggests a purely secular use for one of the ruling families of the Uí Néill dynasty. But while many of the cashels are obviously purely secular, one is justified

in asking whether they all were, because a glance at some of those in Kerry might suggest otherwise.

The stone fort or cashel at Leacanabuaile, Cahirciveen (Fig. 77), excavated in 1939-40, proved to have a number of buildings inside it, including an almost square structure giving access to a round one behind it, making them look something like a keyhole in ground plan. The almost square house was shown to overlay two round buildings beneath it and to have been later than the round house adjoining it. Thus, all the early buildings on the site appear to have been of the *clochán* variety, even though it was not possible to be sure whether they were originally roofed in stone or with thatch.

A similar scene emerged in Brendan O'Flaherty's excavation at Loher between Waterville and Caherdaniel, also on the Iveragh Peninsula in Kerry. Here, round houses made of wood proved to be the earliest, followed by a *clochán* and finally by a rectangular house akin to that at Leacanabuaile 12 miles (20 kilometres) away. The location of this cashel at Loher might, like Teampull Mancháin on the Dingle Peninsula, have been specially chosen to provide a view of Skellig Michael, which would not have been visible from certain other locations in the surrounding area. Further up the hill slope is an oval dry-wall enclosure containing a *clochán*, a small oratory and some cross-inscribed slabs, including one bearing the alpha and omega symbols. The grouping of *clochán* and cross-inscribed slabs enclosed by a drystone wall higher up the slope, and the stone cashel with *clochán* further down, could well

187

Fig. 77 *The stone 'fort' at Leacanabuaile, County Kerry, encloses a 'key-hole' lay-out of adjoining round and rectangular buildings which may have been used in conjunction with a maritime pilgrimage along the west coast of Ireland*

have functioned in conjunction with seaborne pilgrimage, as it is not very far away from a sheltered sea cove. Perhaps Leacanabuaile, only a little further away from the sea, and even the famed Staigue Fort on the south side of the Iveragh Peninsula, may have done so too.

On the Dingle Peninsula, we find similar cashel walls associated with beehive huts. In the Glenfahan area there is one known as Caherconor, though the *clocháin* within the cashel (Fig. 78) are not very well preserved. More easily comprehensible is Reask, excavated by Tom Fanning. There, the stone wall encloses a roughly circular area with a number of *clocháin*, some of them double, as well as a fine collection of cross-decorated slabs, some preserved *in situ*, others now displayed in the nearby Heritage Centre at Ballyferriter. Reask is clearly a religious site of some kind, perhaps once associated with the pilgrimage traffic to Mount Brandon. It lies some distance from the Saint's Road, but being located on solid ground (despite its name which connotes a somewhat marshy place), it could have acted as a reception area for pilgrims who landed from the sea on nearby White Strand in Smerwick harbour on their way to Mount Brandon. Not far away is the round earthen enclosure at Emlagh, which might once have had a greater significance than it would appear to have now, because, as mentioned earlier (page 80), a line drawn from it to Gallarus oratory continues on straight to the summit of Mount Brandon. At the other end of the country, the earthen enclosure at Drumawark, Donegal, which formerly housed a cross, lay close to the pilgrimage road to Lough Derg, and may legitimately be claimed as having had something to do with the pilgrimage traffic to St Patrick's Purgatory.

Around the coast there are some stone cashels which can arguably also be connected with pilgrimage. The most southerly of these is at Knockdrum, which is not far from the Cork coast near Castletownshend, where a cross-inscribed stone at present inside the entrance would seem to have imbued the cashel with a religious purpose. Those on west coast islands such as the Magharees (Illauntannig), High Island (Ardoileán) with its beehive huts, and Caher Island, which was apparently the last station on the way to Croagh Patrick, can reasonably be linked to pilgrimage traffic.

But further north along the coast we come to a greater enigma: the notable oval stone wall enclosing the religious buildings on the island of Inishmurray off the Sligo coast (Plate XI). Dr Paddy Heraughty's 1982 monograph on Inishmurray explained the role played by the cashel in the rounds of the island's pilgrimage, which was still of importance in County Sligo during the early years of this century. Even though early historical sources make no mention of the island as a place of pilgrimage, the antiquity of the pilgrimage is vouched for by the wooden statue from Teach Molaise of St Molaise, which is now in the National Museum in Dublin. Bringing us back even earlier is the 9th-century crozier and the bell from the island, which Cormac Bourke recently brought to light in the Duke of Northumberland's collection at Alnwick Castle. But was the cashel built as part of the monastery, or was it there long before the monastery, as a recent study by Jenny White Marshall would suggest? Even if we can at present provide no definitive answer to this intriguing question, we can say that there is some likelihood that other stone cashels, as well as earthen enclosures, might have provided accommodation and shelter for those on sea pilgrimage around the Irish coast. But this, of course, does not mean that they *all* did so.

Fig. 78 *An aerial view of Caherconor at Glenfahan on the Dingle Peninsula shows ruined beehive huts nestling within a dilapidated stone cashel wall. Pilgrims may have stayed here on their way to or from Skellig Michael*

Chapter 17

Cross-decorated Stones

IT WAS FROM THE EARTHEN-BANKED ROUND ENCLOSURE OF KILCOLMAN IN THE townland of Maumanorig, overlooking Ventry harbour, that the Saint's Road to Mount Brandon appears to have had its visually detectable starting point. Within it is a bullaun, and beside that a large, low boulder with two crosses carved on it (Fig. 23). One of these crosses, unusually deeply sunk into the surface of the stone, is a large cross of arcs – a series of compass-drawn arcs arranged so as to form a cross. It is surrounded by a circle and stands on a stem with a three-pointed foot. The other, smaller, equal-armed cross is more shallowly carved, has bifurcating terminals and is placed close to the end of an Ogham inscription, which forms two sides of a frame around the large cross. This inscription Macalister read as 'ANM COLMAN AILITHIR' and translated as 'Name of Colman the pilgrim'. But given the pilgrimage context, it might be better to think of it in terms of asking for a prayer for the *soul* of Colman the pilgrim. The use of the formula 'ANM' is generally regarded as being late in the series of Irish Ogham inscriptions, and another instance on a stone at Ratass near Tralee was dated to the 8th or early 9th century by Donncha Ó Corráin, on the basis of the genealogy of the person named in the inscription. The Kilcolman stone may, therefore, not be too far removed in date from the Ratass stone.

The combination of two crosses and an Ogham inscription is repeated on a taller pillar at Arraglen (Fig. 28), located at a height of about 2000 feet (650 metres) in a saddle between Masatiompán and the ridge leading up to Mount Brandon; the crosses placed back to back at Arraglen are but variants of those placed side by side

Fig. 79 *A stele or pillar in the Protestant churchyard at Carndonagh, County Donegal* (OPPOSITE), *showing two possible pilgrim figures beside a* flabellum *(a relic of St Colmcille?) and, below, a cross of arcs or almost-encircled four-point interlace*

191

at Kilcolman. The Ogham inscription refers to Ronan the Priest, whom we could imagine at this lofty spot gathering together his flock of footsore pilgrims, some having come up the western side of the mountain from Tiduff and others having made their way up the more difficult eastern approach from Faha and Cloghane, before joining them all together for the final climb to the summit of Mount Brandon. Faha, the 'base camp' at the eastern foot of the mountain, has two separate stones with a cross of arcs, and when we consider them together with the Kilcolman stone near the start of the Saint's Road, and Arraglen two-thirds of the way to the top, we can scarcely avoid the conclusion that the cross of arcs must have been a cross-type associated with pilgrimage, though not necessarily the only one.

This impression can be reinforced when we plot on a map (Fig. 81) the occurrence of the cross of arcs in stone not only on the Dingle Peninsula but throughout the country, for it occurs at a number of well-known pilgrimage sites such as Clonmacnois, Glendalough and Ballyvourney. What is particularly striking about this distribution is the wide arc it spans around the Irish coast from Cork (Crooha West, near Adrigole) and Kerry (the Dingle Peninsula) to the Aran Islands in Galway, County Mayo (offshore islands and sites in view of Croagh Patrick), Sligo (Inishmurray), Donegal (Glencolmcille, the Inishowen Peninsula and the northernmost island of Inishtrahull), and as far round as Drumnacur in County Antrim. From there the motif can be followed across the North Channel to Whithorn in Wigtownshire, Iona and Cladh a Bhile in Argyll and right up as far as the Shetlands, where it occurs on stones from Bressay (Fig. 80), Papil, and Papa

Fig. 80 *Stone from Bressay on Shetland* (LEFT) *with two possible pilgrim figures under a cross, and an Ogham inscription on the side*

Fig. 81 *Distribution map* (OPPO-SITE) *of the occurrence of crosses of arcs on Irish stones of the Early Christian period*

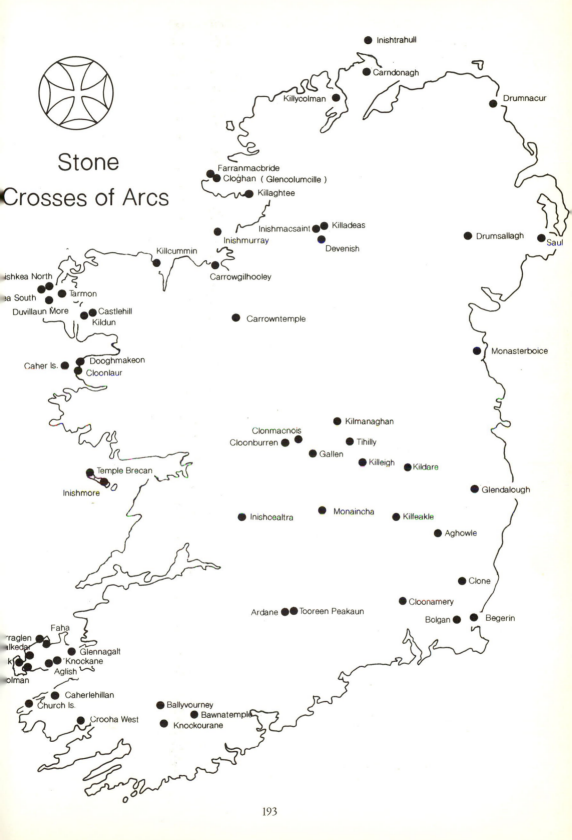

Stone
Crosses of Arcs

Inishtrahull

Carndonagh

Killycolman

Drumnacur

Farranmacbride
Cloghan (Glencolumcille)
Killaghtee

Inishmacsaint   Killadeas
Inishmurray   Devenish

Drumsallagh

Saul

Killcummin

ishkea North
ea South   Tarmon
Duvillaun More
        Castlehill
        Kildun

Carrowgilhooley

Carrowntemple

Monasterboice

Caher Is.   Dooghmakeon
             Cloonlaur

Kilmanaghan
Clonmacnois
Cloonburren   Tihilly
        Gallen
        Killeigh   Kildare

Temple Brecan
Inishmore

Glendalough

Inishcealtra   Monaincha   Kilfeakle

Aghowle

Clone

Ardane Tooreen Peakaun   Cloonamery
                      Bolgan   Begerin

raglen Faha
lkeda
        Glennagalt
k   Knockane
        Aglish
olman

Caherlehillan

Church Is.
Crooha West   Ballyvourney
        Bawnatemple
        Knockourane

193

Westray, as well as on the bottom of one of the beautiful silver bowls from the great religious hoard discovered on St Ninian's Isle (prompting the question as to whether it, and the famous 'hanging bowls', could have contained oil brought back as a relic from holy places). The stone from Papa Westray has a Latin cross above a cross of arcs, very reminiscent of a similar combination on a lost stone from the Aran island of Inishmore, preserved for us in a drawing in the Ordnance Survey letters of 1838.

Such resemblances over vast stretches of water and, more strikingly, the close correspondence in the coastal distribution of crosses of arcs with that for the maritime pilgrimage suggested above as having been associated with the early island hermits and the cult of St Brendan, could easily lead us to presume a connection between pilgrimage and crosses of arcs, stretching all the way from the southwest of Ireland to the Shetland Isles. This connection can probably be traced inland, too, as far as Clonamery, County Kilkenny, where a cross of arcs stands above the door lintel of a church dedicated to St Broondawn, who may be identical with our Kerry navigator. That the cross of arcs may also be related to the relics which pilgrims travelled to venerate is suggested by the Emly house-shaped shrine now in the Museum of Fine Arts in Boston (Fig. 67), which has a silver grille of interlinked crosses of arcs on one side, though how far the Book of Durrow and the Ardagh Chalice should be regarded as relics because their ornamentation includes a cross of arcs is another question.

The cross of arcs is often described as a Maltese cross, but incorrectly, because the arms of the cross of arcs are curved or arched as the name implies, whereas the arms are straight on the Maltese cross. The latter's association with Malta comes

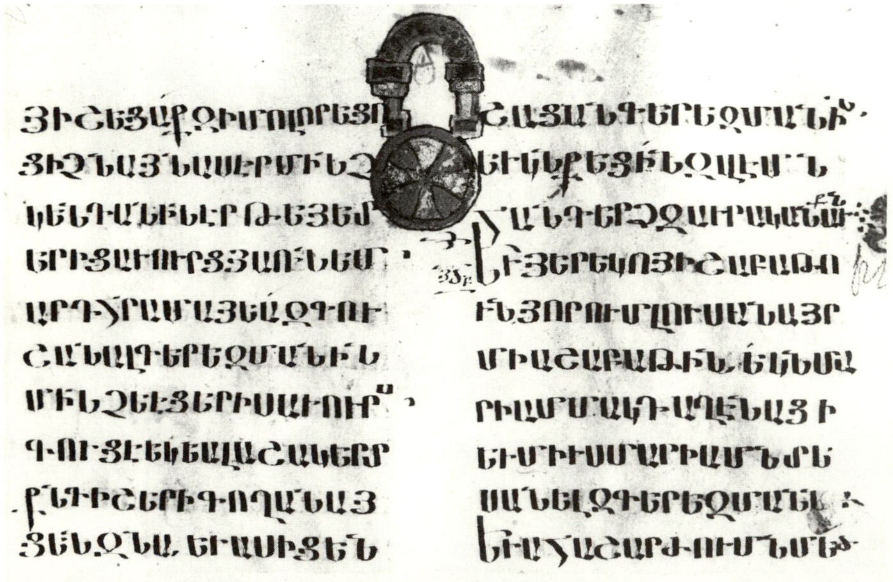

Fig. 82 *An encircled cross of arcs surmounted by an arch with hanging lamp representing the shrine of the Holy Sepulchre in Jerusalem, as depicted in an 11th-century Armenian manuscript*

Fig. 83 *Crosses of Armenian pilgrims in the Church of*
the Holy Sepulchre in Jerusalem

through the Knights Hospitallers of St John of Jerusalem, who found their permanent home there after they had been forced to abandon Jerusalem and Rhodes in turn. The cross of arcs is a neat, compass-drawn variant of the extended family of Greek, or equal-armed, crosses which have the closest connections with Jerusalem. This is demonstrated, for instance on page 70 of an 11th-century Armenian manuscript (Fig. 82) now in the Matenadaran in Erevan, which shows an equal-armed cross, with slightly curving arms, placed directly beneath an arch with lamp hanging over the Tomb of the Saviour – the holiest place of pilgrimage in Christendom.

A variety of other forms of the equal-armed cross can be seen carved on the walls of the stairs leading to the Chapel of St Helena in the Church of the Holy Sepulchre (Fig. 83). Where similar crosses are found in Europe, they suggest an ultimate link with Jerusalem, and probably a more immediate one with pilgrimage activity, which presumably had brought the knowledge and lore of such cross forms from the Orient back to the West. That they were reaching Ireland by around 600 is shown by their presence in the Cathach, the Royal Irish Academy manuscript that may even have been written by the hand of St Colmcille himself. We find much the same kind of cross on the smaller of the two crosses on the Kilcolman stone; it, together with the cross with bifurcating terminals on the pillar beside the slab-shrine at Killabuonia (Fig. 59), also in Kerry, strongly suggest that not only the cross of arcs but also other variants of the equal-armed cross can probably be associated with pilgrimage activity in Ireland, though obviously we have no proof.

There are also indications that upright slabs bearing crosses may have been related to pilgrimage activity. One already discussed (page 95) is the 'VII ROMANI' stone at Temple Brecán on Inishmore, which is most likely to have been commissioned by seven pilgrims who had been to Rome. On the small island of Duvillaun More off the Belmullet peninsula in Mayo there is an upright slab bearing on one face an encircled cross of arcs and on the other a Crucifixion scene for which a 9th- or 10th-century date has recently been argued. It stands at the head of a long rectangular setting of stones, which probably mark the grave of one of those early hermits venerated by pilgrims whose name has long since been forgotten. A number of smaller cross-decorated pillars are found further south on Caher Island, which is alleged to have been the last station on the pilgrimage to Croagh Patrick.

County Donegal has a number of interesting cases where cross-decorated stones may be connected with pilgrimage. The most important collection is in the valley of Glencolmcille, where many of the stations on the pilgrimage route have cross-decorated pillars standing on cairns of stones, which down to our own day act as the focal points for prayer for pilgrims doing their rounds. Some (e.g. Fig. 39) show clear traces of ornament derived from metalwork of 8th- or 9th-century type, which provides us with a rough idea of the date of these monuments. This suggests that the pillars are translations into stone either of metal reliquaries which may formerly have been preserved on the site, or perhaps imitations of wooden pillars once ornamented with metalwork.

The Glencolmcille pillars are unlikely to have acted as gravemarkers and were almost certainly erected in connection with pilgrimage activity in the valley. This is also likely to have been the case at Aighan, County Donegal (Fig. 84). There, a stone bearing cross decoration on both faces now lies loose on a cairn of stones which, at least until the last century, was a place of pilgrimage, where the station was held during the nine days following 23 June. Associated with the mound was a curious small brownish stone almost resembling a bone, with its surface pitted with three small holes into which fingers could have been fitted. This stone used to be borrowed temporarily to be brought to the house of a sick person, as it was believed to cure all kinds of diseases; tradition has it that it was even lent to a patient in America and duly returned safely to its place on the cairn of stones.

One interesting Donegal cross-decorated stele which may be associated with the veneration of Colmcille stands in the grounds of the Church of Ireland Church at Carndonagh on the Inishowen peninsula. One face of this stone bears the figure of the crucified Christ on a cross, the stem of which is flanked on each side by a standing figure with an equal-armed cross carved on the breast; beneath them is another equal-armed cross with the arms filled with interlace. The other face (Fig. 79) has near the bottom what can be interpreted as a cross of arcs, or alternatively a four-pointed interlace almost enclosed within a circle. Above it stand two figures on either side of an object with a long handle, and a circular head enclosing a marigold pattern. This has been described as a *flabellum*, an ecclesiastical object of uncertain use, but which was used, at least in Mediterranean countries, to keep flies away from host and celebrant at Mass. The word has been used by the eminent Celtic scholar Whitley Stokes to translate the Irish word *cuilebaidh*, which was a relic of St Colmcille brought to the Columban foundation at Kells, County Meath, in 1090 (precisely where it was before that is not known). Another *cuilebaidh* is mentioned

Fig. 84 *Cross-decorated stone lying on the old Midsummer pilgrimage Station at Aighan, near Bruckless, County Donegal*

in the *Annals of Ulster* as having been lost at sea in the year 1034. Perhaps the *flabellum* on the Carndonagh stele was modelled on one or other of these. It has at the bottom of the handle two loops, which may imitate leather thongs designed to hold the *flabellum* upside down when not in use. The carving may, therefore, represent a movable object, which was probably smaller than the carving itself. The fact that a *cuilebaidh* was regarded as a relic of St Colmcille could suggest, furthermore, that the *flabellum* illustrated at Carndonagh may imitate a relic of the Donegal saint, whose island monastery on Iona lay not too far away by sea. While the dating of this stone has varied between the 7th and the 9th centuries, it is not impossible that the *flabellum* could have imitated a *cuilebaidh* which may have been among the relics removed from Iona to Ireland at some stage during the 9th century to prevent them falling into Viking hands, such transferral of relics being mentioned in the *Annals of Ulster* under the years 830, 848 and 877. The figure to the right of the *flabellum* as we look at it can clearly be seen to carry a drop-headed staff, and to carry a satchel by his side. Perhaps he, and his opposite number whose attributes are less well preserved, may be regarded as pilgrims flanking a relic of St Colmcille.

These cross-decorated stones which have been linked to pilgrimage activity are of the standing variety: most of them are decorated on both faces, and can still be seen standing upright on their respective sites. But there is also a range of cross-decorated slabs which are more likely to have been laid flat on the ground, as they bear a cross on only one side, whereas the other is left rough or at least undecorated. Sometimes, only one such slab is known from a site, as is the case with Kilmacduagh. But there are some instances where sizeable collections of such stones are found on a single site as, for instance, at Clonmacnois, Glendalough,

Inishcealtra, Nendrum and Saul in County Down, Temple Brecán on the Aran Islands, Durrow (another Columban foundation), Gallen and Lemanaghan in Offaly, Clonmore in Carlow, Lismore in Waterford, Clonfert in Galway, St Berrihert's Kyle (Ardane) and Toureen Peakaun both in Tipperary, and Tullylease in north Cork, to name but the most important.

By far the most significant of these is Clonmacnois, where hundreds of such stones survive, all too many of them sadly only in fragments; many have disappeared since George Petrie attempted the first inventory way back in 1822. Of the sixty or so complete or fragmentary slabs that vanished between then and 1909, when Macalister published his updated corpus, many were considered to have been put in graves by local people as a kind of talisman for the dead. Some of these have, fortunately, reappeared in the meantime, while others have been stolen in recent years. The surviving specimens have now all been brought indoors for security reasons, the better examples being displayed in the present site buildings by the Office of Public Works.

The Clonmacnois slabs, some of which are illustrated in Figs. 85a-f, show a considerable variety in design. Many have Greek or, more frequently, Latin crosses, some of the latter having elaborate decoration in a central roundel and in the semicircular expanded terminals. Inscriptions, where present, contain a single personal name, often preceded by the formula 'Ōr do', meaning 'a prayer for', and only in the rarest instances is the name of the person's father given. With the exception of two bishops, the rank or standing of the individual is not stated. Petrie (as posthumously edited by Margaret Stokes), Macalister and Lionárd built up a chronology for the slabs ranging from the 8th to 12th century on the basis that the names inscribed on the stones allowed their identification with those in the well-documented list of abbots and other prominent members of the monastic community, whose graves they presumed were marked by the stones. But the equation of the names on the slabs with those known from historical sources, and the notion that the slabs were grave-markers are both assumptions that cannot be verified, and which are here called into question.

Looking first at the question of the equation of names, we should note that many of the names on the stones were so common in early historic Ireland that they need not necessarily be identified with those of documented office-holders and other monastic personnel at Clonmacnois. Only two names on the slabs seem to present little problem in being identified with historically known persons. One of these is Suibine mc [son of] Mailae Humai, whose name is recorded on a beautiful but long-since vanished slab illustrated by Petrie, and whose patronymic helps to identify him as the Clonmacnois scribe and anchorite who was 'the most learned Irishman of his day' before he died around 890. The other is Odrán háu Eolais, whose unusual name is identical with that of a Clonmacnois lector who died in 994. His stone (Fig. 85c) is of much poorer quality, suggesting that the craftsmanship of a century earlier was of a much higher standard, as witnessed by Suibine's stone, and perhaps also that of an otherwise unidentified wright (saer) named Tuathal (Fig. 85d). But two reliable identifications are a very small percentage of the 250 inscribed stones known from Clonmacnois, and even if we subtract from that number those where the full name has not been preserved on the slab, it is still a very small statistical sample on which to base the identification of the rest of the names on the stones with those of personages historically documented as having been associated with Clonmacnois. In addition, many names on the slabs do not occur in the historical roll-call of Clonmacnois, and equally many names in that roll-call do not occur on the slabs. There would, therefore, appear to be reasonable grounds for querying the assumption that many of the names inscribed on the Clonmacnois slabs were necessarily those of abbots or other prominent members of the monastic community.

What, then, of the assumption that the stones marked the graves of those named on the slabs? This might appear to be reasonable, given the fact that the stones were finished smooth on one side only and left rough on the other and, thus, presumably placed flat on the ground, although not a single stone remains in its original position on the site. One stone (Fig. 85b) asking for a prayer for Fe[idil]mid in the usual *Ōr do* formula also bears in Latin the interesting words *occisus est sine ca[usa]*, 'he was killed without ca[use]'. But these words in Latin would appear to be a later addition, as they are in smaller and rougher lettering, so there is no indication that the stone was set up to mark the unfortunate Feidilmid's grave after he was murdered. On the contrary, it would suggest that the original *Ōr do* inscription was carved before his death. The fact that the additional words about his death are in Latin sets this inscription apart from almost all the others, which use only Irish. The use of Latin, the language of the Church and otherwise used on the Clonmacnois slabs only to describe the titles of bishops, would suggest that this text was inscribed at the behest of the religious community, which would have known the language, rather than of a lay person, who would not. It is as if the information about Feidilmid's death were only to be recorded for the benefit of the monastic community.

The use of Latin on cross-inscribed slabs elsewhere in Ireland is rare, informative yet also problematical. The stone asking for a prayer ('Ōr do') for Muredach hú Chomocain on the island of Inishmurray (Fig. 38) adds the words *hic dormit* (sleeps here) in the same lettering, giving us the impression that this really is a tombstone. Two other instances are both from Tullylease, County Cork. One fine stone requests in Latin that 'whosoever should read this inscription should pray for Berechtuine' (*quicumquae hunc titula[m] legerit orat pro Berechtuine*). The other inscription is fragmentary, and was reconstructed by Harold Leask to read *quorum corpora hic requiescunt et nomina st [for sunt] scripta . . .*, meaning 'whose bodies lie here and whose names are written [in the book of the dead]'. Yet one other slab, which is now in the Ulster Museum in Belfast, bears the inscription *Fratres orent p[ro]nobis Ogrechu et Ugen*, meaning, 'Brothers pray for us, Ogrechu and Ugen'.

Of these inscriptions, only that of Muredach on Inishmurray indicates that it marks the grave of a single individual. The Berechtuine inscription has been variously interpreted either as commemorating a Berichter of Tullylease who is recorded as having died in 839, or another Berichter, the son of a Saxon prince, who came to Ireland in the 7th century but whose name is not linked with Tullylease in historical sources. The formula of the inscription does not, in either case, indicate that it was applied to a stone serving as a grave-marker. In contrast, the other inscription from Tullylease does state specifically that it is asking for a prayer for the dead – not one, but all who are buried in the graveyard. The inscription in Belfast, of uncertain date, is not sufficiently clear to indicate whether the two people mentioned were alive or dead when the stone was carved. It may be noted here that the Latin inscriptions on two upright stones, that at Kilnasaggart, County Armagh

Fig. 85: a) *Alas poor Colman, whose name on this Clonmacnois slab is accompanied by a single word in Ogham script – bocht, meaning poor; b) Fragmentary cross-inscribed slab at Clonmacnois, County Offaly, asking a prayer for Feidilmid, 'who was killed for no reason'; c) The poorly-carved slab of Odrán háu Eolais at Clonmacnois. He died in 994; d) The well-preserved (9th-century?) slab of Tuathal Saer (the wright) at Clonmacnois, County Offaly; e) Cross-decorated slab at Clonmacnois with the cross complete, but lacking an inscription, perhaps because it was never sold; f) Cross-decorated slab at Clonmacnois, County Offaly – a blank that was never completed*

and the 'VII ROMANI' stone at Temple Brecán on Inishmore give no indication that they were carved as grave inscriptions.

Thus, the Latin inscription on Inishmurray is the only one that can be taken to mark the grave of an individual. If it is of the Early Christian period, as seems likely, it is a rare monument, for gravestone inscriptions are virtually unknown in Europe during the later first millennium. Not even Charlemagne had an inscription carved on his tomb at Aachen. Latin inscriptions on the surviving early slabs in Ireland can be seen to be so rare that they must be regarded as exceptional.

They may also be set apart from, and may even have served a different function from, the vast majority of inscribed slabs at Clonmacnois and elsewhere, where a prayer for an individual is asked for through the medium of the Irish formula '*Ōr do*': they can scarcely be perceived as having served the function of grave-markers on the sole evidence of a single Latin inscription on Inishmurray.

One notable characteristic of the Clonmacnois slabs is the awkward way in which the inscriptions are fitted on to the stones, giving the impression that the crosses were cut first, and that the stones were kept in stock until a client came and asked for a name to be put on the stone (as is the case with the monumental masons of today), whereupon the name would be added where there was space for it. There are one or two examples that look like blanks (e.g. Fig. 85f), and others (e.g. Fig. 85e) where the cross has been completed but there is no inscription, suggesting that they had been kept in stock without ever finding a buyer. This circumstance is scarcely in keeping with the theory that such inscriptions marked the graves of monastic personnel: to commemorate a beloved abbot who had just died, one would have expected cross and inscription to have been formally integrated in design, and executed at the same time, rather than the inscription being added to a stone in stock. The notion that the slabs were kept in stock until such time as a client came to have his name suitably inscribed (the names all seem to be male) would, on the contrary, suggest that the buyers or clients are more likely to have come from outside the monastery, and to have commissioned a stone asking for a prayer for themselves on the occasion of their visit to the monastery, and not in expectation of their death and burial there at some later date.

But in suggesting that the Clonmacnois slabs could have been commissioned by people from outside the monastery, it is necessary to provide a motive and an occasion for them to have done so. Perhaps a clue can be found in the very fact that Clonmacnois has by far the largest collection of such slabs in the country. Why was this so, and just what made Clonmacnois so special? Was it simply the availability of a good workshop which could churn out high-quality stones over one or more centuries? Or could it also have had something to do with the fact that Clonmacnois was not only the oldest recorded place of pilgrimage in Ireland but also one of the most popular, and could the slabs best be explained as having been bought and the inscriptions commissioned by pilgrims who wanted to commemorate their pilgrimage made to Clonmacnois, without any suggestion that they were going to be buried there? Pilgrims buying stones from the workshop would have increased the material wealth of the monastery, though it is difficult to ascertain what the method of payment would have been before the introduction of coinage to Ireland at the end of the first millennium.

Such a hypothetical explanation for the creation of the Clonmacnois slabs could find support in the presence of the smaller collections of cross-inscribed slabs at other sites known to have been places of pilgrimage, such as Glendalough, Inishcealtra, Inishmurray, Saul (County Down), Clonfert and Temple Brecán on the Aran Islands. The presence of known relics would help to explain the slabs at places like Clonmore in County Carlow and Lemanaghan in Offaly. Though not historically documented, we would expect relics at Nendrum, County Down (where there is a round tower), Lismore (from where a famous crozier of c.1100 came), and Durrow. More enigmatic are Tullylease and the County Offaly site at Gallen, near Ferbane. If pilgrimage is not the causative factor in the existence of slabs at all of these sites, it is difficult to explain why only they have so many slabs, and why there are no such slabs at hundreds of other smaller monastic sites throughout the country where no early pilgrimage activity has been recorded.

One smaller site with a number of slabs is Toureen Peakaun in the Glen of Aherlow in Tipperary, where an early saint named Peakaun was venerated, and where in addition to the slabs, there is a high cross, a Romanesque church, and a sundial. Further westwards in the same glen is Ardane, otherwise known as St Berrihert's Kyle, where there is another high cross in addition to slabs. The name would suggest veneration of a saint, though he was not necessarily buried there, as there is neither church nor graveyard, only a lovely grove with a holy well that is still visited annually by pilgrims. The lack of any burials here, where there was no monastery, reinforces the idea that cross-inscribed slabs were the product of pilgrimage activity to a site. The slab found beside the old well at St Patrick's Cathedral in Dublin may represent a similar case, and in a largely forgotten site at Clonaltra West, in County Westmeath, there are two fragmentary slabs which were found beside a bullaun, with nothing else – not a sign of a burial or a graveyard in sight. And at Clonmacnois, about a quarter of a mile from the main monastic complex and close to St Ciarán's Well is a cross-inscribed slab asking for a prayer for Fechtnach; it differs little in design from many of the more decorative slabs at Clonmacnois itself. The existence of such a stone at a holy well, the presence of large collections of others at known pilgrimage sites, and their absence from the many monasteries where early pilgrimage is not recorded, all argue that many inscribed cross-decorated slabs may have been commissioned in conjunction with pilgrimage activity. The feet on the Cosgrach Laighnech slab at Inishcealtra (Fig. 49) might also support such a tentative conclusion. It and other Inishcealtra slabs may also have had their inscriptions secondarily supplied but, unlike Clonmacnois, they are applied upside down to the cross.

But the fact that the Suibine and Odrán slabs can, with a high degree of probability, be linked to monastic personnel shows us that we cannot glibly ascribe all the Clonmacnois slabs to pilgrimage activity. Perhaps the names on the stones are those of people both inside and outside the monastery. But, if that were so, we should be more wary of the chronology which Petrie, Macalister and Lionárd built up for the Clonmacnois slabs by equating the names of the stones almost exclusively with similarly named people known to have been members of the monastic community at Clonmacnois.

What, then, of the stones mentioned in the Middle Irish poem written in praise of Clonmacnois perhaps around 1400, and probably wrongly attributed to Aengus O Gilláin? Two of its verses run as follows, in the charming translation by T. W. Rolleston:

In a quiet water'd land, a land of roses,
  Stands Saint Kieran's city fair;
And the warriors of Erin in their famous generations
  Slumber there.
There beneath the dewy hillside sleep the noblest
  Of the clan of Conn,
Each below his stone with name in branching Ogham
  And the sacred knot thereon.

These stanzas give the impression that many an Irish warrior buried in an earlier age at Clonmacnois had his grave marked by a stone bearing an interlace (knot) with his name written in Ogham. There is indeed one intriguing stone at Clonmacnois which has the word *bocht*, meaning poor, inscribed in Ogham beneath the name Colman in normal script (Fig. 85a) – though this was scarcely the same 'Colman the pilgrim' whose name is writ in Ogham in the boulder at Maumanorig in the Dingle Peninsula. The story behind that single adjective in Ogham we shall never know. But the fact that this is the only one of many hundreds of cross-inscribed slabs at Clonmacnois to bear an Ogham inscription would scarcely support an interpretation of the slabs as marking the graves of warriors. Rather, it would suggest that the poet may have had a distinctly rose tint in his non-existent spectacles when looking back at an heroic Ireland which had already been dead for centuries when he wrote.

Nevertheless, we should not entirely neglect Macalister's report that Ogham stones were rumoured to have been present in the Clonmacnois area in around 1861. That this may not have been entirely without foundation is suggested by a few lightly scored Ogham letters in an otherwise undecorated stone that came to light as recently as the summer of 1990. According to Mrs Heather King, who kindly brought the stone to my attention, it was discovered about three feet deep in the course of digging a grave near an excavation she was conducting in the new cemetery extension at Clonmacnois. Its location only a few dozen yards from the old Pilgrims' Way could suggest a link between Ogham and pilgrimage, which is discussed further in Chapter 18.

CHAPTER 18

OGHAM STONES

‘OGHAM', OR 'OGAM', PRONOUNCED VARIOUSLY AS *OG-ham* or *Oam*, is a word derived from Ogmios, the Celtic god of writing, and is used to denote a system of letters or ciphers often found inscribed on Irish pillar-stones. The letters are composed of between one and five notches, which are placed on, at either side of, or diagonally across a central line (Fig. 86) which, on the Ogham stones, is usually (though not always) a sharp corner on the stone. The inscriptions are normally read from bottom to top, and sometimes they continue from top to bottom down the other side of a stone (Fig. 87).

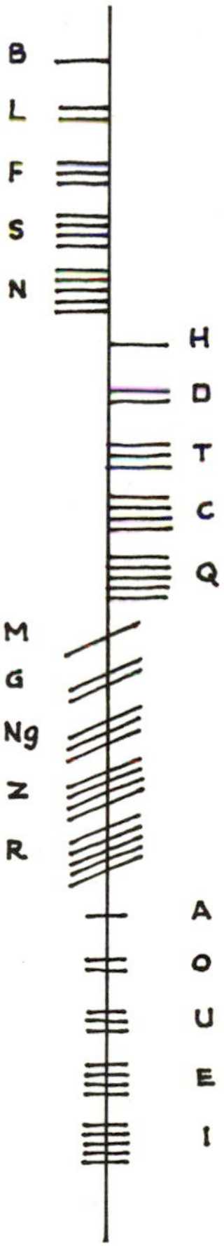

Over 300 such inscribed stones are known from Ireland, with concentrations in counties Kerry (more than 120), Cork (more than 80) and Waterford (around 50); the numbers in other counties do not rise above single figures, and they are overwhelmingly distributed in the southern half of the country. Much ink has flowed during the last two centuries on discussing the meaning, date and use of Ogham stones, but much still remains unclear. The first volume of Macalister's *Corpus Inscriptionum Insularum Celticarum* of 1945 provides us with the readings of the Ogham inscriptions known to him at the time, but in the realisation that his interpretations may leave much to be desired, efforts are now underway to provide a more up-to-date corpus, which will, it is to be hoped, help to clarify at least some of the obscurities surrounding these stones.

It would seem to be generally agreed that the invention of the Ogham script predates the time of St Patrick in the 5th

Fig. 86 *The Ogham alphabet*

205

Fig. 87 *The Ogham stone at Ardmore, County Waterford is unusual in having one inscription carved on two corners, and a separate one carved on a third*

century, and that it is probably based on the Roman alphabet. The numerous Ogham inscriptions in parts of Wales and Cornwall, where some of the Déisi tribe of County Waterford are known to have settled in around the 4th or 5th century, may have played a role in transmitting a knowledge of this Roman-based script to Ireland, where a considerable number of Ogham stones are known from County Waterford. The use and knowledge of Ogham continued to flourish undiminished after the introduction of Christianity (it is impossible in most instances to differentiate between pagan and Christian Oghams, because we cannot identify any of the names given in the inscriptions). Names are usually given in the genitive case, and should be imagined as having been preceded by a word not written on the stone, so that it should be read as (stone or monument of) X, often followed by the name of a father, an ancestor or a patron. We are provided with one clue as to dating because the form of the word used in denoting the relationship of these people to the person commemorated on the stone is of such an archaic form that it is considered to be earlier than the corresponding forms used in the Irish language in manuscripts dating from the 8th century.

For this reason, Ogham stones are often considered to have been gradually fading from use around the year 700. That this was not necessarily so is intimated by one stone from Ratass in Kerry, which Donncha Ó Corráin has recently dated to the 8th/9th century from genealogical information provided on it. Furthermore, a cross fragment discovered at Killaloe in County Clare in 1916 bears both an Ogham and a Runic inscription giving the Irish and Norse versions of the same name, and as the few known Irish Runic inscriptions are unlikely to be earlier than the year 1000, the Killaloe Ogham is almost certainly later than this date.

For the decipherment of the Ogham script, Ireland's equivalent of the Rosetta Stone was the Book of Ballymote, of around 1400, which provided the key to the values of the individual scores, thus enabling scholars to give readings of the inscriptions, though because of weathering and damage, these have not always agreed with one another. Knowledge of Ogham was still common among the people as late as the 19th century, when it is found occasionally on gravestones. John Windele recorded a more unusual use of Ogham at that time by a man named Collins, from near Kinsale in Cork, who had a poem on the zodiac painted in white Ogham letters on his favourite walking-stick. The same man was brought before the magistrate at Petty Sessions and accused of not having his name written on the shaft of his cart, as the law obliged him to do. The court did not believe his protestations to the contrary, until a parish priest from another part of the county was summoned and gave evidence that his name really was written on the cart – but in Ogham, whereupon Collins was discharged by the magistrate with the recommendation that he provide a translation on his cart!

Around thirty Irish Ogham stones are known to bear a cross as well as an Ogham inscription. In almost all cases, there is no way of knowing whether both are contemporary, because cross and inscription do not overlap to show which was earlier, as on the example at Teampull Mancháin/Templemanaghan in Kerry. One instance where they do impinge on one another is the stone from Knockourane/Mount Music, now in University College, Cork, which has a deeply carved cross at one end and a much shallower Ogham inscription abutting on to it. The light scoring on the Ogham could suggest that it is secondary, but – unless the Ogham inscription is unusual in going from top to bottom – it would seem that the stone was turned upside down and the cross inscribed secondarily on to it. This was presumably one of the instances that convinced Macalister, and others before him, that crosses had been added to earlier Ogham-inscribed stones in order to Christianise what were essentially pagan monuments. But one stone discovered after Macalister's death disproved the theory. This was found in M. J. O'Kelly's excavation at Church Island, Valentia in County Kerry, on a site with a round hut probably with a thatched roof, and an oratory (with stone finials) that overlay an earlier wooden structure. The stone, now placed in the Cork Public Museum, clearly shows that the Ogham inscription is later than the encircled cross which, in essence, is a cross of arcs with additional circles in the centre.

Another certainly Christian Ogham stone where the inscription can be no earlier than the cross is the oft-mentioned boulder at Kilcolman in Maumanorig (Fig. 23). There, an encircled cross of arcs takes up the major part of one face of the stone, and the Ogham inscription of Colman the pilgrim, which forms half a rectangular frame around it, must be either contemporary with, or later than, the cross. The Ogham-inscribed pillar at Arraglen (Fig. 28), also in the Dingle Peninsula, has a cross on each of the two broad faces, and an inscription in Ogham asking a prayer for Ronan the priest. Being at a height of about 2000 feet (650 metres) on the slopes of the Mount Brandon ridge, there can be little doubt about this obviously Christian monument having had some connection with the pilgrimage to Mount Brandon. In this context, it is perhaps worth recalling that the Dingle Peninsula has been tentatively identified by some as the location of Srub Brain, where Bran wrote in Ogham the quatrains about his voyage (see page 38), according to the old Celtic tale *Immram Brain*. Away far to the north in the Shetlands, the stone from Bressay (Fig. 80) bears an Ogham inscription on one side; on each face it displays a variation of the cross of arcs which was tentatively linked above (page 192) with pilgrimage activity.

It is remarkable that about one-sixth of all the Ogham stones known from Ireland, and half of those from County Kerry, are or were in the Dingle Peninsula. Given the obvious links between pilgrimage and the stones mentioned above from Kilcolman and Arraglen, the question must inevitably arise as to whether some other – though certainly not all – Ogham stones may have had something to do with pilgrimage.

One other cross-inscribed Ogham stone on the peninsula almost certainly did, as it stands outside Teampull Mancháin/Templemanaghan, situated on a slope where views can be had of both Mount Brandon and the Skelligs. Another Ogham stone (Plate XII), with a hole near the top but without any cross, stands in front of the Romanesque church at Kilmalkedar on the Saint's Road to Mount Brandon. In the neighbouring county of Cork, we find that the grave of St Abbán (page 136) close to Ballyvourney is marked by a small mound of stones flanked by three Ogham stones (Fig. 10) and with a bullaun placed upon it. Surmounting the grave is a recent

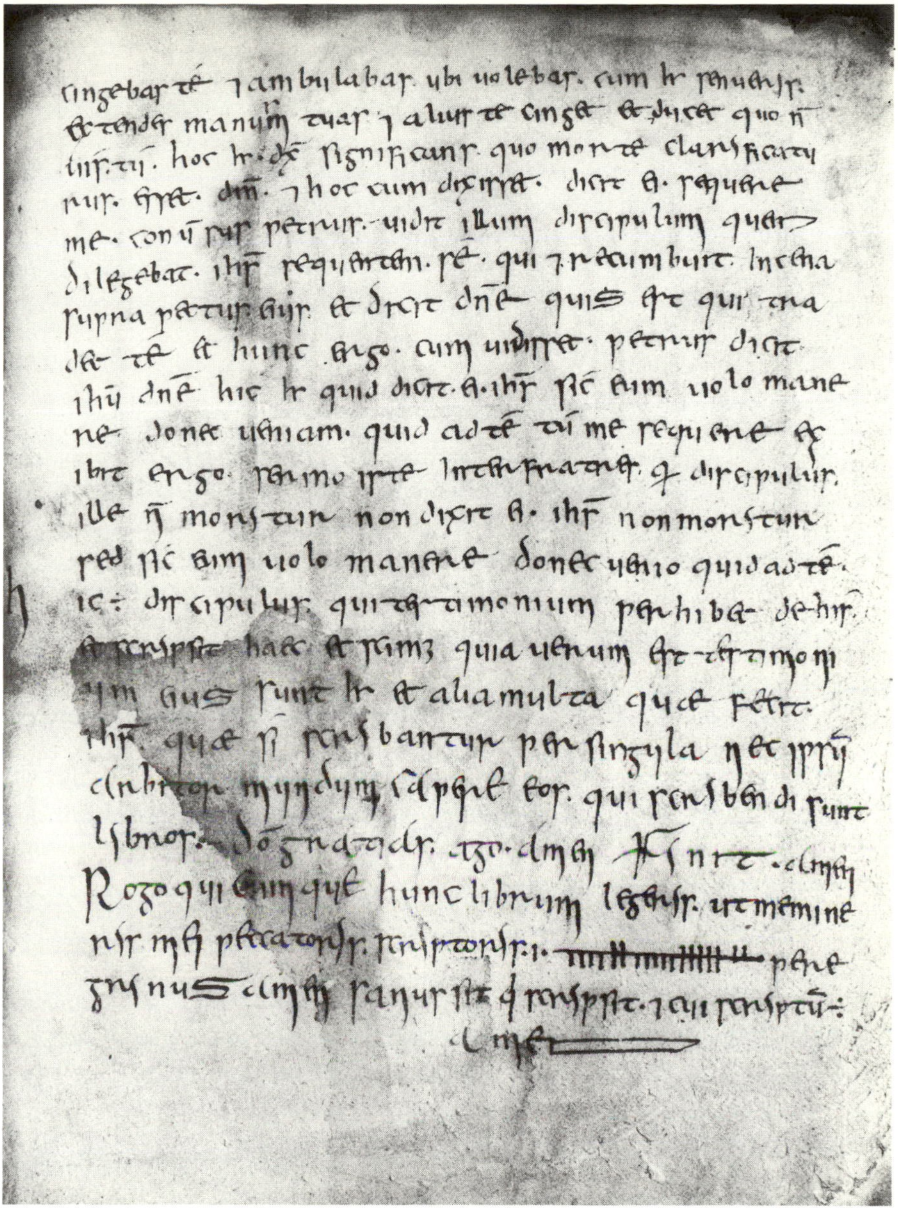

Fig. 88 *An unusual link between Ogham and pilgrimage is found in a fragment of St John's Gospel where the scribe's name (Sonid or Dinos?) in Ogham is followed immediately by the Latin word* peregrinus, *meaning a pilgrim*

cement cross bedecked with the usual rosary beads, plastic crucifixes and other signs of modern devotion, as well as a blue ribbon of the kind used to 'measure' the medieval statue of St Gobnait on her feast day. While the cairn of stones could, of course, be a pagan burial mound under which three people may have been buried, the presence of the Ogham stones in conjunction with a modern 'pattern' could suggest a further pilgrimage connection. About 15 miles (25 kilometres) to the east lies Aghabullogue, where a number of Ogham stones have been found in a small area where Olann, another early Cork saint, is still venerated. In the grounds of the ruined Protestant church is an Ogham stone known as 'St Olann's Cap', which had a large rounded pebble resting on its cupped top. This upper stone 'was borrowed as a talisman for lying-in ladies', in the words of the Victorian Ogham scholar Richard Rolt Brash, but when it was removed by a clergyman of the parish because of the suspicion with which he regarded it (doubtless because of its phallic appearance), it was very quickly replaced by another. Lest it wander away again, its modern successor has been cemented into place. This association of an Ogham stone with the curing of female ailments, together with the concentration of Ogham stones in an area where an early saint is venerated, could once again suggest the idea of Ogham being linked with early pilgrimage to the site.

According to Ann Hamlin, two-thirds of all Irish Ogham stones have no connection with any site having religious connotations. One might well pose the question as to whether some, at least, of these may possibly have been erected by a pilgrim somewhere near his house to commemorate a pilgrimage undertaken to a cult centre some distance away, in the same way that Moslems today in certain parts of the Islamic world indicate on their house-fronts that they have undertaken the pilgrimage to Mecca. Whilst there can obviously never be any proof for this suggestion, and whilst the majority of Ogham stones probably never had anything to do with pilgrimage, it may be that the remaining one-third of Ann Hamlin's stones that were found at sites with religious connections may indeed have been linked with pilgrimage. Religious sites with Ogham stones include Ardfert, County Kerry, a centre for the cult of St Brendan the Navigator, Ardmore, County Waterford (Fig. 87), burial-place of St Declan and Clonmore, County Carlow, where Onchu's collection of relics rest along with him. It may not be irrelevant to mention that the Ogham stone at Island (Bracklaghboy), much further north in County Mayo, is located on a hillock where it has a fine view of Croagh Patrick.

One further small, but significant, piece of evidence that helps to cement the link between pilgrimage and Ogham, comes from an unexpected source. On folio 11 recto (Fig. 88) of a fragment of St John's Gospel, manuscript D.II.3 in the Library of the Royal Irish Academy in Dublin, one small word of Ogham, which can be transliterated either as 'Sonid' or 'Dinos' and probably denotes the name of the scribe, is followed in normal Latin script by the significant word *'Peregrinus'*, meaning a pilgrim.

Chapter 19

Sundials

W E TEND TO THINK OF SUNDIALS NOWADAYS AS GARDEN ORNAMENTS MORE decorative than useful, or as a feature in the walls of 17th-18th century buildings, where many people would scarcely notice them were it not for the gnomon projecting outwards to cast its shadow on hours carved handsomely in Roman numerals. Less well known is the fact that a number of pre-Norman sundials survive both in Britain and in Ireland. One of the most graceful of the Irish examples is that standing almost – but, obviously, not quite – in the shadow of the west gable of the Romanesque church at Kilmalkedar in the Dingle Peninsula (Figs.89-90). It has the shape of a budding flower: a rectangular shaft expanding outwards into a semicircular cup-shape, on one face of which the dial is carved. The half-circle is divided into four roughly equal parts, as is commonly the case with the Anglo-Saxon sundials. Back to back with the dial is a stylised cross of arcs found also on other Dingle Peninsula stones such as at Kilcolman and Arraglen, and therefore in contexts that suggest some connection with pilgrimage activity. Kilmalkedar itself was, as we have seen, an important stopping place on the Saint's Road to Mount Brandon, and this must give rise to speculation that the Kilmalkedar sundial – and perhaps others as well – may have had something to do with pilgrim ritual. St Brendan's *Navigatio*, which specifically describes itself as a pilgrimage, pays great attention to the liturgical division of the days and the hours – for instance, terce, sext and nones (third, sixth and ninth) – at which certain prayers should be said. Although the Kilmalkedar sundial may be as many as three centuries later than the *Navigatio*, it may nevertheless follow the Navigatio's attention to liturgical subdivisions of the day, and its long-lost gnomon may have helped to indicate certain hours at which the pilgrims on the Saint's Road should pray.

If location on the Saint's Road and its cross of arcs decoration were not justification enough for relating the Kilmalkedar sundial to pilgrimage activity on the Dingle Peninsula, then the cross of arcs found on the dial at Monasterboice

Fig. 89 *The north-west face of the sun-dial at Kilmalkedar, County Kerry, decorated with a cross of arcs*

ought to connect it with pilgrimage to this site which preserved a founder's relic until the 16th century. The Monasterboice sundial (Fig. 91), which is in a railed enclosure close to the North Cross, is on the top of one face of a tall, rectangular pillar, where it is divided into four sections. The encircled cross of arcs stands in false relief lower down the shaft, separated from the dial by another very weathered circle containing what may have been a cross with semicircular terminals.

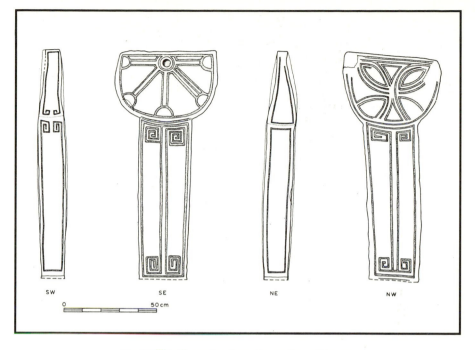

SW   SE   NE   NW

0   50 cm

Fig. 90 *This illustration shows the two faces of the sun-dial at Kilmalkedar. Left, the southeast face with the sun-dial, and, right, the northwest face with the cross of arcs* (SEE ALSO FIG. 89)

Some of the other Irish sundials are on sites where we know pilgrimages took place in earlier centuries. There was one at Saul, County Down, a site which was visited by Heneas MacNichaill on his penitential pilgrimage. That sundial, now lost, was fortunately drawn by G. V. du Noyer, and reproduced in an article by Albert Way in the *Archaeological Journal* of 1868, which still remains our only record of it. We do not know how high it was, as it was partially buried in the ground when du Noyer drew it but, like the Monasterboice sundial, it was placed on top of an upright, rectangular pillar. In contrast, however, it was divided up into eight separate time segments. Another known place of earlier pilgrimage that had not one but two sundials is Inishcealtra; neither is still preserved *in situ*. One of them was a slab little more than 2 feet (60 centimetres) wide; it divides the face into two halves, an upper and a lower, by a horizontal line, in the middle of which the gnomon rested. The upper half has twelve notches, as if to indicate the daylight hours. The lower half has the same number, but with the addition of only three radial lines, located in positions equivalent to twenty-past, twenty-five-past and half-past on a modern clock. The larger Inishcealtra dial is on a slab with a pointed top; it is 4 feet 9 inches (1.40 metres) high, and its dial is marked as an incised half-circle with four divisions.

The remaining six old Irish sundials are on sites where pilgrimage may have been practised, even though this is not documented in early historical sources. Two are accompanied by the remains of a Romanesque church and a slab bearing a cross of arcs. These are at Clone, County Wexford and Toureen Peakaun in County

Fig. 91 *The sun-dial at Monasterboice, County Louth*
(LEFT), *bears a cross of arcs on the shaft*

Fig. 92 *Ireland's tallest sun-dial at Nendrum in
County Down* (RIGHT) *has been reassembled from
many fragments, which show that it has a hammer-
headed cross on the shaft*

Tipperary; both expand flower-like at the top, as on the one at Kilmalkedar,
suggesting that this shape may be typical of the 12th century. Another site,
Nendrum in County Down, preserves the stump of a round tower. Its sundial (Fig.
92) has been reconstructed from a number of fragments discovered in H. C.
Lawlor's excavation of the site in 1922-4. This is one of the most decorative of all
the Irish sundials. Its features are carved in relief, and the dial is no wider than the 6
feet 3 inches (almost 2 metres) high pillar, which makes it the tallest surviving
example in Ireland. Beneath the dial is a tall rectangular panel, and the surviving
fragments indicate that it contained a narrow cross with a hammer-headed terminal
to the uppermost limb.

A small dial at Kilcummin, County Mayo, close to the Atlantic shore, is of the same width as its pillar (now largely sunk into the ground), and has a fourfold division. Two further northern sundials expand at the top, that at Clogher in Tyrone having a fourfold division but differing from the others in having an interlace and well-carved fish of the trout or salmon variety carved beneath it. The interlace could indicate that this may be the earliest of the surviving Irish sundials, dating from anywhere between the 7th and the 9th centuries. Finally, there is the sundial now preserved on the terrace in front of Bangor Castle in County Down. This is likely to have originally stood at the old monastic site in Bangor, and probably once had twelve divisions on its dial.

Dr Ann Hamlin, who has recently discussed the subdivisions of the northern Irish sundials, has argued cogently in favour of seeing these sundials in a monastic context, in which the subdivisions could have corresponded with the times at which the monastic offices – such as terce, sext and nones – would have been recited. But whether the sundials located further south in Ireland should all be seen in a purely monastic context ought, perhaps, to remain an open question, as some of them, such as those at Clone and Kilmalkedar, lack evidence for the presence of an early monastery on the site. The existence of the Kilmalkedar sundial on the Saint's Road to Mount Brandon, the presence of the cross of arcs on it and on the Monasterboice dial, and the two examples formerly on the old pilgrimage site of Inishcealtra, could argue in favour of our seeing them in a more purely pilgrimage context, in which they could have served on sunny days to indicate to pilgrims the hours at which they should carry out certain religious activities and recite particular prayers.

CHAPTER 20

POSSIBLE REPRESENTATIONS OF EARLY
IRISH PILGRIMS

S TANDING AT PRESENT BESIDE THE HIGH CROSS AT THE SOUTHERN END OF
Carndonagh in Donegal is a small pillar. Carved on one of its faces (Fig.
93) is a figure bearing a bell in one hand, perhaps a book or a bag in the
other; lying horizontally beneath is a drop-headed staff or crozier. As we
have seen earlier, croziers were, along with bells, the attributes of early Irish saints
(as represented by what have been presumed to have been their enshrined relics),
so that one might suppose that the Carndonagh figure shows us an early Irish saint.
But the staff was not just the symbol of a saint; it was also the sign of the pilgrim: in
the old Irish annals, the expression used of someone who went on pilgrimage was
that 'he took the staff' (*bachall*).

However we interpret this figure on the Carndonagh pillar, we may more
probably identify as a pilgrim one or probably both of the figures on a stele (Fig.
79) just over the wall in the Church of Ireland graveyard. As we have already seen
(page 196), they flank the shaft of a *flabellum* that may copy a relic of St Colmcille.
Though the surface of the left-hand figure is worn, both figures carry in the right
hand a small staff with drop head, and around the neck or falling from the shoulder
of each would appear to be a small satchel shown at waist height. The satchel is the
sign of the traveller, and when bearing a shell, it was the symbol of the pilgrim to
Santiago, though transferred to the Christ figure on the carving at Santo Domingo
de Silos (Fig. 8) in northern Spain. The presence of two figures on either side of
what may be taken to represent a relic would make it unlikely that both figures
represent saints, so they may reasonably be presumed to show us pilgrims to the
site, dressed in knee-length robes.

Fig. 93 *The figure with bell, book or satchel, and drop-
headed staff or crozier, on a pillar at Carndonagh,
County Donegal* (OPPOSITE), *may represent a pilgrim*

The same robe is worn by a charming little figure on an upright slab standing about a mile to the east of the pilgrimage site of Ballyvourney in County Cork (Fig. 51). He lacks a satchel, but carries in front of him a staff, with the head facing outwards and away from him, unlike the Carndonagh figures. It is only a break in the stone surface which makes the staff look as if it were T-shaped. He struts with such vigour that the wind seems to part his hair into two separate halves, so that he resembles the St Matthew figure in the Book of Durrow. That the ground he treads upon is the circle surrounding a cross of arcs would create the presumption that he, too, is a pilgrim.

The outward-facing staff is also a feature found on a pediment-shaped stone (Fig. 46) found in the 18th century on the ground outside the Priest's House at Glendalough. It is now built in over the south door of the building which, as argued above (page 120), is almost certainly the tomb-shrine of the monastic founder, St Kevin. If the staff-bearing figure is taken to be a pilgrim, there would be all the more reason to interpret the bell-bearing figure on the opposite side in the same way, as he is bowing towards the central figure between the two who, in the circumstances, is most likely to represent St Kevin. The two flanking figures wear ankle-length robes, in contrast to the knee-length robes worn by the Carndonagh and Ballyvourney figures. If these two Glendalough figures are correctly interpreted as pilgrims, one carrying a staff and the other a bell, it could help us to see the figure with bell and staff on the small Carndonagh pillar as a pilgrim rather than a saint.

The staff and bell are borne by a figure on a stone at Killadeas not far from Lough Erne in County Fermanagh (Fig. 94), which stands close to a large slab with a cross of arcs on a stem. On the narrow side of the stone there is a single protruding head, with interlace beneath it. The figure itself is carved in false relief on the main face of the stone. Because of the shape of the stone, he bends slightly forward like the figure on the right of the Glendalough lintel who, however, is constrained from standing upright by the sloping roof of the pediment above him. Here, too, the figure carries his staff facing outwards, and the clear representation of shoes could support his identification as a pilgrim rather than a cleric, as is usually suggested. As at Ballyvourney and Carndonagh, he wears a knee-length garment.

Only about 2 miles from Killadeas, and close to the eastern shore of Lough Erne, lies White Island, where a number of curious stone figures (Figs. 95-6) are attached to the interior north wall of a Romanesque church. One of them is dressed like a nun, and may therefore be female. She wears a long robe to the ankles, and in her small hands she carries a bell and a drop-headed staff facing inwards, like those on the Carndonagh pillar, so that she, too, could be interpreted as a pilgrim. The other full-length figures at White Island also wear long robes, but are more likely to be male. One of them carries in each hand a rather curious animal with the (winged?) body of a quadruped, yet the head of a bird. Composite animals often have a symbolic meaning, such as the winged griffin that, with the body of a lion as king of the earth and the head of an eagle as lord of the skies, can symbolise Christ as King of Heaven and Earth. It is not easy to read such a symbolic significance into these two White Island animals, and one wonders if they might not be the sculptor's naïve way of expressing farmyard animals and poultry, which a pilgrim could be imagined to have brought to a shrine as an offering in the days before coinage became current in Ireland. One of the figures has his or her hands covered in a muff,

Fig. 94 *The hunched figure at Killadeas, County
Fermanagh, bearing staff and bell, wears a fine pair of
shoes which may help to identify him as a pilgrim*

like the presumed St Kevin figure at Glendalough, and another carries in his right
hand a stick (or staff?), and has seemingly a bag or satchel hanging from a belt. The
only other figure with a hairstyle like that of the animal-bearer is one which can
only be taken to be a warrior, for he carries in front of him a sword and shield.
Because of these attributes of war, it might be difficult to see him as a pilgrim, but

Fig. 95 *These unique stone figures at White Island,*
County Fermanagh, may be explained in the context of
pilgrimage to Devenish in Lower Lough Erne

his sword and shield, which are really too small to have been of any use in defence or attack, may be a simplistic representation of his status as a member of the ruling classes.

The only other attribute borne by this figure is a penannular brooch worn on his left shoulder. Its details, in as far as they can be made out, suggest that it belongs to a style likely to have been common around the 8th or 9th centuries. A more developed example of this kind of brooch was found at Ballyspellan, County Kilkenny, and is now in the National Museum in Dublin. Scratched on its back (though possibly as late as the 19th century, in the opinion of Siobhán de hÓir)

Fig. 96 *Another example of the stone figures at White Island, this one carrying two animals by the neck*

are what appear to be four personal names inscribed in Ogham script, which in Chapter 18 I have tentatively associated with pilgrimage activity. Ogham was also found on a stone from St Ninian's Isle in Shetland, where an apparently ecclesiastical treasure of around 800 was found to contain, among other things, a silver bowl decorated with a cross of arcs, and a dozen penannular brooches – ten more than were discovered with the famous chalice bearing a cross of arcs found at Ardagh in County Limerick. Dating from roughly a century earlier is the Hunterston Brooch, possibly of Irish origin though found in Scotland and now in the National Museums in Edinburgh, which has a cross shape in the central panel

Fig. 97 *A penannular brooch of c600 bearing an equal-armed cross on each terminal*

which Robert Stevenson interpreted as having been modelled on a reliquary. Some zoomorphic penannular brooches of an earlier generation bear equal-armed crosses on their terminals, including one (Fig. 97) of *c*.600 in the Craggaunowen Project in the Hunt Museum at Limerick University. The same type of cross, which like Ogham has been linked with pilgrimage activity, is found on a hand-pin of roughly the same period from Treanmacmurtagh in County Sligo. Scattery Island in the Shannon estuary, with its round tower and Romanesque church, and another probable island pilgrimage site, Inishkea North in Mayo, have both produced brooches, while a brooch of a rather different kind, now sadly lost, bearing a Latin cross with squared terminals on both faces of its kite-shaped appendage, came to light at Clonmacnois, which has also given us a number of other brooches and pins. When combined together, this material makes an interesting case for the ecclesiastical (and perhaps liturgical) connections of certain brooches, but also for their use in conjunction with pilgrimage, so that the brooch worn by the White Island figure would be quite compatible with his being portrayed in a dual role as both warrior and pilgrim.

Helen Hickey (Lanigan-Wood) has suggested that the White Island figures might have formed the sides of a pulpit-like ambo, which would make them into some of the few surviving pieces of church furniture known from early historic Ireland. They could, however, have been the legs of a raised reliquary-shrine. It is curious that neither White Island nor Killadeas are mentioned in the early Irish historical sources, so that the presence of the figures at both places presents us with something of a mystery. Perhaps the best explanation is that both sites were out-stations for the major pilgrimage site on the island of Devenish, further south in Lough Erne, where there are the remains of two round towers and a stone-roofed Romanesque church dedicated to the patron saint, Molaise.

CHAPTER 21

ODDS AND ALMOST ENDS: BULLAUNS, CURSING STONES AND HOLED STONES

THE PRESENCE OF BULLAUN STONES AT A NUMBER OF EARLY IRISH PILGRIMAGE
sites has been mentioned above without any adequate description being
given of them. Here I shall discuss them in a little more detail, though
without providing any adequate explanation for them – simply because
there is none, in the absence of any early source material which could tell us what
they were used for.

The word 'bullaun', according to Sir William Wilde, derives from the Latin word
'*bulla*', meaning a bowl. Wakeman, in his book on Inishmurray, offers a more
plausible derivation, namely that it comes from the Irish word '*bullaun*' meaning
'little pool'. Bullauns are natural boulders, often of very considerable size, into
which one or more depressions, ranging between 3 inches (7.5 centimetres) and 15
inches (37.5 centimetres) in diameter, have been ground by the action of human
hand. Usually there is only a single depression in each boulder, but some have two,
three, or four (Fig. 98); in rare instances as many as seven or nine depressions are
encountered. The depressions were explained as saints' pillows (in the case of
single depressions) or the marks of a saint's knees while praying (double
depressions). But it would have needed a lot of saints to explain the bullauns with
up to nine depressions. Serious students have been inclined to see bullauns as
ancient grinders of food, especially corn, or even iron ore. But food grinders are
known in other, more practical forms in the shape of querns. One stone of a saddle
quern from Inishtrahull – Ireland's most northerly point – had a cross of arcs carved
into its grinding surface. A number of rotary querns bear cross decoration,
including one from Clonmacnois which bears the name 'Sechnasach' (Fig. 99)
accompanied by a Latin cross (both it and the Inishtrahull stone are now in the
National Museum of Ireland in Dublin). Another decorative quern stone, bearing
neither cross nor inscription, now lies close to a Crucifixion slab, perhaps of 9th- or
10th-century origin, on the Atlantic island of Inishkea North, County Mayo, where
a church was dedicated to St Colmcille (Columba).

Fig. 98 *Bullaun stone with four depressions at Aghowle,*
County Wicklow

Oral tradition does not link bullauns to any normal domestic activity, though Crozier and Rea suggested that the word may have had a connotation as a drinking vessel or a milk pail. Interestingly, the story is told about one Glendalough bullaun stone, known as the Deer Stone, that when St Kevin's master mason lost his wife as she gave birth to twins, a doe came down from the hills and gave her milk every day into the stone for as long as the children were in need of it. In folk tradition, bullauns are, if anything, associated with the healing properties of the water that gathers in the basins, and this may be the real reason behind their frequency and popularity. Ailments are said to have been cured when water from them was rubbed on eyes, for instance, and a number are known as 'wart stones' because water from them is said to be helpful in healing these blemishes. As healing aids, they fit into the framework of small local pilgrimages or patterns held on particular days of the year at hallowed local sites, where occasionally pilgrims are known to have inscribed crosses on them, as is the case on the stone from Adrigole, County Cork, illustrated here (Fig. 100). Two separate accounts written of different parts of County Kerry around the turn of the century illustrate the link with local patterns. The first was written by the noted Belfast antiquary F. J. Bigger, about Temple Feaghna near Tuosist:

A Patron is held here on Good Friday, Saturday, and Easter Sunday. A visitor commences his devotions at a low stone in the middle of the south wall of the old church, where he makes a cross with the pebble on the slab (which is quite worn with such marking), then he goes around the church three times, then halts at a rude shrine in the east wall, after which he goes to the graves of his relatives, then to the holy well, and finally to the bullán stone to the south of the church. The well, Toberfeaghna, almost dry when I saw it, lies to the east of the church across the road, but by far the most interesting feature of the place is the bullán rock, if I may so describe it. This rock appears to be in its natural site on a sloping bank, the north side is level with the earth, and the south side about 3 feet 6 inches high above the earth. Upon its surface are eight holes or depressions varying in size, two or three of them being very slight, and three or four of them good sized basins. In each cavity is a worn oval pebble resembling and locally known as 'butter lumps'. In the centre is the upper half of a quern, found not long ago in a neighbouring field, but having nothing to do with other stones. When the devotees arrive at this rock they sometimes move these stones and otherwise use them, but do not take them away, in fact it is firmly believed that they could not be taken away. Several have tried to do so but always failed, the stones being found in their places next morning. One time a young shopboy from Kenmare took one of them, but his horse would not cross the bridge out of the parish, so he deemed it wise to leave it back again. As I only had a bicycle I tried no such tricks, and had a smooth passage home. This rock is 7 feet 2 inches by 6 feet 10 inches on its surface, and the larger basins are about 13½ in diameter by about 5 inches or 6 inches deep . . . The present bullán seems to me to be a very remarkable example.

Fig. 99 *An early Christian quernstone from Clonmacnois, inscribed with the name Sechnasach*

The second account is that of John Cook, who describes thus his visit of around 1906 to a traditional place of pilgrimage:

> *At Kilclogherane, up an old by-road, off the main road from Aghadoe to Milltown, two miles from the latter, is a spot still frequented as a place of pilgrimage. On the left-hand side, about a quarter of a mile up, is a bullán stone set in a hole in the ditch, about breast-high, an unusual place in my experience. A number of bottles, a dozen or so, small and medium size, lay about the stone. Immediately, and off the left side of the bohreen, is an old hawthorn-tree, surrounded by bushes, brambles, and ferns, growing in wild and luxuriant confusion, and through which a tangled pathway runs. There is no trace of any building or ruin of any old church here or in the immediate vicinity; but here the pilgrims say their rounds, and tie bits of rags on the hawthorn-tree and bushes. It is a curious, old-world, out-of-the-way spot, and I could find no cause why it was frequented. Another bullán stone, the water of which cures, lies some yards further on in the bottom of the ditch, on the right-hand side, with rags hung about, where prayers are also said. Notwithstanding the long spell of dry weather preceding my visit, both the stones had water in them, received from the droppings off the bank and bushes above, and to which due superstition is attached. That the stones are never without water is due to the fact of their being set well into the banks and practically covered, so that there is very little evaporation from them.*

A similar scene greets the visitor today at the grave of St Abbán near Ballyvourney (see page 208). There is a magical charm in this clearing in a small wood, where a small cairn of stones, flanked by three Ogham stones, is surmounted by a loose bullaun which gathers water from the leaves of trees above (Fig. 10). In a more prominent location, a bullaun lies flush with the ground only about 20 metres from the front of St Ciarán's tomb-shrine at Clonmacnois, suggesting a link between bullauns and the more important places of pilgrimage. This impression is strengthened at Glendalough which, as H. S. Crawford and Liam Price have noted, has the greatest collection of bullauns anywhere in Ireland. There are thirty at Glendalough itself, including the Deer Stone mentioned above, and almost the same number on the lands formerly owned by the monastery, whither Price thought that they may have been introduced from Britain for the purpose of grinding food. Interestingly, the largest group of bullauns in the Glendalough area lies close to St Kevin's Road, the pilgrimage road, on both sides of the river leading from the Wicklow Gap down to the monastery. There would thus appear to be a reasonable case for seeing some of the bullauns as being related to pilgrimage activities; probably pilgrims sought cures by applying water from bullauns to afflicted parts of the body. But, since bullauns are found widely throughout Ireland in differing contexts – on hills, in raths or ring-forts, as well as associated with churches and monastic sites – this suggestion could not be extended to all bullauns; it is relevant only to those bullauns associated with places of pilgrimage, or places where local patterns are known to have taken place. Bullauns would, indeed, appear to have had a variety of purposes.

One curious bullaun stone is that known as St Brigid's Stone in a field beside the church at Killinagh, west of Blacklion in County Cavan. In it there are nine basins, each filled with a rounded stone, in the centre of which is a larger stone, which has no basin. Wakeman recorded the tradition that the stones were used for cursing. The practice is the same as that recorded for the Clocha Breacha, the 'speckled stones', on Inishmurray (see page 103). The stones were turned by someone

Fig. 100 *A bullaun stone recently inscribed with a cross*
at Adrigole, County Cork

wishing to curse another; if his reasons for doing so were justified, the curse would
have its effect; if not, the curse would rebound on the person who turned the stones.

The same tradition is recorded at the Pass of Keimaneigh near the famed Cork
pilgrimage spot Gougane Barra, where there are five basins, and at Kilcummin,
County Mayo, where there was a set of cursing stones, now long since disappeared.
In 1839 Caesar Otway recorded the turning of 'the stones of Duan McShaun' at

Louisburgh in County Mayo against the local parish clerk, which resulted in the window of the church being blown in, and the Great Wind of 1838 is even reputed to have been caused by a malignant old woman turning the stones. According to Westropp, the Leac na Naomh, or Saint's Stone, a mass of conglomerate on the altar of the oratory on Caher Island, was similarly used: the wronged person would go out to the island, fast and pray, and call down the wrath of God, Patrick and the saints, who had blessed the stone, if he was in the wrong. John O'Donovan, in the Ordnance Survey letters of 1839, was told by Geraghty, one of his informants on the island, that if the turner of the stone was in the right, a storm arose and boats and men were lost. When O'Donovan suggested that the loss of innocent men's lives seemed a questionable proof of divine justice, Geraghty triumphantly silenced him by citing the miracles of Joshua. But O'Donovan's other informant, a man by the name of O'Toole, took a more Christian view in that, whilst unable to deny the power of the relic, he had little regard for its decisions, and would prefer to see it destroyed. Both men agreed that it punished perjurers who appealed to it.

Cursing stones were also recorded on Tory Island in County Donegal, where they are said to have been used successfully in 1884 against the British gunboat *Wasp*, which was wrecked with loss of life when it attempted to land police and troops to collect rates from the islanders. Precisely what cursing stones should have to do with sites having religious and even pilgrimage connotations such as Inishmurray, Caher Island and Tory Island it is difficult to know; perhaps they were part of some pagan rite that was taken over and given a Christian gloss.

The same may be true also of holed stones, which are occasionally found on sites related to pilgrimage. One instance is at Kilmalkedar on the Saint's Road in the Dingle Peninsula, where the hole is at the top of an Ogham stone (Plate XII). Not far away, the cross-decorated slab at Reask (Fig. 27) had a hole high up near the edge, which was still intact when du Noyer sketched it in about the middle of the last century, but it has since been broken out. A larger hole occurs near the top of a cross-decorated stone at Mainistir Chiaráin on the Aran Islands, though this may have been made to hold a gnomon for a sundial. An upright slab with traces of a ringed cross carved on both faces, and with the centre of the cross perforated by a broad hole, exists at Castledermot, County Kildare, where there is a round tower and remains of a Romanesque church, as well as the hogback mentioned earlier (page 155). At Glencolmcille, the stone carved with cross-decoration at the station at Farranmacbride has a hole at the centre of the cross (Fig. 40), and the pilgrim is told that he or she may see heaven through it. Some holed stones were used by young people to plight their troth by having their fingers meet through the hole. On Inishmurray, mothers-to-be knelt in front of a holed stone near the Women's Church and passed their fingers into two side openings in the stone in the hope of averting a calamity at childbirth; the islanders maintained that death at childbirth was unknown among them.

CHAPTER 22

HOLY WELLS AND SACRED TREES

F MANY OF THE PILGRIMAGE SITES HAD MORE THAN SIMPLY REGIONAL SIGNIFICANCE, and can almost be described as national in character, the holy wells were their local counterparts. There, we still feel the survival of religious practices whose origins go back so far that they disappear into the mists of time. Even in the 19th century, few wells would have attracted visitors from a distance of more than about twenty miles around; this is understandable when we realise that there were anything up to 3,000 such wells in Ireland. Many visits were undertaken not solely to perform religious exercises and duties; they were also festive social occasions where people from surrounding areas could meet to exchange views and settle personal matters once a year on the local saint's feast day. In this, they were Christian successors to old pagan festivals such as those in honour of the god Lug on Croagh Patrick and Mount Brandon. Indeed, some of the patterns on patron days held at wells in the last fortnight in July, or the first fortnight in August, were probably Christianised versions of just those same pagan rites.

The practice of visiting holy wells certainly did not begin with the introduction of Christianity. The pagan Celts had a great respect for wells, as witnessed by the wooden statues excavated some decades ago at the well that was the source of the River Seine in France. And anyone who has seen the force of the water gushing up from the earth close to the road below St Feichín's church at Fore 'of the Seven Wonders' (see page 136) will understand how fascinating these life-giving sources must have been to a prehistoric community. It may well be that the presence of a venerated well was one of the major reasons for choosing the location of many an Early Christian monastery, in order to achieve a felicitous and frictionless continuity from pagan to Christian cult. Certainly, there is very often a 'saint's well' within or immediately outside the bounds of an early monastery; one instance is recorded in County Limerick of a well dedicated to St Molua (My Lua) where the pagan predecessor was associated with Lugaid or Lua, a clear instance of name transfer from pagan to Christian worship.

Fig. 101 *The Well of St Moling's Tree at Mullenakill,
County Kilkenny, combines a well, tree, cross-slab,
altar and a pile of stones which each pilgrim adds to*

Scarcely any early references survive concerning practices at holy wells, though Giraldus Cambrensis refers to a few in the 12th century. It is only in the 18th and early 19th centuries that we begin to learn a little more, particularly from those who found the form of piety practised at the wells quite abhorrent to their own religious beliefs, and it is often from those hostile writers who complain about the 'superstitions' and 'idolatry' at the wells that we glean most. It is fortunate, too, that the activities of the Ordnance Survey in the 1830s brought men like John O'Donovan out into the field to record antiquities and folk traditions before the Catholic Church acted to quell the pattern days at holy wells because of the 'drunkenness and debauchery' and the faction fights which took place in the evenings after the pious practices of the day had been completed. The eating, drinking and gambling at Ardmore in Waterford horrified a correspondent writing in Philip Dixon Hardy's *The Holy Wells of Ireland* in 1836. He wrote of two women there handing out water from the well as fast as they could, and receiving a halfpenny from each person in return for about half a pint. He saw:

> *many persons on their knees before the well, and many more within the walls of the old chapel, with their faces opposite the extreme gable, on the stone of which were several crosses. Some walked on their knees up to those crosses, then rose and kissed the stone most affectionately; others knelt on one spot and rose, advanced on their feet, repeating as usual, and removing the beads, kissed the crosses, went out another entrance, and all walked round the premises three times – at intervals bowing to the walls, continually repeating Aves, and Pater Nosters, and removing beads.*

Most wells did not have a chapel beside them as Ardmore did. Dr Patrick Logan, in his excellent book *The Holy Wells of Ireland*, tells how the pilgrims at holy wells generally started by reciting five decades of the rosary, then approached the well and knelt beside it saying more prayers, subsequently walking three times around the well before finally drinking some water from it and filling a bottle with the holy water to bring home. Often associated with the wells were bullauns and sacred trees, as well as piles of stones, to which each pilgrim would add a new stone. 19th-century commentators often expressed shock at seeing devotees walking around the well or the stones or the tree on their knees, until these were bruised and bloodied. Such a spectacle prompted Hardy to ask: 'Why allow him to try to save himself by such painful performances as could only please a deity who delighted in the misery of his creatures?'

The trees that often exist beside a well still have rags tied to them, as seen strikingly at Seir Kieran, County Offaly, or at the Well of Doon, County Donegal, which may have only become a place of pilgrimage as late as the 18th century. These rags – often red or white – are probably placed on the tree so that any ailment the pilgrim might have will be left at the holy well, and he or she will be cured. At Clonenagh, County Laois, the rags have been replaced by thousands of coins hammered into the tree by passers-by; legend has it that when the neighbouring well dried up, the water rose and formed a pool in the branches of the tree (Fig. 102). Crutches are known to have been left at wells by those who felt cured at the spot, and the modern pilgrim often deposits a medal or rosary beads or even coins in the hope of obtaining the intercession of the saint in curing whatever ails him.

In trying to find out what motivated a pilgrim to go to a holy well, Rev Charles O Conor of Bellanagare, a noted 18th-century antiquary – according to his 'Third Letter to Columbanus', addressed to his brother The O Conor Don – pressed an old man named Owen Hester who had visited wells in Roscommon to:

> . . . state what possible advantage he expected to derive from the singular custom of frequenting in particular such wells as were contiguous to an old blasted oak or an upright unhewn stone and what the meaning was of the yet more singular custom of sticking rags on the branches of such trees and spitting on them - his answer, and the answer of the oldest men, was that their ancestors always did it: that it was a preservative against Geasu-Draoidacht, i.e. the sorceries of the druids: that their cattle were preserved by it, from infections and disorders: that the daoini maethe, i.e. the fairies, were kept in good humour by it: and so thoroughly persuaded were they of the sanctity of those pagan practices that they would travel bareheaded and barefooted from ten to twenty miles for the purpose of crawling on their knees round these wells, and upright stones and oak trees westward as the sun travels, some three times, some six, some nine, and so on, in uneven numbers until their voluntary penances were completely fulfilled.

So, penance was one of the purposes of pilgrimage to holy wells. Another, not specifically mentioned by Hester, was search for a personal cure, and individual wells were famed for curing particular ailments: eye problems, headaches, backache, toothache, sprains, rheumatism etc. Even madness is known to have been cured. At one holy well at Kilbarry in Roscommon, where the patient spent three nights in a darkened house, and slept on stone slabs, called 'saints's beds', in search of a cure, the regime was reminiscent of the treatment provided for the ancient Greek clients of the healing god Asclepius at Epidauros and elsewhere.

In the same way that the larger pilgrimages fulfilled a psychological and religious need for those taking part, the holy wells did the same at local level for

those unable to spend possibly weeks going on the larger pilgrimages. But a recent thesis by Elisabeth Walther on holy wells in Counties Galway and Mayo has demonstrated that, even in rural areas, attendances at holy wells have been steadily declining, to such an extent that a number have been abandoned, and in certain cases even the location of the well has been forgotten by all but the older inhabitants. Local initiative, based on old traditions, has, it would seem, been allowed to decline in favour of the larger and nationally recognised pilgrimages to places such as Croagh Patrick and Lough Derg, and in favour of the more recent Marian pilgrimage to Knock in County Mayo, where the Catholic Church is in a better position to supervise the religious practices and to provide the necessary facilities for those wanting to continue Ireland's age-old pilgrimage tradition.

As we have seen, during the 18th and the first half of the 19th century the Catholic Church closed down pattern days at a number of holy wells because of the drunkenness and debauchery so often recorded. But it has allowed the purely religious aspect of the pilgrimage to survive and prosper, and priests can often be found leading the faithful at prayers on the site. One case of a successful rural pilgrimage revival of recent years is that to St Patrick's Well at Mauméan, about 1200 feet up a mountain in Connemara, where the 19th-century pilgrimage was revived during the last decade.

The Mauméan well is one of a number of holy wells, particularly in the northern half of the country, dedicated to the most famous of Ireland's three national apostles. A great number of wells also are dedicated to St Brigid of Kildare, another of the trio. Logan has pointed out that at some of them her cult has replaced that of earlier saints, a process analogous to what seems to have happened at some of the major national pilgrimage sites such as Lough Derg and the Dingle Peninsula.

But in general, the holy wells of the Irish countryside are dedicated to the saint who lived, died and is venerated in the locality. Nevertheless, Caoimhín Ó Danachair's study of the holy wells in the Dingle Peninsula showed that this was not universally the case. There is no longer any tradition there of a well dedicated to the local saint, Malkedar, from whom the main church of the peninsula gets its name. Instead, Ó Danachair found that dedications in the peninsula were not exclusive even to Kerry saints; the dedications included, not unnaturally, St Brendan who had a total of five, but also St Manchán and Fionan, who had one each. The Deity had one fewer dedications than Brendan, and Our Lady two fewer (perhaps, as with the case of church dedications, well dedications to the Virgin may not be much earlier than about the 12th century). The non-Kerry saints represented included St Gobnait of Ballyvourney in three dedications, St Ciarán of Clonmacnois (or possibly of Seir?) in two, while Saints Brigid of Kildare, Enda of Aran and Molaga of Labbamolaga in Cork each had a well dedicated to them.

These latter saints are interesting in the present context as they are saints to whose tombs pilgrims are known to have resorted in ancient or modern times, or both. One gets the impression that in the Dingle Peninsula, itself a highly

Fig. 102 *When St Fintan's Holy Well ran dry at Clonenagh, County Laois, on the road from Mountrath to Portlaoise, the water climbed to a hollow in the tree, into the bark of which thousands of coins have been hammered. The priest is in the hollow*

significant area of pilgrimage, wells were dedicated to saints to whose tombs pilgrims might be expected to go at other times, and the same would appear to have been the case with church dedications at pilgrimage sites such as Glendalough, where there was traditionally a total of 'Seven Churches'. Both wells and churches may thus, in certain instances, have belonged to a network of pilgrimage sites that were interlinked with one another. There may, indeed, have been a number of such networks covering particular parts of the country, which may have been largely, though not entirely, exclusive of one another.

An interesting case in point is revealed along the west and northern coast of Ireland, where we find wells dedicated to St Brendan and St Colmcille (Columba), dedications which extend far into Scotland where their cults were also widespread. St Brendan's wells were already noted in the Dingle Peninsula, but their distribution on the Irish west coast extends northwards to include the pilgrimage road to Croagh Patrick and the island of Inishglora off the Belmullet Peninsula in County Mayo. The next-door island to the south is Inishkea North, where a church (and, if we only knew, probably originally a well also) was dedicated to St Colmcille, as was also the case on the island of Inishturk further south in the same county of Mayo. St Colmcille does not seem to have been represented in well dedications in the Dingle Peninsula, but is most popular in his native county of Donegal, where St Brendan was apparently not the subject of old well dedications, though one of the 'beds' at Lough Derg still bears his name. It looks as if the islands off the west coast of Mayo may have been the territory where the cults of the two saints crossed (and even clashed?) with one another, that of St Colmcille being stronger further north, and that of St Brendan further south, where it may also have included a network associated with St Enda of Aran, who was one of the saints to whom a well was dedicated on the Dingle Peninsula.

CHAPTER 23

CONCLUSION: THE GOLDEN PILGRIM AGE

'THE HISTORY OF A NATION WAS', THE POET W. B. YEATS SAID, 'NOT IN parliaments and battlefields but in what the people say to each other on fair-days and high days, and in how they farm and quarrel, and go on pilgrimage'. For Ireland, that pilgrimage is a pious exercise that has helped to fulfil religious needs and yearnings for more than 1400 years. St Colmcille's departure from the country in 563 and his subsequent voyage to Iona was interpreted at the time as a pilgrimage, and our first historical reference to someone dying on pilgrimage within Ireland dates from as early as the first decade of the 7th century. Other than the forty or fifty similar instances that have been laconically recorded in the old Irish annals, we really have very little factual information about early Irish pilgrimage, so it has been neglected when compared to the incomparably better-documented monastic aspect of religious life in Early Christian Ireland.

Pilgrimage was, of course, a constituent part of that religious experience, yet one that was undertaken not by the whole monastic community in unison, but by individual clerics, probably often towards the end of their lives, when they would have been more interested in securing a place in heaven than in setting down in writing how they were going to get there – Celedabhaill (or whoever wrote the poem attributed to him) being the only articulate exception. A further factor contributing to our lack of information on the subject is that it was, in the poet Seamus Heaney's words, a 'peasant pilgrimage', and therefore an activity practised in much greater numbers by a lay majority, who were also a silent majority because they never wrote about their experiences – or, if they did, their accounts have not survived the intervening centuries. But the comparative scarcity of references to Irish pilgrimage in the early historical sources should not lull us into neglecting it or thinking that it scarcely existed, for we know that pilgrimage played an important role in Europe during the medieval period, and why should Christian Ireland have been an exception?

Indeed, in a number of ways, Ireland is likely to have followed the lead of other European countries. Its pilgrims travelled to Rome where they would have followed the circuit of the 'seven churches' – an epithet that was subsequently associated with a number of important Irish pilgrimage sites, where the proliferation of small churches probably represents an international imitation of the Roman model. In Rome, too, the Irish pilgrims would have learned to collect secondary relics: earth from the martyrs' tombs and *brandea* (or rags) that would have come into physical contact with them. The Irish pilgrims would almost certainly have brought such relics back home with them, and would have begun to collect relics in a similar fashion from the tombs of their own native saints.

But, in other respects, pilgrimage in and from Ireland differed significantly from the European norm. In the first place, the early Irish Church was differently organised, led by the abbots of scattered monasteries and not, as elsewhere, by bishops based in large urban centres inherited from the late Roman Empire. Secondly, the earliest Irish pilgrims appear to have been clerics who went abroad on pilgrimage for the sake of the Lord and their own immortal souls, but with the avowed intention of staying away permanently and never returning home. In time, these Irish *peregrini* wandering on the Continent became a thorn in the side of the order-loving Carolingian administrators, until, during the final years of Charlemagne's life, they were finally forbidden to circulate freely in his empire.

Soon after this tide had begun to turn against the Irish *peregrini* during the second half of the 8th century, a profound change took place in the character of Irish pilgrimage. The guiding hand of the Church turned pilgrims' thoughts away from travel abroad, and encouraged the flock instead to stay at home and heed the advice, 'to go to Rome, much labour, little profit.'

This reversal in pilgrimage practice came at a time when the cult of relics was experiencing a remarkable expansion, and it is the combination of these two factors which provides the vital, if now largely vanished, clues to our understanding of pilgrimage development in Ireland in the decades around 800. After the siege of Rome in 756, the papacy started to exhume the relics of early martyrs from the catacombs, and distributed them to Roman churches in the hope that they would assist in preventing future destruction of the city. Before the end of the century, relics had become a requirement for the dedication of new church altars, and the catacombs ensured that the Eternal City was able to meet the growing demand for them. Relics were sent in caravan-loads northwards across the Alps, and sold there to gullible buyers rapacious to enlarge their collections. That Ireland, too, looked for its share is suggested by two Irish (or 'Hiberno-Scottish') house-shaped shrines recently discovered in Italy, which were probably brought there empty so that they could transport Roman relics homewards on a return journey that never took place. Just such house-shaped shrines were probably created to house the relics of Conlaed and Ronan mentioned in the annals in 800-1; at around the same time some of the more important Irish monasteries, such as Clonmacnois, began to build permanent stone shrines around the tombs of their founding saints. If the reason for their construction was to prevent excessive touching of the holy person's relics, and if the house-shaped and other shrines were designed to assist in the reverent display, parade and transport of sacred bones and belts, we would have good grounds for thinking that lay participation in Irish pilgrimage may have expanded considerably in the period around 800, whereby increased visits to, and veneration of, relics would have had the beneficial result of enriching the people spiritually – and the monasteries materially. The recommendation that pilgrims should stay in Ireland, and the provision of new reliquaries, certainly suggest that something new was stirring on the Irish religious scene in around 800, in the wake of the spiritual reforms initiated by the Culdee (Servants of God) movement, which vigorously discouraged pilgrimage outside the bounds of Ireland.

In search of a suitable replacement for the journey across the Irish Sea to Rome, the Church must have looked westwards, where the difficult waters of the Atlantic coast could provide as much physical and penitential hardship as any pilgrimage to Italy. There, too, the Lughnasa festival gatherings on mountains such as Croagh Patrick and Mount Brandon provided an annual framework that could easily be adapted for Christian pilgrimage by subtly transforming the cult of the Celtic god Lug into that of a nationally popular saint. The offshore islands of the south-west, west and north coasts of Ireland would already have been endowed with a spiritual aura through the hermits who would have sought the solitary life on them in previous centuries. Islands such as Skellig and the Magharees (Illauntannig) in Kerry, the Aran Islands, St MacDara's and Ardoileán (High Island) in County Galway, Caher, Duvillaun, the Inishkeas and Inishglora off the Mayo coast, Inishmurray in Sligo and Rathlin O'Birne and Tory in Donegal, all preserve ecclesiastical monuments that could be interpreted as the result of possible new pilgrimage activity revolving around veneration of the graves of hermits who had lived and died there.

The west of Ireland was also the starting-point for the *Navigatio Brendani*, probably a creation of the 9th century which expands on earlier stories of ocean adventures. It is an imaginative tale about what is specifically stated to have been a pilgrimage undertaken by St Brendan from the west coast of Ireland to a host of wondrous islands in search of the Promised Land of the Saints. The *Navigatio* can be interpreted simply as a pilgrimage of the mind, designed by the Church as an armchair substitute for a real pilgrimage to Rome. But it can also be taken to provide what may be our only literary reflection of genuine pilgrimages to islands off Ireland's western shores, not only direct from the mainland, but also hopping from island to island, as the *Navigatio* portrays St Brendan doing. Seaborne pilgrimage traffic up and down the coast can be deduced from the spread of the cult of maritime saints like Brendan and Colmcille, which is reflected in church and holy well dedications on islands along the Atlantic coasts of Ireland and Scotland, and which also found a foothold on mainland locations such as the Dingle Peninsula and Glencolmcille. It is the Dingle Peninsula that provides our most striking archaeological confirmation of the former existence of a western maritime pilgrimage in that its pilgrimage road to the cult centre on Mount Brandon starts not at the landward end of the peninsula but near a fine landing place close to its western extremity. The wide variety of the peninsula's stone monuments such as beehive huts, cross-bearing pillars and Ogham stones really only begins to make sense when seen in conjunction with the pilgrimage to Mount Brandon in honour of St Brendan, and Kilmalkedar presents us with a microcosm containing the great majority of what we might describe as 'pilgrimage monuments'.

There is very little historical documentation concerning sites on the Dingle Peninsula and on the islands off the western and northern coasts, and certainly nothing that would warrant the presumption that they were inhabited permanently by anything other than small communities, who may have been responsible for organising the maritime pilgrimages and providing shelter for their participants. Some of the islands only come into the light of history when they are mentioned as places raided by the Vikings in the early decades of the 9th century. The sudden appearance of these Norsemen on the Atlantic seaways may have curbed the maritime pilgrimage just as it was getting into its stride, so that subsequent pilgrimage to islands may have been largely undertaken from the mainland.

The Viking raids may have taken a similar toll on mainland pilgrimage. This can be inferred from the absence of references to pilgrims' deaths in the Irish annals between the years 834 and 950, a period which opened with a noticeably increased frequency and ferocity of Viking raids on inland monasteries. The pilgrim deaths recorded by the annals prior to 834 all took place at Clonmacnois, but this circumstance may reflect a strong Clonmacnois contribution to annal-writing, rather than suggesting that Clonmacnois was the only place of pilgrimage in Ireland before that date. References to pilgrims' deaths in the annals start to increase again after 950, and a much greater variety of (pilgrimage) sites at which pilgrims die is recorded. It is scarcely a coincidence that at almost exactly the same time we begin to find annalistic entries concerning round towers, some of them on documented pilgrimage sites. These towers, therefore, were probably built by the monks not for their own protection but in conjunction with the new wave of pilgrimage traffic which was presumably restarted with renewed vigour after the Vikings had begun to settle down and even intermarry with the Irish.

To judge by the annalistic entries for pilgrim deaths, the two hundred years after the turn of the millennium are likely to have been the centuries that experienced the greatest lay pilgrimage activity in Ireland. In this, they mirror the pattern on the European continent, where pilgrimage was accompanied by the construction of a myriad of beautiful churches in the Romanesque style, particularly on the road to Santiago. The location of Irish churches in the same style makes a strong case for associating their introduction into the country in the 1120s with the increasing pilgrimage traffic. Even where churches do not display the decorative elements of the Romanesque style, they may have been erected to cater for pilgrimage traffic, as on the Aran Islands where the almost featureless churches – and the high crosses – are likely to date from the 11th to 12th centuries.

Where we know that monastic communities existed on sites which still preserve such monuments, we can presume that it was the monks who built them. But consideration of why a community would have built a round tower or pilgrimage road would suggest that many ecclesiastical monuments surviving on ancient monastic sites were constructed not just for the internal use of the communities themselves, but more probably in order to service the lucrative pilgrimage traffic as well. Even where monastic communities are not recorded in the historical sources, as on the Dingle Peninsula, we ought to presume that the Church and its personnel would have been responsible for constructing the monuments. How else could one envisage the provision of the extensive terracing necessary to support the beehive huts on Skellig Rock?

The extensive activity of the 12th century gave Ireland the pilgrimage which has made it best known internationally – Lough Derg in County Donegal, where we can still see many 'a pilgrim bent and whispering on his rounds', in the words of Seamus Heaney. Lough Derg sprang to fame through the influence of the

Normans, who invaded Ireland in 1169. Their arrival is unlikely to have had the same devastating effect on pilgrimage traffic that Ireland experienced under their Nordic predecessors more than three centuries earlier. They even used relics to bolster up their own importance, as we can see from John de Courcy's 'discovery' of the relics of Saints Patrick, Brigid and Colmcille at Downpatrick in 1185. They would have curbed pilgrimage in the old Irish tradition within their newly won territories, but it must have continued during the later medieval period in the Gaelic parts of Ireland not under their domination. Adequate testimony for this is provided by the wooden statues surviving from Inishmurray and Ballyvourney, as well as by others known to have existed at Lough Derg, on St MacDara's Island and Inishkea North, and also by the houses at Temple Brecán, Kilmacduagh, Kilmalkedar and Banagher. The sites visited by Heneas MacNichaill on his penitential tour of Ireland in the 1540s show, too, the number of pilgrimages that must have been still very much alive in his day. But the destruction of some of Ireland's most sacred relics by the Reformation zealots of the same period provides an indication that the state authorities must have been trying to abolish the pilgrimage 'idolatry' which they would have associated with them. The Counter-Reformation responded in the early 17th century by granting special indulgences to chosen pilgrimage locations: that 15,000 people were recorded as having participated in the annual pilgrimages to Inishcealtra and Monaincha in 1609-11 is a number that speaks for itself.

In the medieval period, Lough Derg was the only Irish pilgrimage that was well documented – thanks to the foreign correspondents who wrote accounts of their experiences. After 1600, observations made about Irish pilgrimages are often much more critical, because they emanated from commentators with a very different religious background who found Irish practices at these annual events abhorrent to their principles. But, by the beginning of the 19th century, even the Catholic Church in Ireland had become cynical about these 'pilgrimages'. In 1877, Thomas Johnson Westropp records a boatman describing the Inishcealtra pilgrimage of an earlier generation as 'flotillas of boats from every side of the great lake, the villages of tents, and the crowds of beggars, devotees and merrymakers'; something of the festive atmosphere of a midsummer fair is evident, too, from Peacock's painting of the Glendalough pilgrimage of 1813 (Plate VIII).

Already, the penitential aspects of these 'pilgrimages' were taking second place to the 'drunkenness and debauchery' and faction-fighting described in contemporary sources, so the Catholic Church finally felt constrained to suppress the pilgrimages it had instituted and organised more than a thousand years before. The more religious aspect of pilgrimage has continued unabated to today at Croagh Patrick and Lough Derg, and they are among the few surviving pilgrimages where the strict regime gives any idea of the harshness of their medieval predecessors. Otherwise, it is only at the patterns held at holy wells that the age-old customs are still preserved at local level, though these are, sadly, fast disappearing.

Pilgrimage can thus be seen to have had a virtually unbroken tradition in Ireland for almost 1500 years, despite ups and downs. It has helped to keep the faith of a nation alive even in the darkest times, but its most active and innovative period is likely to have been the years between 800 and 1200. Most of the ancient monuments on old monastic sites which could be associated with pilgrimage are most likely to belong to these years. They could therefore be appropriately entitled the Golden Pilgrim Age in Ireland.

BIBLIOGRAPHY

To avoid footnotes, I have listed reference works consulted in the preparation of this book below, chapter by chapter; specific works concerning particular places or things are also included. The order of these works in the bibliography is determined by the relative position of their subject matter in the text, except for those listed at the beginning of a chapter, which refer to works already cited in previous chapters. Where the title of a work does not suggest any obvious association with the text, an indication of its relevance is given in brackets at the end of the reference. In certain instances, only the relevant pages, and not the full pagination of the article, are quoted.

The following abbreviations are used:

ed. or eds.	editor or editors
JCHAS	Journal of the Cork Historical and Archaeological Society
JCKAS	Journal of the (County) Kildare Archaeological Society
JGAHS	Journal of the Galway Archaeological and Historical Society
JRSAI	Journal of the Royal Society of Antiquaries of Ireland
MDI	Journal of the Society for the Preservation of the Memorials of the Dead, Ireland
NMAJ	North Munster Antiquarian Journal
PRIA	Proceedings of the Royal Irish Academy
UJA	Ulster Journal of Archaeology

CHAPTER 1

Kötting, Bernhard, *Peregrinatio Religiosa, Wallfahrten in der Antike und das Pilgerwesen in der alten Kirche.* Forschungen zur Volkskunde 33/34/35, Regensburg/Münster, 1950 (reprinted 1980).

Sumption, Jonathan, *Pilgrimage, an Image of medieval Religion*, London, 1975.

Rollason, David, *Saints and Relics in Anglo-Saxon England*, Oxford, 1989.

Geary, Patrick J., *Furta Sacra, Thefts of Relics in the Central Middle Ages*, Princeton, 1978.

Kriss-Rettenbeck, Lenz, and Gerda Möhler (eds.), *Wallfahrt kennt keine Grenzen*, Munich, 1984.

Stalley, Roger, 'Sailing to Santiago: medieval pilgrimage to Santiago de Compostela and its artistic influence in Ireland', in John Bradley (ed.), *Settlement and Society in Medieval Ireland, Studies presented to F. X. Martin, o.s.a.*, Kilkenny, 1988, pp. 397-420.

Clyne, Miriam, 'A medieval pilgrim: from Tuam to Santiago de Compostela', *Archaeology Ireland* 4 (3), 1990, pp. 21-2.

CHAPTER 2

See the first five items listed above under Chapter 1.

McDonald, Eddie, 'Riches of Clonmore (Part 2)', *Carloviana*, 1981, pp. 13-14.

FitzGerald, Lord Walter, 'Father Moore's Well at Rathbride, Co. Kildare', *JCKAS* 7, 1912, pp. 329-32.

Henry, P. L., *The Early English and Celtic Lyric*, London, 1966.

Meyer, Kuno (ed. and transl.), *Liadain and Curithir, An Irish Love-story of the Ninth Century*, London 1902.

O'Donovan, John (ed.), *Annals of the Kingdom of Ireland, by the Four Masters*, 7 vols., Dublin, 1851 (reprinted Dublin, 1990).

CHAPTER 3

Bede, The Venerable, *Ecclesiastical History of the English People* (translated by Leo Sherley-Price), Harmondsworth, 1955 (latest paperback reprint London, 1990).

Kenney, James F., *The Sources for the Early History of Ireland: I, Ecclesiastical*, New York, 1929 (latest reprint Dublin, 1979).

Costello, Con, *Ireland and the Holy Land*, Dublin, 1974.

Tierney, J. J. (ed.), *Dicuili Liber de Mensura Orbis Terrae*, Scriptores Latini Hiberniae VI, Dublin, 1967.

Meehan, Denis (ed.), *Adomnan's* De Locis Sanctis, Scriptores Latini Hiberniae III, Dublin 1958 (reprinted 1983).

Mac Airt, Seán, *The Annals of Inisfallen (Ms. Rawlinson B. 503)*, Dublin, 1944 (reprinted 1988).

Lynn, C. J., 'Some fragments of exotic porphyry found in Ireland', *Journal of Irish Archaeology* 2, 1984, pp. 19-32.

Ó Laoghaire, Diarmuid, 'Irish spirituality', in Próinséas Ní Chatháin and Michael Richter (eds.), *Ireland and Europe, The Early Church*, Stuttgart, 1984, pp. 73-82 (*rómh*).

Meyer, Kuno, *Betha Colmáin Maic Lúacháin, Life of Colmán son of Lúachan*, Royal Irish Academy, Todd Lecture Series XVII, Dublin, 1911 (reprinted 1943).

Gougaud, Louis, *Christianity in Celtic Lands*, London, 1932.

CHAPTER 4

See Kötting, 1950 (Chapter 1); Bede, 1955, and Kenney, 1929 (Chapter 3).

Hennessy, William M. (ed.), *Annals of Ulster*, 4 vols., Dublin, 1887-1901.

Mac Airt, Seán, and Gearóid Mac Niocaill (eds.), *The Annals of Ulster (to A.D 1131)*, Dublin, 1983.

Charles-Edwards, T. M., 'The social background to Irish *peregrinatio*', *Celtica* 11, 1976, pp. 43-59.

Byrne, Mary E., 'On the punishment of sending adrift', *Ériu* 11, 1932, pp. 97-102.

MacDonald, A. D. S., 'Aspects of the monastery and monastic life in Adomnan's Life of Columba', *Peritia* 3, 1984, pp. 292-3.

Angenendt, Arnold, 'Die irische Peregrinatio and ihre Auswirkungen auf dem Kontinent vor dem Jahre 800', in Heinz Löwe (ed.), *Die Iren und Europa im früheren Mittelalter*, vol. I, Stuttgart, 1982, pp. 52-79.

Leclercq, Jean, 'Mönchtum und Peregrinatio im Frühmittelalter', *Römische Quartalschrift* 55, 1960, pp. 212-25.

Hughes, Kathleen, 'The changing theory and practice of Irish Pilgrimage', *Journal of Ecclesiastical History* 11, 1960, pp. 143-51.

Pochin Mould, Daphne D. C., *Irish Pilgrimage*, Dublin, 1955.

CHAPTER 5

See Kenney, 1929, and Tierney, 1967 (Chapter 3); Hughes, 1960 (Chapter 4).

Selmer, Carl (ed.), *Navigatio Sancti Brendani Abbatis from Early Latin Manuscripts*, Publications in Medieval Studies, Notre Dame, 1959 (reprinted Blackrock, 1989). See also the review by James Carney in *Medium Aevum* 32, 1963, pp. 37-44.

O'Meara, John J., *The Voyage of Saint Brendan: journey to the Promised Land*, Dublin, 1978.

Dillon, Myles, *Early Irish Literature*, Chicago, 1948, pp. 101-31 (adventure and voyage tales).

Dumville, D., '*Echtrae* and *Immram*: some problems of definition', *Ériu* 27, 1976, pp. 73-94.

Mac Mathúna, Séamus, *Immram Brain, Bran's Journey to the Land of the Women*, Tübingen, 1985.

Meyer, Kuno and Alfred Nutt (eds.), *The Voyage of Bran Son of Febal*, 2 vols., London, 1895-7.

MacCana, P., 'On the "prehistory" of Immram Brain', *Ériu* 26, 1975, pp. 33-52.

Oskamp, Hans Pieter Atze, *The Voyage of Máel Dúin*, Groningen, 1970.

Stokes, Whitley, 'The Voyage of Snedgus and Mac Riagla', *Revue Celtique* 9, 1988, pp. 14-25.

Stokes, Whitley, 'The Voyage of the Húi Corra', *Revue Celtique* 14, 1893, pp. 22-69.

Plummer, Charles, *Irish Litanies*, Henry Bradshaw Society LXII, London, 1925, pp. 60-75 (Litany of Irish Saints – II).

Harbison, P., 'St Kilda and St Brendan', *St Kilda Mail* 13, April 1989, pp. 27-8.

Severin, Tim, *The Brendan Voyage*, London, 1978 (latest paperback reprint London, 1990)

Wallace, J. N. A., 'Carved stone pillar at Bantry, Co. Cork', *NMAJ* 2, 1940-1, pp. 153-5.

Macalister, R. A. S., 'A drawing in the Pepysian Library', *JRSAI* 56, 1926, 119-20.

Farrell, A. W., S. Penny and E. M. Jope, 'The Broighter Boat: a reassessment', *Irish Archaeological Research Forum* II (2), 1975, pp. 15-28.

Ellmers, Detlev, 'Keltischer Schiffbau', *Jahrbuch des Römisch-Germanischen Zentralmuseums Mainz* 16, 1969, pp. 108-12 (Broighter boat).

MacCana, Proinsias, 'The voyage of St. Brendan: literary and historical origins', in John De Courcy Ireland and David C. Sheehy (eds.), *Atlantic Visions*, Dun Laoghaire, 1989, pp. 3-16.

Anderson, Alan Orr and Marjorie Ogilvie, *Adomnan's Life of Columba*, London, 1961 (2nd revised edition 1991).

Lethbridge, T. C., *Herdsmen and Hermits, Celtic Seafarers in the Northern Seas*, Cambridge, 1950.

Donaldson, Gordon, *A Northern Commonwealth: Scotland and Norway*, Edinburgh (The Saltire Society), 1991.

Eldjárn, Kristján, 'Papey, Fornleifarannsóknir 1967-1981', *Árbók Hins Íslenzka Fornleifafélags* 1988 (1989), pp. 35-88 (with English summary).

Ó Caoimh, Tomas, 'St Brendan sources: St Brendan and early Irish hagiography', in John De Courcy Ireland and David C. Sheehy (eds.), *Atlantic Visions*, Dun Laoghaire, 1989, pp. 17-24.

Heist, W. W., *Vitae Sanctorum Hiberniae ex codice olim Salmanticensi nunc Bruxellensi*, Brussels, 1965, pp. 324-31 (first life of St Brendan).

Hughes, Kathleen, 'On an Irish litany of pilgrim saints compiled c.800', *Analecta Bollandiana* 77, 1959, pp. 305-31.

Sanderlin, Sarah, 'The date and provenance of the "Litany of Irish Pilgrim Saints – II" (the Irish Litany of Pilgrim Saints)', *PRIA* 75 C, 1975, pp. 251-62.

MacKinlay, James Murray, *Ancient Church Dedications in Scotland, Non-scriptural Dedications*, Edinburgh, 1914, pp. 65-7.

Stokes, Whitley, *Lives of Saints from the Book of Lismore*, Anecdota Oxoniensia, Oxford, 1890, pp. 99-116 and 247-61 (Life of St Brendan).

Dunraven, Edwin, Third Earl of, *Notes on Irish Architecture* (ed. Margaret Stokes), vol. I, London, 1875, pp. 40-4 (Inishglora).

Best, Richard Irvine and Hugh Jackson Lawlor, *The Martyrology of Tallaght*, Henry Bradshaw Society LXVIII, London, 1931.

Bowen, E. G., *Saints, Seas and Settlements in the Celtic Lands*, Cardiff, 1969 (latest paperback reprint, 1988).

CHAPTER 6

See O'Donovan, 1851 (Chapter 2); Mac Airt, 1944 (Chapter 3); Hennessy, 1887-1901, Hughes, 1960 and Pochin Mould, 1955 (Chapter 4); and Hughes, 1959 (Chapter 5).

Ní Chearbhaill, Máire, *Places of Pilgrimage in Continental Europe, Ireland and the United Kingdom*, Killala, 1984.

MacCana, Proinsias, 'Placenames and mythology in Irish tradition: places, pilgrimages and things', in Gordon W. MacLennan (ed.), *Proceedings of the First North American Congress of Celtic Studies*, Ottawa, 1988, pp. 319-41.
Plummer, Charles, *Bethada Náem nÉrenn, Lives of Irish Saints*, vol. ii, Oxford, 1922, p. 156 (Life of St Kevin).
Murphy, Denis (ed.), *The Annals of Clonmacnoise*, Dublin, 1896.
Stokes, Whitley, 'The Annals of Tigernach', *Revue Celtique* 16-18, 1895-7 (in various parts).
Best, R. I., 'The Leabhar Oiris', Ériu 1, 1904, 103 (Cork).
Hennessy, William M. (ed.), *The Annals of Loch Cé*, 2 vols., London 1871.
Gwynn, Aubrey, *The Medieval Province of Armagh, 1470-1545*, Dundalk, 1946, pp. 268-70 (Heneas MacNichaill).
Hogan, J., 'Miscellanea Vaticano-Hibernica, 1580-1631', *Archivium Hibernicum* III, 1914, p. 263 (indulgences granted by Pope Paul V).

CHAPTER 7

See above O'Donovan, 1851 (Chapter 2), and Hennessy, 1871 (Chapter 6).
Wagner, Margit, 'Tradition der Askese bei Wallfahrten in Irland', in L. Kriss-Rettenbeck and Gerda Möhler (eds.), *Wallfahrt kennt keine Grenzen*, Munich, 1984, pp. 45-54.
Leslie, Shane, *Saint Patrick's Purgatory, A Record from History and Literature*, London, 1932.
Picard, Jean-Michel, and Yolande de Pontfarcy, *Saint Patrick's Purgatory; a twelfth-century tale of a journey to the Other World* (with a foreword by Joseph Duffy), Blackrock, 1985.
Gerald of Wales (Giraldus Cambrensis), *The History and Topography of Ireland* (translated by John J. O'Meara), London, 1982 (reprinted 1988).
Gwynn, A., review of Alice Curtayne, *Lough Derg: St. Patrick's Purgatory, Studies* 33, 1944, pp. 550-4.
Ryan, John, 'Saint Patrick's Purgatory', *Studies* 21, 1932, pp. 443-60 (reprinted in *Clogher Record Album*, 1975, pp. 13-26).
Hennig, John, 'Studies in the Latin texts of the *Martyrology of Tallaght*, of *Félire Oengusso* and of *Félire húi Gormáin*', *PRIA* 69 C, 1970, pp. 45-112.
Haren, Michael, and Yolande de Pontfarcy (eds.), *The Medieval Pilgrimage to St. Patrick's Purgatory, Lough Derg and the European Tradition*, Clogher, 1988.
Stokes, Whitley (ed.), *The Tripartite Life of St Patrick*, 2 vols., London, 1887.
Gwynn, Aubrey, and R. Neville Hadcock, *Medieval Religious Houses, Ireland*, London, 1970 (reprinted Blackrock, 1988).
O'Donovan, John, *Ordnance Survey Letters . . . Co. Mayo*, vol. I, Bray, 1927 (islands off the Mayo coast).
Hanson, R. P. C., *The Life and Writings of the Historical Saint Patrick*, New York, 1983.
Tóchar Phádraig, Patrick's Causeway from Ballintubber to Croagh Patrick, A Pilgrim's Progress, Ballintubber, 1989.
Mannion, Brian, 'Togher Patrick', *Cathair na Mart, Journal of the Westport Historical Society* 7 (1), 1987, pp. 78-84.
Keville, John, 'Aughagower', *Cathair na Mart, Journal of the Westport Historical Society* 2, 1982, pp. 3-22.
MacNeill, Máire, *The Festival of Lughnasa*, Oxford 1962 (reprinted Dublin, 1982).

CHAPTER 8

See Selmer, 1959, Heist, 1965, and Hughes, 1959 (Chapter 5); Gwynn, 1946 (Chapter 6); Gerald of Wales, 1982, and Gwynn and Hadcock, 1970 (Chapter 7).
Lacy, Brian, *et al.*, *Archaeological Survey of County Donegal*, Lifford, 1983, 243, no. 1519 (Slieve League).
Meyer, Kuno, *Cath Finntrága – The Battle of Ventry*, Anecdota Oxoniensia, Oxford, 1885.
Cuppage, Judith, *et al.*, *Archaeological Survey of the Dingle Peninsula*, Ballyferriter, 1986.
MacDonagh, Steve, *A Visitor's Guide to the Dingle Peninsula*, Dingle, 1985.
O Conchúir, Doncha, *Corca Dhuibhne, Its People and Their Buildings*, Baile 'n Fhirtéaraigh 1977.
Macalister, R. A. Stewart, 'On an ancient settlement in the south-west of the Barony of Corkaguiney, County of Kerry', *Transactions of the Royal Irish Academy* 31, 1899, pp. 209-344 (beehive huts).
Barry, T. B., 'Archaeological excavations at Dunbeg promontory fort, County Kerry, 1977', *PRIA* 81 C, 1981, pp. 295-329 (radiocarbon date for beehive hut).
Harbison, Peter, 'How old is Gallarus Oratory?', *Medieval Archaeology* 14, 1970, pp. 34-59.
Fanning, T., 'Excavation of an Early Christian cemetery and settlement at Reask, County Kerry', *PRIA* 81 C, 1981, pp. 3-172.
Todd, James Henthorn, and Reeves, William (eds.), *The Martyrology of Donegal, A Calendar of the Saints of Ireland* [by Michael O'Clery], translated from the original Irish by John O'Donovan, Dublin, 1864.
Leask, H. G., *Early Irish Churches and Monastic Buildings*, vol. I, Dundalk, 1955 (reprinted 1977).
Bieler, Ludwig, 'Insular palaeography, present state and problems', *Scriptorium* III, 1949, 271 (Kilmalkedar alphabet stone).
Hamlin, Ann, 'A Chi-rho-carved stone at Drumaqueran, Co. Antrim', *UJA* 35, 1972, pp. 22-8 (Arraglen).
Macalister, R. A. S., *Corpus Inscriptionum Insularum Celticarum*, vol. I, Dublin, 1945 (Ogham inscriptions).
Macalister, R. A. S., 'The Ogham inscription at Maumanorig, Co. Kerry', *PRIA* 44 C, 1938, pp. 241-7.
Ó Danachair, Caoimhín, 'The holy wells of Corkaguiney, Co. Kerry', *JRSAI* 90, 1960, pp. 67-78.
de Paor, Liam, 'A survey of Sceilg Mhichíl', *JRSAI* 85, 1955, pp. 174-87.

Henry, F., 'Early Monasteries, Beehive huts, and dry-stone houses in the neighbourhood of Caherciveen and Waterville (Co. Kerry)', *PRIA* 58 C, 1957, pp. 45-166.

Harbison, Peter, 'John Windele's visit to Skellig Michael in 1851', *Journal of the Kerry Archaeological and Historical Society* 9, 1976, pp. 125-48.

Lavelle, Des, *Skellig, Island Outpost of Europe*, Dublin, 1976.

Sitwell, Sacheverell, *Dance of the Quick and the Dead*, London, 1936, p. 110.

Berger, Rainer, 'Radiocarbon dating of early medieval Irish monuments', forthcoming.

Horn, Walter, Jenny White Marshall and Grellan D. Rourke, *The Forgotten Hermitage of Skellig Michael*, Berkeley/Los Angeles/Oxford, 1990.

Westropp, T. J., 'The coast and islands of Co. Galway', in *Illustrated Guide to the Northern, Western and Southern Islands, and Coast of Ireland*, Dublin, 1905, pp. 45-53 (High Island), 54-5 (St MacDara's Island), 60-96 (Aran Islands).

Killanin, Lord, and Michael V. Duignan, *The Shell Guide to Ireland*, 2nd ed, London, 1967 (3rd edn Dublin 1989), pp. 58-63 (Aran Islands).

Robinson, T. D., *Oileáin Árann, the Aran Islands, Co. Galway, Eire: a map and a guide*, Kilronan, 1980.

Robinson, Tim, *Stones of Aran: pilgrimage*, Dublin, 1986 (reprinted Dublin/London, 1990).

O'Donovan, John, *Ordnance Survey Letters . . . County Galway*, vol. III, Bray, 1928; pp. 151-5 (St Colmcille's Farewell), 417-30 (Temple Coemháin).

Ryan, John, *Early Irish Monasticism*, Dublin, 1931 (reprinted Dublin, 1986).

Roderick O'Flaherty, *A Chorographical Description of H-Iar Connaught* (Hardiman, James [ed.]), written in 1684, Dublin, 1846.

O'Sullivan, Anne, 'Saint Brecán of Clare', *Celtica* 15, 1983, pp. 128-39.

Waddell, John, 'An archaeological survey of Temple Brecán, Aran', *JGAHS* 33, 1972-3, pp. 5-27.

Hughes, Kathleen, and Ann Hamlin, *The Modern Traveller to the Early Irish Church*, London, 1977 (reprinted New York, 1981, under the title *Celtic Monasticism*).

Macalister, R. A. S., *Corpus Inscriptionum Insularum Celticarum*, vol. II, Dublin, 1949 (half-uncial inscriptions).

Higgins, J. G., *The Early Christian Cross Slabs, Pillar Stones and Related Monuments of County Galway, Ireland*, BAR International Series 375, 2 vols., Oxford, 1987.

de Paor, Liam, 'The limestone crosses of Clare and Aran', *JGAHS* 26, 1955-6, pp. 53-71.

Waddell, John, 'Kilcholan: an early ecclesiastical site on Inishmore, Aran', *JGAHS* 35, 1976, pp. 86-8.

O'Donovan, John, *Ordnance Survey Letters . . . County Galway*, vol. III, Bray, 1928, pp. 116-25 (St MacDara's Island).

Caponigro, Paul, 'Saint MacDara's Church', *Ireland of the Welcomes* 39, no. 3, May-June 1990, pp. 26-30.

Wakeman, W. F., *A Survey of the Antiquarian Remains on the Island of Inishmurray*, London/Edinburgh, 1893.

Stokes, Whitley, *The Martyrology of Oengus the Culdee*, Henry Bradshaw Society XXIX, London, 1905 (reprinted Dublin, 1984).

Heraughty, Patrick, *Inishmurray, Ancient Monastic Island*, Dublin, 1982.

Marshall, Jenny White, *The spread of mainland paruchia to the Atlantic islands of Illauntannig, High Island and Inishmurray*. Ph.D. dissertation, Los Angeles, University of California, 1989.

O'Farrell, Fergus, 'The Inishmurray statue of St Molaise: a re-assessment', in E. Rynne (ed.), *Figures from the Past; studies on Figurative Art in Christian Ireland in honour of Helen M. Roe*, Dun Laoghaire, 1987, pp. 205-8.

Price, Liam, 'Glencolumbkille, County Donegal, and its early Christian cross-slabs', *JRSAI* 71, 1941, pp. 71-88.

McGill, P. J., 'Glencolmkille: its early Christian monuments and pilgrimages', *The Donegal Annual* 3 (3), 1957, pp. 120-7.

Herity, Michael, 'The antiquity of an *Turas* in Ireland', in Albert Lehner and Walter Berschin (eds.), *Lateinische Kultur im VIII. Jahrhundert, Traube-Gedenkschrift*, St Ottilien, 1989, pp. 95-143.

Herity, Michael, *Gleanncholmcille*, 2nd edn Glencolmcille, 1990.

Walsh, Paul, 'The monastic settlement on Rathlin O'Birne Island, County Donegal', *JRSAI* 113, 1983, pp. 53-66.

O'Kelleher, A., and G. Schoepperle (eds.), *Betha Colaim Chille, Life of Columcille, compiled by Manus O'Donnell*, Chicago, 1918.

CHAPTER 9

See Plummer, 1922 (Chapter 6); Gerald of Wales, 1982 (Chapter 7); Leask, 1955, Killanin and Duignan, 1967 and Wakeman, 1893 (Chapter 8).

Macalister, R. A. Stewart, *The Latin and Irish Lives of Ciaran*, London, 1921.

Ryan, John, *Clonmacnois, A Historical Summary*, Dublin, 1973.

Westropp, Thomas Johnson, 'A description of the ancient buildings and crosses at Clonmacnois, King's County', *JRSAI* 37, 1907, pp. 227-306 and 329-40.

Macalister, R. A. Stewart, *The Memorial Slabs of Clonmacnois, King's County*, Dublin, 1909.

Tubridy, Mary (ed.), *The Heritage of Clonmacnoise*, Dublin, 1987.

de Paor, Liam, 'The high crosses of Tech Theille (Tihilly), Kinnitty, and related sculpture', in E. Rynne (ed.), *Figures from the Past, Studies on Figurative Art in Christian Ireland in honour of Helen M. Roe*, Dun Laoghaire, 1987, pp. 131-58.

Otway, Caesar, *A Tour in Connaught: comprising sketches of Clonmacnoise, Joyce Country, and Achill*, Dublin, 1839, pp. 76-7.

Logan, Patrick, *The Holy Wells of Ireland*, Gerrard's Cross, 1980, pp. 23-4.

Barrow, Lennox, *Glendalough and St. Kevin*, Dundalk, 1972.

Leask, H. G., *Glendalough, Co. Wicklow* (no date).

Wilde, William, 'Memoir of Gabriel Beranger, and his labours in the cause of Irish art, literature and antiquities from 1760 to 1780', *JRSAI* 12, 1872-3, pp. 445-85 (Glendalough).

Petrie, George, 'The Ecclesiastical architecture of Ireland anterior to the Norman invasion, comprising an essay on the origin and uses of the round towers of Ireland', *Transactions of the Royal Irish Academy* 20, 1845, pp. 1-521 (also published separately), (pp. 245-8, Glendalough).

'Historical and descriptive notes with ground plans, elevations, sections and details of the ecclesiastical remains at Glendalough, Co. Wicklow', extract from the *80th Annual Report of the Commissioners of Public Works in Ireland* 1911-12.

Crawford, W. H., 'The patron, or festival of St Kevin at the Seven Churches, Glendalough, County Wicklow 1813', *Ulster Folklife* 32, 1986, pp. 37-47.

Bremer, W., 'Note on the Holywood stone', *JRSAI* 56, 1926 pp. 51-4 (with further references).

'Ancient pilgrim road excavated at Turlough Hill', *Electrical Mail*, August 1972, p. 1.

'Some notes on the investigations at St Kevin's Road', *Electrical Mail*, September 1972, p. 6.

Ryan, M., and P. Wallace, 'St Kevin's Rd (Brockagh td)', in Delaney, T. (ed.), *Excavations 1972* 29, no. 33.

Price, Liam, 'Glendalough: St Kevin's Road', in É. Ua Riain (ed.), *Féil-Sgríbhinn Eóin Mhic Néill*, Dublin, 1940, pp. 244-71.

O'Donovan, J., *Ordnance Survey Letters . . . County Galway*, vol. II, Bray 1928, pp. 118-69 (Kilmacduagh).

Colgan, J., *Acta Sanctorum . . . Hiberniae*, Louvain 1645, 244-7 (St MacDuagh)

Keating, Geoffrey, *The History of Ireland*, vol. III, Irish Texts Society, London, 1908, pp. 64-7.

Macalister, R. A. S., 'The history and antiquities of Inis Cealtra', *PRIA* 33 C, 1916, pp. 93-174.

de Paor, Liam, 'Saint Mac Creiche of Liscannor', *Ériu* 30, 1979, pp. 93-121 (Inishcealtra).

de Paor, Liam, section on 'Mountshannon' in Killanin, Lord, and Michael V. Duignan, *The Shell Guide to Ireland*, 3rd ed., Dublin/London, 1989, pp. 250-1 (Inishcealtra).

O'Conor, T., *Ordnance Survey Letters . . . County Galway*, Vol. II, Bray, 1928, pp. 561-82 (Inishcealtra).

Bigger, Francis Joseph, 'Inis Chlothrann (Inis Cleraun), Lough Ree: its history and antiquities', *JRSAI* 30, 1900, pp. 69-90.

Ledwich, Edward, *Antiquities of Ireland*, 2nd ed., Dublin, 1804, pp. 102-20 (Monaincha).

McNeill, C., and H. G. Leask, 'Monaincha, Co. Tipperary', *JRSAI* 50, 1920, pp. 19-35.

Cunningham, George, *Roscrea and District*, Roscrea, 1976, pp. 19-30 (Monaincha).

Harris, Dorothy C., 'Saint Gobnet, Abbess of Ballyvourney', *JRSAI* 78, 1938, pp. 272-7.

Articles on Ballyvourney by M. J. O'Kelly, F. Henry and D. Ó hEaluighthe in *Journal of the Cork Historical and Archaeological Society* 57, no. 185, 1952, pp. 18-61.

Hackett, William, 'The Irish Bacach, or professional beggar, viewed archaeologically', *UJA* 9, 1861-2, pp. 256-71.

Westropp, Thomas Johnson, 'Notes on the antiquities of Ardmore', *JRSAI* 33, 1903, pp. 353-80.

Fitzgerald, E., 'On St Declan's Oratory at Ardmore, County of Waterford, and the old Irish inscription built into its east end', *JRSAI* 3, 1854-5, pp. 223-31.

Power, Canon P., *Ardmore-Deaglain, A Popular Guide to the Holy City*, Waterford, 1919.

Smith, J. T., 'Ardmore Cathedral', *JRSAI* 102, 1972, pp. 1-13.

Fore, Co. Westmeath, Dublin (no date given).

CHAPTER 10

See also the bibliography for chapters 7-9.

Graves, James, 'The church and shrine of St Manchán', *JRSAI* 13, 1874-5, p. 139.

Devine, Joe, *Down the Great Road, A Journey to Lemonaghan*, 1989.

Wilde, William, *Loch Corrib*, Dublin, 1867, p. 148 (Inchagaoill).

Westropp, T. J., 'Clare Island Survey, Part 2: history and archaeology', PRIA 31, 1911: pp. 45-52 (Inishturk), 52-6 (Caher Island), 56-72 (Inishbofin) and 72-4 (Inishark).

Mulcahy, Michael, 'St. Declan's Road', *Ardmore Journal* 5, 1988, pp. 16-21.

CHAPTER 11

See Dunraven, 1875, pp. 105-7 (Chapter 5) for Termon Cronan; Henry, 1957, pp. 96-104 for Illaunloughan, Killoluaig and Killabuonia; Waddell, 1976, Wakeman, 1893 and Heraughty, 1982 (Chapter 8); Bigger, 1900 (Inchcleraun) and works on Glendalough, Inishcealtra and Ardmore cited above for Chapter 9.

Lynch, P. J., 'Leaba Molaga', *Journal of the North Munster Archaeological Society* 1, 1909, pp. 35-6.

ffrench, J. F. M., 'St Mullins, Co. Carlow', *JRSAI* 22, 1892, pp. 377-88.

O'Sullivan, T. F., 'Pattern Day at St Moling's', *Carloviana* 1976/77, p. 28.

O'Kelly, M. J., *Archaeological Survey and Excavation of St Vogue's Church, Enclosure and other monuments at Carnsore, Co. Wexford*, Dublin, 1975.

Macalister, R. A. S., 'The antiquities of Ardoileán, County Galway', *JRSAI* 26, 1896, pp. 197-210.

Herity, Michael, 'The High Island Hermitage', *Irish University Review* 7 (1), 1977, pp. 52-69.

Hill, Arthur, *Monograph of Cormac's Chapel, Cashel, Co. Tipperary*, Cork, 1874.

de Paor, Liam, 'Cormac's Chapel: the beginnings of Irish Romanesque', in E. Rynne (ed.), *North Munster Studies: essays in commemoration of Monsignor Michael Moloney*, Limerick, 1967, pp. 133-45.

St Patrick's Rock, Cashel (official guide, no date).

Thomas, Charles, *The Early Christian Archaeology of North Britain*, Oxford/London, 1971, pp. 132-66.

Westropp, T. J., ' "Slane in Bregia", County Meath: its friary and hermitage', *JRSAI* 31, 1901, p. 418.

Harbison, Peter, 'Some Romanesque heads from County Clare', *NMAJ* 15, 1972, pp. 3-5 (Termon Cronan).

Rourke, Grellan D. and White Marshall, Jenny, 'Illaunloughan – an Early Christian hermitage in County Kerry', forthcoming.

Waterman, D. M., 'Early Christian mortuary house at Saul, Co. Down', *UJA* 23, 1960, pp. 82-8.

Wakeman, W. F., 'On the ecclesiastical antiquities of Cluain-Eois, now Clones, County Monaghan' *JRSAI* 13, 1874-5, pp. 327-40.

Lang, J. T., 'The Castledermot Hogback', *JRSAI* 101, 1971, pp. 154-8.

Cogitosus, 'Sanctae Brigidae Virginis Vita', in J.-P. Migne (ed.), *Patrologiae cursus completus, Series Latina Prior* LXII, Paris 1878, pp. 775-90 (pp. 788-90, description of Kildare church and sarcophagi; English translation in L. Bieler, *Ireland, Harbinger of the Middle Ages*, London/New York/Toronto, 1963, p., 28).

CHAPTER 12

See Geary, 1978, pp. 141 and 183 (Chapter 1) for Killabban; Meyer, 1911 (Chapter 3); Mac Airt and Mac Niocaill, 1983 (Chapter 4); Stokes, 1887 (Chapter 7); Colgan, 1645, p. 276 (Chapter 9) for Onchu; Cogitosus, 1878 (Chapter 11) for Kildare.

Doherty, Charles, 'The use of relics in early Ireland', in Próinséas Ní Chatháin and Michael Richter (eds.), *Ireland and Europe, the Early Church*, Stuttgart, 1984, pp. 89-101.

Bourke, Cormac, 'Early Irish hand-bells', *JRSAI* 110, 1980, pp. 52-66.

Bourke, Cormac, 'Early Irish bells', *Journal of the Dromore Historical Society* 4, 1986, pp. 27-38.

Duignan, Michael, 'The Moylough and other Irish belt-reliquaries', *JGAHS* 24, 1951, pp. 83-94.

O'Kelly, Michael J., 'The belt-shrine from Moylough, Co. Sligo', *JRSAI* 95, 1965, pp. 149-88.

Harbison, P., 'The date of the Moylough belt shrine', in Donnchadh Ó Corráin (ed.), *Irish Antiquity: essays and studies presented to Professor M. J. O'Kelly*, Cork, 1981, pp. 231-9.

Bourke, Cormac, 'On the "crozier of Glendalough"', *Archaeology Ireland* 4 (4), 1990, pp. 10-11.

Lucas, A. T., 'The social role of relics and reliquaries in Ancient Ireland', *JRSAI* 116, 1986, pp. 5-37.

Gwynn, L., 'The reliquary of Adamnán', *Archivium Hibernicum* 4, 1915, pp. 199-214.

Cone, Polly, (ed.), *Treasures of Early Irish Art 1500 BC to 1500 AD*, New York, 1977, pp. 62 (St Lachtin's Arm), 185-6 (Clonmacnois Crozier) and 214-16 (Cross of Cong).

Harbison, Peter, 'The double-armed Cross on the church gable at Killinaboy, Co. Clare', *NMAJ* 18, 1976, pp. 3-12.

Raftery, Joseph, *Christian Art in Ancient Ireland*, vol. II, Dublin, 1941 (St Patrick's Relics).

Crawford, Henry S., 'A descriptive list of Irish shrines and reliquaries', *JRSAI* 53, 1923, pp. 74-93 and 151-76.

Youngs, Susan, (ed.), *The Work of Angels: masterpieces of Celtic metalwork, 6th-9th centuries AD*, London 1989, pp. 134-40 (house-shaped shrines).

Blindheim, Martin, 'A house-shaped Irish-Scots reliquary in Bologna, and its place among the other reliquaries', *Acta Archaeologica* 55, 1984, pp. 1-53.

Kendrick, T. D., and Elizabeth Senior, 'St Manchan's Shrine', *Archaeologia* 86, 1937, pp. 105-18.

Harbison, Peter, 'Early Irish reliquary-shrines in bronze and stone', *Würzburger Diözesangeschichtsblätter* 51, 1989, pp. 37-50.

O'Farrell, Fergus, '"The cross in the field", Kilfenora – part of a 'Founder's Tomb'?', *NMAJ* 26, 1984, pp. 8-12.

CHAPTER 13

Lucas, A. T., 'The plundering and burning of churches in Ireland, 7th to 16th century', in E. Rynne (ed.), *North Munster Studies: essays in commemoration of Monsignor Michael Moloney*, Limerick, 1967, pp. 172-230.

Barrow, George Lennox, *The Round Towers of Ireland; a study and gazetteer*, Dublin, 1979.

Stokes, Margaret, *Early Christian Architecture in Ireland*, London, 1878.

Hamlin, Ann, 'Documentary evidence for round towers', appendix to Michael Hare and Ann Hamlin, 'The study of early Church architecture in Ireland: an Anglo-Saxon viewpoint', in L. A. S. Butler and R. K. Morris (eds.), *The Anglo-Saxon Church: papers on history, architecture and archaeology in honour of Dr H. M. Taylor*, CBA Research Report 60, 1986, pp. 131-45.

Grimaldi, Giacomo, *Descrizione della Basilica Antica di S. Pietro in Vaticano, Codice Barberini Latino 2733* (edited by Reto Niggl), Vatican City, 1972.

Tronzo, William, 'Setting and structure in two Roman wall decorations of the Early Middle Ages', *Dumbarton Oaks Papers* 41, 1987, 477-92 (reference thanks to Professor Eamonn Ó Carragáin).

Rynne, Etienne, 'The round towers of Ireland – a review article', *NMAJ* 22, 1980, pp. 27-32.

Hennessy, William M., (ed.), *Chronicum Scotorum*, London, 1866.

CHAPTER 14

See Leask, 1955, p. 79ff. (Chapter 8) and de Paor 1967 (Chapter 11) for Romanesque churches.

Stalley, Roger, *The Cistercian Monasteries of Ireland*, London/New Haven, 1987.

Stalley, Roger, 'Three Irish buildings with west country origins', in N. Coldstream and P. Draper (eds.), *Medieval Art and Archaeology in Wells and Glastonbury*, British Archaeological Association 1981, pp. 62-80 (Cormac's Chapel).

Henry, Françoise, and George Zarnecki, 'Romanesque arches decorated with human and animal heads', *Journal of the British Archaeological Association* 3rd series, 20-1, 1957-8, pp. 1-34 (Dysert O'Dea).

Harbison, Peter, 'Two Romanesque carvings from Rath Blathmaic and Dysert O'Dea, Co. Clare', *NMAJ* 29, 1987, pp. 7-11.

Stalley, Roger, 'Architectural review and Proposed Programme of Restoration' in *The Restoration of Ardfert Cathedral, Feasibility Study* 1989, pp. 19-27.

Crawford, Henry S., 'The Romanesque doorway at Clonfert', *JRSAI* 42, 1912, pp. 1-7.

CHAPTER 15

See Dunraven, 1875 (Chapter 5); Macalister, 1899, de Paor, 1955, and Killanin and Duignan, 1967 (p. 310, Clonamery) (Chapter 8), and Westropp, 1911, pp. 45-52 (Chapter 10) for Inishark.

Rohlfs, Gerhard, 'Primitive Kuppelbauten in Europa', *Bayerische Akademie der Wissenschaften, Phil.-Hist. Klasse, Abhandlungen*, N.F., 43, 1957, pp. 1-37.

Ó Ríordáin, Seán P., and J. B. Foy, 'The excavation of Leacanabuaile stone fort, near Caherciveen, Co. Kerry', *JCHAS* 46, no. 164, 1941, pp. 85-99.

O'Flaherty, Brendan, 'Loher', in C. Cotter (ed.), *Excavations 1985, Summary Accounts of Archaeological Excavations in Ireland*, Dublin, 1986, pp. 26-7.

Graham, Angus, 'Some illustrated notes from Kerry', *JRSAI* 81, 1951, pp. 139-45 (beehive huts).

Aalen, F. H. A., 'Clochans as transhumance dwellings in the Dingle Peninsula, Co. Kerry', *JRSAI* 104, 1964, pp. 39-45.

Carrigan, William, *The History and Antiquities of the Diocese of Ossory* vol. IV, Dublin, 1905, p. 120.

FitzGerald, Lord Walter, 'County of Kilkenny, Parish of Clonamery, Clonamery Churchyard', *MDI* V, 1901, pp. 80-1.

Stell, Geoffrey P., and Mary Harman, *Buildings of St Kilda*, Edinburgh, 1988.

Waterman, D. M., 'Banagher Church, County Derry', *UJA* 39, 1976, pp. 25-41.

CHAPTER 16

See Lacy, 1983, Cuppage, 1986, Fanning, 1981, Macalister, 1949, Marshall, 1989, and O'Farrell, 1987 (Chapter 8); Ó Ríordáin and Foy, 1941 and O'Flaherty, 1986 (Chapter 15).

Somerville, Boyle, ' "The Fort" on Knockdrum, West Carbery, County Cork', *JRSAI* 61, 1931, pp. 1-14.

Henry, Françoise, 'The antiquities of Caher Island (Co. Mayo)' *JRSAI* 77, 1947, pp. 23-38.

Bourke, Cormac, 'A crozier and bell from Inishmurray and their place in ninth-century Irish archaeology', *PRIA* 85 C, 1985, pp. 145-68.

CHAPTER 17

See above Stokes, 1895-7, *sub anno* 1090 (Chapter 6) for *cuilebaidh*; Macalister, 1938, Price, 1941, and Herity, 1989 (Chapter 8), and Devine, 1989 (Chapter 10).

Ó Corráin, Donncha, 'Appendix: The Ogham inscription', *Journal of the Kerry Archaeological and Historical Society* 10, 1977, pp. 17-18 (Ratass).

Crawford, Henry S., 'A descriptive list of early cross-slabs and pillars', *JRSAI* 42, 1912, pp. 217-44; 43, 1913, pp. 151-69, 261-5 and 326-34; 46, 1916, pp. 163-7.

Henry, Françoise, 'Early Christian slabs and pillar-stones in the West of Ireland', *JRSAI* 67, 1937, pp. 263-79.

O'Brien, D. Maddison, 'Two crosses at Crooha West, Adrigole', *JCHAS* 73, no. 217, 1968, p. 71.

Crozier, Isabel, and Dorothy Lowry-Corry, 'Some Christian cross-slabs in Co. Donegal and Co. Antrim', *JRSAI* 68, 1938, pp. 219-25 (Drumnacur).

Anderson, J. Romilly, *The Early Christian Monuments of Scotland*, Edinburgh, 1903.

Close-Brooks, Johanna, and Robert B. K. Stevenson, *Dark Age Sculpture*, Edinburgh, 1982, pp. 34-5 (Papil and Bressay).

Small, Alan, Charles Thomas and David M. Wilson, *St Ninian's Isle and its Treasure*, 2 vols., London, 1973.

Roth, Uta, 'Studien zur Ornamentik frühchristlicher Handschriften des insularen Bereichs', *Bericht der Römisch-Germanischen Kommission* 60, 1979, pp. 73-5 (Cathach).

Harbison, Peter, 'The date of the Crucifixion slabs from Duvillaun More and Inishkea North, Co. Mayo', in E. Rynne (ed.), *Figures from the Past: Studies on Figurative Art in Christian Ireland in honour of Helen M. Roe*, Dun Laoghaire, 1987, pp. 73-91.

Herity, Michael, 'Cathair na Naomh and its Cross-slabs', *Catnair na Mart, Journal of the Westport Historical Society* 9(1), 1989, pp. 91-100 (Caher Island)

Patterson, W. H., in *JRSAI* 11, 1870-1, pp. 466-70 (Aighan).

Harbison, Peter, 'A group of Early Christian carved stone monuments in County Donegal', in J. Higgitt (ed.), *Early Medieval Sculpture in Britain and Ireland*, BAR British Series 152, 1986, pp. 49-85 (Carndonagh).

Olden, Thomas, 'On the Culebath', *PRIA* 16, 1879-88, pp. 355-58.

Gógan, Liam S., *The Ardagh Chalice*, Dublin, 1932, pp. 75-78 (*flabellum*).

Lawlor, H. C., *The Monastery of Saint Mochaoi of Nendrum*, Belfast, 1925.

An Archaeological Survey of County Down, Belfast, 1966, pp. 287-9 (Saul).

Williams, Sterling de Courcy, 'The old graveyards in Durrow parish', *JRSAI* 27, 1897, pp. 128-47.

Kendrick, T. D., 'Gallen Priory excavations', *JRSAI* 69, 1939, pp. 1-20.

Crawford, Henry S., 'A descriptive list of early cross-slabs and pillars', *JRSAI* 43, 1913, pp. 264-5 (Lemanaghan).

Kelly, Dorothy, 'Cross-carved slabs from Latteragh, County Tipperary', *JRSAI* 118, 1988, pp. 93-5 (Lemanaghan).

Harbison, Peter, 'Early Christian antiquities at Clonmore, Co. Carlow', *PRIA* forthcoming.

Ó hÉailidhe, Pádraig, 'The crosses and slabs at St Berrihert's Kyle in the Glen of Aherlow', in E. Rynne (ed.), *North Munster Studies; Essays in commemoration of Monsignor Michael Moloney*, Limerick, 1967, pp. 102-26.

Waddell, John, and Patrick Holland, 'The Peakaun site: Duignan's 1944 investigations', *Tipperary Historical Journal*, 1990, pp. 165-86.

Petrie, George, *Christian Inscriptions in the Irish Language* (ed. M. Stokes), vol. I, Dublin, 1872 (Clonmacnois).

Macalister, R. A. S., *Corpus Inscriptionum Insularum Celticarum* II, Dublin, 1949, pp. 43-71 and 198-200 (Clonmacnois).

Lionard, Pádraig, 'Early Irish grave-slabs', *PRIA* 61 C, 1961, pp. 95-169.

Leask, H. G., 'Tullylease, Co. Cork: its church and monuments', *JCHAS* 43, no. 158, 1938, pp. 101-8.

Lionárd, Pádraig, 'A reconsideration of the dating of the slab of St Berichter at Tullylease, Co. Cork', *JCHAS* 58, no. 187, 1953, pp. 12-13.

Ó hÉailidhe, 'Early Christian graveslabs in the Dublin region', *JRSAI* 103, 1963, pp. 51-64 (St Patrick's, Dublin).

Fanning, Thomas, and Pádraig Ó hÉailidhe, 'Some cross-inscribed slabs from the Irish midlands', in H. Murtagh (ed.), *Irish Midland Studies; essays in commemoration of N. W. English*, Athlone, 1980, pp. 12-13 (Clonaltra West).

CHAPTER 18

See above Macalister, 1945 (Chapter 8); Ó Corráin, 1977, and Close-Brooks and Stevenson, 1982 (Chapter 17).

MacWhite, Eoin, 'Contributions to a study of Ogam memorial stones', *Zeitschrift für Celtische Philologie* 28, 1960/61, pp. 294-308.

Jackson, Kenneth, *Language and History in Early Britain*, Edinburgh, 1953.

Carney, James, 'The invention of the Ogam Cipher', *Ériu* 26, 1975, pp. 53-65.

Macalister, R. A. S., 'On a runic inscription at Killaloe Cathedral', *PRIA* 33 C, 1917, pp. 493-8.

MacManus, Damian, *A Guide to Ogam*, Maynooth, 1991.

Ferguson, Sir Samuel, *Ogham Inscriptions in Ireland, Wales and Scotland*, Edinburgh 1887, 12 (Windele's account of Mr Collins).

O'Kelly, Michael J., 'Church Island near Valencia, Co. Kerry', *PRIA* 59 C, 1958, pp. 57-136.

Brash, Richard Rolt, *The Ogam Inscribed Monuments of the Gaedhil*, London, 1879 (Aghabullogue).

Hamlin, Ann, 'Early Irish stone carving: content and context', in S. M. Pearce (ed.), *The Early Church in Western Britain and Ireland, Studies presented to C. A. Ralegh Radford*, BAR British Series 102, 1982, pp. 283-96.

CHAPTER 19

See above Cuppage, 1986, pp. 309-11 (Chapter 8) for Kilmalkedar; Macalister, 1916 (Chapter 9); Waddell and Holland, 1990 (Chapter 17).

Way, Albert, 'Ancient sun-dials', *Archaeological Journal* 25, 1868, pp. 206-23.

Atkinson, G. M., 'Description of antiquities under the conservation of the Board of Public Works, Ireland', *JRSAI* 18, 1887-88, pp. 249-53 (Kilmalkedar sundial).

Macalister, R. A. S., *Monasterboice, Co. Louth*, Dundalk, 1946, pp. 69-71 (Sundial).

Hore, Philip Herbert, *History of the Town and County of Wexford* vol. VI, London, 1911, pp. 587-8 (Clone sundial).

Hamlin, Ann, 'Some northern sun-dials and timekeeping in the Early Irish Church', in E. Rynne (ed.), *Figures from the Past; studies on figurative art in Christian Ireland in honour of Helen M. Roe*, Dun Laoghaire, 1987, pp. 29-42.

CHAPTER 20

See above Macalister, 1909, Barrow, 1972, and articles on Ballyvourney (Chapter 9); Youngs, 1989, pp. 103-4 for Ballyspellan brooch (Chapter 12); Small, Thomas and Wilson, 1973, and Harbison, 1986 (Chapter 17).

Hickey, Helen, *Images of Stone*, Belfast, 1976 reprinted 1985, (Killadeas and White Island).

Lowry-Corry, Lady Dorothy, 'A newly discovered statue at the church on White Island', *UJA* 22, 1959, pp. 59-66 (with further references).

Stevenson, Robert B. K., 'The Hunterston Brooch and its significance', *Medieval Archaeology* 18, 1974, pp. 16-42.
Kilbride-Jones, H. F., *Zoomorphic Pennannular Brooches*, London, 1980.
Duignan, Lasairiona, 'A hand-pin from Treanmacmurtagh Bog, Co. Sligo', *JRSAI* 103, 1973, pp. 220-3.
Westropp, Thomas J., 'Descriptive sketch of places visited, Part I. – Scattery Island and Canons' Island, Co. Clare', *JRSAI* 27, 1897, pp. 273-90 (Scattery Island brooch).
Henry, F., 'A wooden hut on Inishkea North, Co. Mayo', *JRSAI* 82, 1952, pp. 168-9 (brooch).

CHAPTER 21
See above Lacy, 1983, and Wakeman, 1893 (Chapter 8); Otway, 1839 (Chapter 9); Wilde, 1867, p. 164, and Westropp, 1911 (Chapter 10).
Weir, Anthony, *Early Ireland: a field guide*, Belfast, 1980, pp. 55-6 (bullauns).
Crozier, Isabel R., and Lily C. Rea, 'Bullauns and other basin-stones', *UJA* 3, 1940, pp. 104-14.
Bigger, Francis Joseph, 'The lake and church of Kilmakilloge, the ancient church, holy well, and bullán-stone of Temple Feaghna, and the holy well and shrine at Saint Finan's, County Kerry', *JRSAI* 28, 1898, pp. 314-23.
Cooke, John, 'Antiquarian remains in the Beaufort District, County Kerry', *PRIA* 26 C, 1906, pp. 1-14.
Crawford, Henry S., 'Notes on stones used as a cure at Killerry, near Dromahair, and on certain bullauns', *JRSAI* 43, 1913, pp. 267-9.
Price, Liam, 'Rock-basins, or 'bullauns', at Glendalough and elsewhere', *JRSAI* 89, 1959, pp. 161-88.
Wakeman, W. F., 'On certain markings on rocks, pillar-stones, and other monuments, observed chiefly in the County Fermanagh', *JRSAI* 13, 1875, pp. 445-74.
O'Donovan, J., *Ordnance Survey Letters . . . Co. Mayo* vol. I, Bray 1927, pp. 471-5 (Caher Island).
Brash, Richard Rolt, 'On holed stones', *The Gentleman's Magazine*, December 1864, pp. 686-700.
Frazer, W., 'On "holed" and perforated stones in Ireland', *JRSAI* 26, 1896, pp. 158-69.
Allen, J. Romilly, 'Notes on the antiquities in Co. Kerry visited by the Royal Society of Antiquaries of Ireland and the Cambrian Archaeological Association, August 1891, Part II', *JRSAI* 22, 1892, pp. 255-84 (Reask).
Macalister, R. A. S., 'The cross-inscribed "holed stone" at Mainistir Chiaráin, Aran Island', *JRSAI* 52, 1922, p. 177.
Comerford, Dr M., 'Castledermot: its history and antiquities', *JCKAS* 1, 1895, p. 377 (holed cross).

CHAPTER 22
Walther, Elisabeth, 'Wallfahrten im Westen Irlands', in Kriss-Rettenbeck, Lenz and Möhler, Gerda (eds.), *Wallfahrt kennt keine Grenzen*, Munich 1984, pp. 396-406 (Chapter 1); Gerald of Wales, 1982 (Chapter 7); Ó Danachair, 1960 (Chapter 8) and Logan, 1980 (Chapter 9).
Hardy, Philip Dixon, *The Holy Wells of Ireland*, Dublin, 1836.
Lynch, P. J., 'Topographical notes on the Barony of Coshlea, Co. Limerick etc.' *JRSAI* 50, 1920, p. 117 (St Molua's Well).
Lucas, A. T., 'The sacred trees of Ireland', *JCHAS* 68, nos. 207-8, 1963, pp. 16-54.
FitzGerald, Lord Walter, 'St Columbkill's Well and the Rock of Doon, Parish of Kilmacrenan', *MDI* 9, 1913, pp. 31-2.
FitzGerald, Lord Walter, 'Clonenagh (Church-ruins) Graveyard', *MDI* 8, 1910, p. 155.
O'Conor, C., *Columbanus's Third Letter on the Liberties of the Irish Church*, London, 1810, p. 83 (Hester's account).
Walther, Elisabeth, *Modernes Wallfahrtswesen in Westirland – Am Beispiel von sechs Dörfern der Grafschaften Galway und Mayo*, Köln, 1980. (Mauméan 314-15).
Shannon, Pat, 'A pattern for St Patrick', *Ireland of the Welcomes* 39, no. 2. March-April 1990, pp. 13-15 (Mauméan).

CHAPTER 23
See Giraldus Cambrensis 1988, 105 (Chapter 2) for John de Courcy.
Yeats, William Butler, in *Stories from Carleton*, with an introduction by W. B. Yeats, London, 1889, xvi.
Heaney, Seamus, *Station Island*, London, 1984.
Westropp, Thomas Johnson, 'Collectanea. A folklore survey of County Clare', *Folklore* XXII, no. 3, 1911, pp. 333-34.

INDEX

PICTURE CREDITS

ACKNOWLEDGEMENTS

This book has benefited greatly from assistance I have received from many friends, of whom I would particularly like to single out the following: Gerry Bracken, Con Brogan and John Scarry (OPW), Paul Caponigro, Seamus Cashman, Bill Doyle, Brendan Doyle and Valerie Dowling (National Museum), Walter Horn, John Kennedy, Harvey Kenny, Brian Lynch and Derek Cullen (Bord Fáilte), Tom Lawlor, Cian O'Carroll (SFADCO), Jacobus van Hespen and John Waddell for providing photographs, Brigid Dolan, Ida Ní Thuama and Siobhán O'Rafferty (Royal Irish Academy), Michael Ryan, Raghnall Ó Floinn, Mary Cahill and Nessa O'Connor (National Museum), Pat Donlon (National Library) and Siobhán de hÓir (Royal Society of Antiquaries) for providing information; Cormac Bourke, Jim Donnelly, Heather King, Jenny White Marshall and Frank Mitchell for permission to quote their personal comments; Rainer Berger especially for allowing me to refer, prior to publication, to his fascinating new mortar datings, in which he was assisted by Aighleann O'Shaughnessy and Grellan D. Rourke; Cróine and the late Michael Magan for hospitality in the Dingle Peninsula, as well as Hugh Cheape, George Cunningham, Gordon Donaldson, Michael Gorman, Ann Hamlin, Ben Kiely, Eamonn Ó Carragáin and Michael Williams, P.P. for help of various kinds. The George Campbell drawings are reproduced here for the first time in respectful memory of a great artist. Finally, my thanks to Bord Fáilte, The Irish Tourist Board, which, through the good offices of Matt McNulty, made possible the colour plates of this book.

I would like to thank the following for permission to quote from works published by them:

Burns & Oates, London for extracts from Shane Leslie's *St Patrick's Purgatory*
Dominick Press, Dublin for an extract from Liam Price's article in *Féilsgríbhinn Eoin Mhic Néill*
Faber & Faber Ltd for extracts from Seamus Heaney's *Station Island*; Sacheverell Sitwell's *Dance of the Quick and the Dead*; and Jonathan Sumption's *Pilgrimage*
Gill & Macmillan for an extract from Lord Killanin and Michael V. Duignan's *Shell Guide to Ireland*
Institute of Advanced Studies, Dublin, for an extract from Anne O'Sullivan's article in *Celtica*
HarperCollins for three poem translations from P.L. Henry's *The Early English and Celtic Lyric*
Octagon Books and Columbia University Press, New York, for extracts from J.F. Kenney's *Sources for the Early History of Ireland*
Princeton University Press for the Paschasius Radbertus translation from Geary, *Furta Sacra*
Royal Irish Academy, Dublin, for the Cook extract from its *Proceedings* of 1906
Royal Society of Antiquaries of Ireland, Dublin, for O'Donovan's translation from the Irish poem and Bigger's description of Temple Feaghna in Vols 28 & 30 respectively of its *Journal*; also Lucas quote
Colin Smythe, Gerrard's Cross, for an extract on Clonmacnois from Patrick Logan's *The Holy Wells of Ireland*
Syracuse University Press for Maire Mac Neill's translation in Maureen Murphy and James McKillop's *Irish Literature, A Reader*